MICHIGAN BUSINESS PAPERS

Number 65

MICHIGAN BUSINESS
PAPERS Number 65

Information Economics and Accounting Research

A Workshop Conducted by Joel S. Demski

Edited by

GERALD LOBO and MICHAEL MAHER

A publication of the
Division of Research
Graduate School of Business Administration
The University of Michigan
Ann Arbor, Michigan

Printed in the United States of America
ISBN 0-87712-204-0

Library of Congress Cataloging in Publication Data
Main entry under title:

Information economics and accounting research.

(Michigan business papers; no. 65)
Includes bibliographies.
1. Managerial accounting—Addresses, essays, lectures. 2. Financial statements—Addresses, essays, lectures. 3. Information theory in economics—Addresses, essays, lectures. I. Demski, Joel S. II. Lobo, Gerald, 1947- III. Maher, Michael, 1946- IV. Series.
HF5006.M46 no. 65 [HF5635] 330s [658.1'511] 80-19369 ISBN 0-87712-204-0

CONTENTS

PREFACE

This monograph, an outcome of an intensive three-day research seminar conducted by Professor Joel S. Demski of Stanford University at the University of Michigan Paton Accounting Center, is intended for students of information economics. We have included three lectures by Professor Demski, eight papers which constituted a key part of the seminar, and summaries of discussions about a number of the papers.

As editors, we found ourselves in the unfortunate position of having to omit a number of relevant articles for space and copyright reasons. However, the entire list of readings suggested for use by seminar participants appears at the end of the monograph. This list, in combination with the reference lists accompanying each article, provides the reader with an introduction to the field of information economics.

Acknowledgments. First and foremost, we acknowledge the invaluable contribution of Professor Demski. He will be remembered as one who assured the success of an experiment. The firm of Coopers & Lybrand provided the financial support for the seminar; we greatly appreciate their risk-taking posture in supporting an uncertain venture. Our student and faculty colleagues at the University of Michigan provided helpful input to the seminar. The staff of the Division of Research of the Graduate School of Business Administration were most helpful in translating notes into print and in obtaining reprint permissions from far-flung authors and editors. Finally, grateful acknowledgment is made to the copyright owners who gave permission to reproduce these articles from the following publications:

The Accounting Journal
Joel S. Demski, "A Simple Case of Indeterminate Financial Reporting" (in press)

The Accounting Review

Joel S. Demski and Gerald A. Feltham, "Economic Incentives in Budgetary Control Systems" (April 1978)

The American Economic Review

Milton Harris and Artur Raviv, "Some Results on Incentive Contracts with Applications to Education and Employment, Health Insurance, and Law Enforcement" (March 1978)

Martin Loeb and Wesley A. Magat, "Success Indicators in the Soviet Union: The Problem of Incentives and Efficient Allocations" (March 1978)

The International Economic Review

Richard Kihlstrom, "A Bayesian Model of Demand for Information about Product Quality" (February 1974)

Jacob Marschak and Koichi Miyasawa, "Economic Comparability of Information Systems" (June 1968)

The Journal of Accounting Research

William H. Beaver and Joel S. Demski, "The Nature of Financial Accounting Objectives: A Summary and Synthesis" (1974 Supplement)

Gerald Lobo
Michael Maher

I

Basic Ideas in the Economic Analysis of Information

FIRST LECTURE

JOEL S. DEMSKI

Our goal in this opening session of the seminar is to examine the assumptions behind, and the nature of, the "economic analysis of information." The story has a technical nature because information arises and has "value" only in a world of uncertainty. Thus, uncertainty must be present in our *formal* thinking, and our behavioral assumptions must, in one way or another, accommodate the use of "information."

We begin with a quick review of the behavioral assumptions (expected utility representation and Bayesian revision), next formally consider the possibility of acquiring and using "information," and then consider the only theorem in the area (a series of equivalence statements largely due to Blackwell[1]). We then examine the precise meaning of some casual terminology ("cost and value of information") and conclude with the economist's ritual of constructing a demand curve.

Measurement

The idea of *measurement* is deceptively simple: we associate numbers with some attribute of a class of objects in such a way that some property of the attribute is faithfully represented as a numerical property. To make this precise, we begin with some (primitive) relational system $\langle A, \succcurlyeq \rangle$, where A is some set of objects and $\succcurlyeq$ is a binary relation defined on A ($\succcurlyeq \subset A \times A$).* We then

*Throughout the three lectures we use the symbols $\succ$ and $\succcurlyeq$ to mean "preference relationship."

introduce a numerical relational system, such as $\langle Reals, \geq \rangle$. Measuring the distinguished property of the class of objects A amounts to finding a function $f: A \rightarrow Reals$ such that $a \succcurlyeq a'$ if and only if $f(a) \geq f(a')$ for all $a, a' \in A$. For example, a "as heavy as" a' is equivalent to the weight of $a \geq$ the weight of a'. Of course, we are interested in the measurement of preference. A is a set of choices, $\succcurlyeq$ is a given preference relation, and f is a *utility function*.

Two asides are important here. First, measure theory is a deep subject. Mock's recent AAA Monograph #13, *Measurement and Accounting Information Criteria* [1976], is a good reference. And "the" book is Krantz, Luce, Suppes, and Tversky's *Foundations of Measurement* [1971].

Second, at this juncture we part company with a large subset of the accounting literature. We will use measure theory to represent the behavior of users, but we will *not* define accounting as a measurement system or examine the traditional questions of existence, uniqueness, meaningfulness, scaling, and errors.

Preference Measurement

Example: Suppose $A = \{a^1, a^2, a^3, a^4\}$ with $\succcurlyeq \subset A \times A$ given by $a^1 \succ a^2 \succ a^3 \succ a^4$ and transitive (a^1 is strictly preferred to a^2, etc.). Possible utility functions are shown in Exhibit 1.1.

Exhibit 1.1

	u_1	u_2	u_3	u_4
a^1	4	10^6	−50	4.753
a^2	3	99999	−60	4.735
a^3	2	99998.9	−70	4.692
a^4	1	-10^{24}	−71	4.605

From this point it is fairly easy to see what conditions on $\langle A, \succcurlyeq \rangle$ will guarantee the existence of a utility function.

THEOREM 1. *Suppose A is finite, and $\succcurlyeq$ is complete and transitive. Then a utility function exists, and it is unique up to strictly increasing transformations.*

To illustrate the proof, suppose $|A| = 4$. Renumber the alternatives, using completeness and transitivity, so that $a^4 \succcurlyeq a^3 \succcurlyeq a^2 \succcurlyeq a^1$. Any function $U: A \rightarrow Reals$ satisfying $U(a^4) \geq U(a^3) \geq U(a^2) \geq U(a^1)$ will work.[2] As an aside, note the necessity of transitivity here. For example, $a^1 \succ a^2 \succ a^3 \succ a^4$ and $a^1 \prec a^3$ lead to inconsistent inequalities: $U(a^1) > U(a^3)$ and $U(a^3) > U(a^1)$.

Observe that with finite A and a complete and transitive preference structure we can describe our individual's behavior *as though he maximized* $U(\cdot)$. This is important because it allows us to use the theory of optimization to study choice behavior. However, to study information we demand even more. Essentially, we must formally admit to uncertainty, and seek a preference representation that "separates" tastes and beliefs and allows us to represent beliefs with a probability measure.

The first requirement is met by the conventional state-act-outcome paradigm. For example, we may have the outcomes for states s^1 and s^2 and actions a^1 through a^4 as shown in Exhibit 1.2.

Exhibit 1.2

	s^1	s^2
a^1	80	168
a^2	81	160
a^3	70	170
a^4	100	100

In general, we envision $a \in A$, $x \in X$, $s \in S$, and an *outcome function* $p : S \times A \rightarrow X$, where we observe the essentially tautological nature of the state definition.

The second requirement is met by imposing enough structure on $\langle A, \succcurlyeq \rangle$ so that $U(a)$ is an expected value. Continuing our earlier example, suppose that $\phi(s^1) = \phi(s^2) = 1/2$ and $U(x) = ln(x)$. Then

$$E(U|a^1) = 1/2\ ln(80) + 1/2\ ln(168) = 4.753$$
$$E(U|a^2) = 1/2\ ln(81) + 1/2\ ln(160) = 4.735$$
$$E(U|a^3) = 1/2\ ln(70) + 1/2\ ln(170) = 4.692$$
$$E(U|a^4) = 1/2\ ln(100) + 1/2\ ln(100) = 4.605.$$

Observe the decomposition here, $U : X \rightarrow$ *Reals*; and $\phi : \{\text{all events}\} \rightarrow [0,1]$; and the utility of an act is the respective *expected value* of $U(x)$.

The conditions which ensure such a decomposition constitute a deep issue. Von Neumann and Morgenstern [1947] work with an exogenous probability measure. Savage [1954] works with an endogenous probability measure. Anscombe and Aumann [1963] employ a mixture, and Krantz, Luce, Suppes, and Tversky [1971] offer a conditional version of Savage. For the sake of completeness, we will briefly review the Von Neumann and Morgenstern axiomatization. The basic structure of the problem is assumed to consist of a finite set of possible consequences, and an act or alternative is a probability distribution on X (i.e., a lottery). Moreover, all possible gambles or probability distributions on X are conceivable. To illustrate, suppose that $|X| = 4$. Then we assume that $X = \{x_1, x_2, x_3, x_4\}$ and

$$A = \left\{ \phi(x_j) \,\middle|\, \sum_{j=1}^{4} \phi(x_j) = 1 \quad \text{and} \quad \phi(x_j) \geq 0 \right\}.$$

$\langle A, \succsim \rangle$ is now endowed with four axioms.

A1: $\succsim$ is complete and transitive. $\succsim$ is, of course, the ordering we seek to represent. And the presumed richness of A, coupled with *A1*, guarantees that we can also speak of ordering X. So we renumber the outcome so that $x_1 \succsim x_2 \succsim x_3 \succsim x_4$.

A2: Reduction of compound lotteries. Define $L^i = (\phi_1^i x_1, \phi_2^i x_2, \phi_3^i x_3, \phi_4^i x_4)$, for $i = 1, \ldots, m$. Then $(\hat{\phi}_1 x_1, \hat{\phi}_2 x_2, \hat{\phi}_3 x_3, \hat{\phi}_4 x_4) \sim (\phi_1 L^1, \phi_2 L^2, \ldots, \phi_m L^m)$ where

$$\hat{\phi}_1 = \sum_{i=1}^{m} \phi_i \phi_1^i, \text{ etc.}$$

L is, of course, a notational device for describing a particular alternative in A. And the axiom requires that you not care about the gambling procedure at hand:

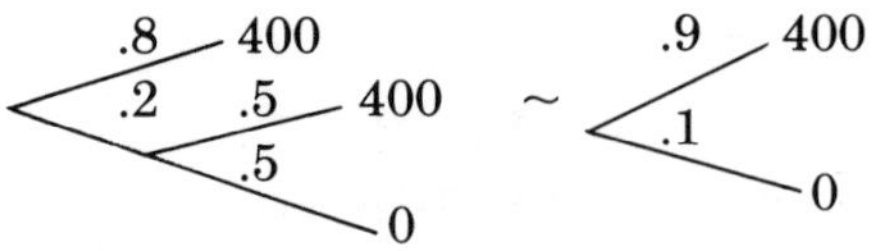

Its role is to allow the use of probability calculus in representing the individual's choice behavior.

A3: Continuity. For all $x_j \in X$, there exists a z_j such that $x_j \sim (z_j x_1, (1 - z_j)x_4) \equiv \tilde{x}_j$, *and* $\tilde{x}_j$ may be substituted for x_j in any lottery.

A4: Monotonicity. $(\phi_1 x_1, (1 - \phi_1)x_4) \succ (\hat{\phi}_1 x_1, (1 - \hat{\phi}_1)x_4)$ if and only if $\phi_1 > \hat{\phi}_1$. This ensures a "sensible" interpretation of the probability measure and is often referred to as the "Did you really mean it?" axiom:

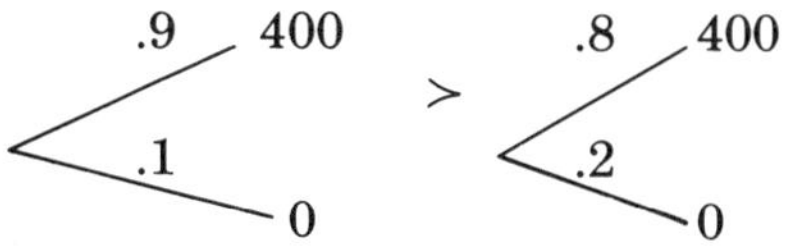

THEOREM 2 (VON NEUMANN AND MORGENSTERN). *With the assumed setting and axioms A1–A4 there exists a function $U : X \rightarrow$ Reals such that $E(U|a^1) \geq E(U|a^2)$ if and only if $a^1 \gtrsim a^2$, for all $a^1, a^2 \in A$. Moreover, U is unique up to positive linear transformations.*

To see the idea behind the proof, which is constructive, consider the $|X| = 4$ case: continuity provides z_2 and z_3 such that

$$x_2 \sim (z_2 x_1, (1 - z_2)x_4) = \tilde{x}_2, \quad \text{and}$$
$$x_3 \sim (z_3 x_1, (1 - z_3)x_4) = \tilde{x}_3.$$

Substituting and employing the reduction axiom then provides, for some act designated a,

$$\begin{aligned} L^a &= (\phi_1 x_1, \phi_2 x_2, \phi_3 x_3, \phi_4 x_4) \\ &= (\phi_1 x_1, \phi_2 [z_2 x_1, (1 - z_2)x_4], \phi_3 [z_3 x_1, (1 - z_3)x_4], \phi_4 x_4) \\ &= ([\phi_1 + \phi_2 z_2 + \phi_3 z_3] x_1, [\phi_2 (1 - z_2) + \phi_3 (1 - z_3) + \phi_4] x_4). \end{aligned}$$

Now define:
$$U(x_1) = 1$$
$$U(x_2) = z_2$$
$$U(x_3) = z_3$$
$$U(x_4) = 0$$

and observe that $E(U|a) = \phi_1 + \phi_2 z_2 + \phi_3 z_3$. Moreover, monotonicity now ensures that $E(U|a^1) \geq E(U|a^2) \leftrightarrow a^1 \gtrsim a^2$.

In turn, uniqueness is quite transparent; the expectation structure must be preserved.

Information Choice Representation

As we are willing to describe our individual as though he maximized his expected utility, we are now ready to introduce information and choice among alternative information structures. We will quickly examine some examples, set the notation, and then consider some general questions.

Examples

All of the examples below are set in a two-state world and concern the possible acquisition of information with the following characteristics:

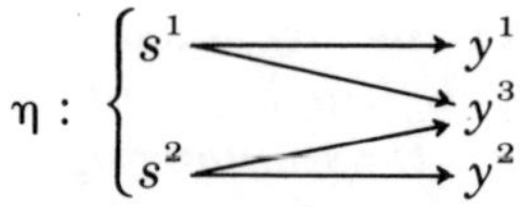

If y^1 is received, we know s^1 will obtain; if y^2 is received we know s^2 will obtain. But y^3 is not informative. To put in specific numbers, the state is revealed with probability .6 (and with probability .4, y^3 will be observed). You should convince yourself that all of the following probabilities are consistent in a Bayesian sense:

$$\phi(s^1) = \phi(s^2) = 0.5$$
$$\phi(y^1|s^1) = \phi(y^2|s^2) = 0.6$$
$$\phi(y^1) = 0.3 = \phi(y^2)$$
$$\phi(s^1|y^1) = \frac{\phi(y^1|s^1)\,\phi(s^1)}{\phi(y^1)} = 1$$
$$\phi(s^1|y^2) = \frac{\phi(y^2|s^1)\,\phi(s^1)}{\phi(y^2)} = 0$$
$$\phi(s^1|y^3) = \frac{\phi(y^3|s^1)\,\phi(s^1)}{\phi(y^3)} = 0.5$$

Example 1. $U(x) = ln(x)$.

	s^1	s^2
a^1	72	160
a^2	73	152

=

	80	168
	81	160

−

	8	8
	8	8

By inspection, if you observe y^1 you will pick a^2; and if you observe y^2 you will pick a^3. If y^3 is observed, $\phi(s^1|y^3) = 1/2$ and:

$$E(U|a^1,y^3) = 1/2\,ln(72) + 1/2\,ln(160)$$
$$= 1/2(4.2767) + 1/2(5.0752) = 4.6759$$
$$E(U|a^2,y^3) = 1/2\,ln(73) + 1/2\,ln(152) = 4.6572.$$

So we have the following optimal policy:

y	$\alpha^*(y,\eta)$
y^1	a^2
y^2	a^1
y^3	a^1

and

$$\begin{aligned} E(U|\eta) &= \sum_y \phi(y)\, E(U|y, \alpha^*(y,\eta)) \\ &= .3\, ln(73) + .3\, ln(160) + .4(4.6759) \\ &= 4.6800 \end{aligned}$$

versus

$$E(U|no\ info) = E(U|a^1) = 4.7530$$

Example 2.

This example is identical to Example 1, except that the information costs seventy instead of eight outcome units. You can readily verify the following optimal policy:

y	$\alpha^*(y,\eta)$
y^1	a^2
y^2	a^1
y^3	a^2

where the outcome structure is:

	s^1	s^2
a^1	10	98
a^2	11	90

and

$$\begin{aligned} E(U|\eta) &= 3.4744 \\ &= .3ln(11) + .3ln\,(98) + .4(3.4489) \end{aligned}$$

while $E(U|no\ info) = 4.7530$.

Example 3.

Continue the same beliefs, tastes, and information structure but the outcome structure is

	s^1	s^2
a^1	80	168
a^2	79	160

and the information will cost eight outcome units. By inspection, the optimal policy is:

y	$\alpha^*(y,\eta)$
y^1	a^1
y^2	a^1
y^3	a^1

Several points are important enough to reinforce at this juncture. The basic and familiar idea here is that information is used to revise beliefs in a Bayesian revision sense. That is, whatever the individual does, we view his reaction to information as Bayesian revision. This "makes sense" in that the only conceivable thing the individual is unsure of is manifested in the state specification, and his unsureness (or "sureness") is represented by a probability measure. Once you buy into the probability calculus, you buy into Bayesian revision. But notice that our representation (Theorem 2) does not directly address acquisition and use of information. Indeed, I do not know of any such theorem.

Several observations emerge when you compare the three examples:

(1) Remember the cost! (Obviously the information is a good buy in example 1 if the cost is zero outcome units.)

(2) The optimal use of the information may depend on what you paid for it (examples 2 and 3).

(3) You may not use the information even though it changes your beliefs (example 3).

Moreover, two central features of the analysis should be kept in mind as we proceed. First, the information can, at most, change your beliefs. It has no consumption value whatever. It is tasteless! Second, consistent behavior, which is the key, requires that the optimal use of the information be the focal point in the analysis. Put differently, one information structure is better than another if (and only if) the outcome lottery it produces is better. To construct this outcome lottery we essentially examine every possible (observable) event and pick the best act in each. (Perhaps you should draw a "decision tree" for the $E(U|\eta)$ calculation in Example 1.)

It is now time to add some generality. To begin, what do we mean, in this specialized world, by the term *information*? The distinguishing feature appears to be the *capability* of altering your probability measure. But you also want to be careful to worry about events that are "important." That is, it appears wise to reserve the term *information* for the capability of revising beliefs "relevant" to the decision at hand. All of this sounds ad hoc (at best) and is meant to motivate a long list of definitions that will both sharpen our thinking and be useful later on.

Definitions

(1) $G = \{g_1, \ldots, g_n\}$ partitions S when $\bigcup_{i=1}^{n} g_i = S$ and $g_i \cap g_j = \phi$ for all $i \neq j$.

(2) Partition G is *as fine as* partition H if it is a subpartition of H.

(3) A partition of S is termed *payoff adequate* if clairvoyance with respect to it will allow selection of an optimal equivalence class of outcomes.

(4) A partition of S is termed *outcome adequate* if clairvoyance with respect to it will reduce the problem to one of choice under subjective certainty.

(5) An adequate partition is termed *relevant* if it is the coarsest partition that is adequate.

(6) Let $G = \{g\}$ be a payoff relevant partition of S. Structure η is termed information (or an information structure) with respect to G if $\phi(g) \neq \phi(g|y, \eta)$ for some probable signal $y \in Y$.

(7) Information structure η is termed
  (a) *noiseless* if it partitions S.
  (b) *perfect* if it is noiseless and the state partition it induces is payoff adequate.
  (c) *complete* if it partitions S into singletons.
  (d) *useless* if (with no alternative optima) $\alpha^*(y, \eta) : Y \rightarrow A$ is a constant function.

Examples

Consider the outcome structure and noiseless information structures in Exhibit 1.3.

Exhibit 1.3

	s^1	s^2	s^3	s^4
a^1	(8,4)	(4,8)	(20,10)	(20,30)
a^2	(10,15)	(15,10)	(40,15)	(15,2)
a^3	(50,1)	(2,25)	(4,4)	(4,4)

$\eta_1 : \{s^1, s^2, s^3, s^4\}$ null

$\eta_2 : \{\{s^1, s^2\}, \{s^3, s^4\}\}$ high-low

$\eta_3 : \{\{s^1, s^2\}, \{s^3\}, \{s^4\}\}$

$\eta_4 : \{\{s^1\}, \{s^2\}, \{s^3\}, \{s^4\}\}$

$\eta_5 : \{\{s^1, H\}, \{s^1, T\}, \{s^2, H\}, \{s^2, T\},$
$\{s^3, H\}, \{s^3, T\}, \{s^4, H\}, \{s^4, T\}\}.$

Suppose $U(x) = ln(x_1 x_2)$:

Structure	Outcome Adequate?	Payoff Adequate?
η_1	no	no
η_2	no	no
η_3	no	yes*
η_4	yes*	yes
η_5	yes	yes

(* = relevant)

(Note the η are ranked [inversely] by *fineness.*)

Suppose $U(x) = x_1 + x_2$:

Structure	Outcome Adequate?	Payoff Adequate?
η_1	no	no
η_2	no	no
η_3	no	no
η_4	yes*	yes*
η_5	yes	yes

(* = relevant)

Now compare the two structures. It is somewhat profound that we are able to say anything in general about the two information structures. It is akin to asking what can be said, in general, about taste for one automobile versus another.

Suppose some information structure is *strictly preferred* to no information. What do you know already? The structure in question is *not* useless! (As an aside, what does this tell you about the "feel better" syndrome? What does it tell you about "bad" information or "misinformation"?)

Now suppose the alternative structures are *costless* and *noiseless.* In this case, "fineness" is the key idea, because you never get "less" and it is costless. This gives rise to the following result that we casually refer to as Blackwell's Theorem:

THEOREM 3 (BLACKWELL). *Let η and η' be two costless and noiseless information structures defined on a fixed, finite S. $E(U|\eta) \geq E(U|\eta')$, regardless of beliefs, tastes, or the outcome structure (in the S environment) if and only if η is as fine as η'.*

To prove sufficiency, let $y_\eta = \{s|\eta(s) = y\}$. Clearly,

$$\phi(y|\eta) = \sum_{s \in y_\eta} \phi(s) \quad \text{and}$$

$$\phi(s|y,\eta) = \begin{cases} \dfrac{\phi(s)}{\phi(y,\eta)} & \text{for all} \quad s \in y_\eta \\ 0 & \text{otherwise} \end{cases}$$

$$E(U|\eta') = \sum_{y \in Y} \phi(y|\eta') \left\{ \max_{a \in A} \sum_{s \in y_{\eta'}} U(s,a) \frac{\phi(s)}{\phi(y|\eta')} \right\}$$

$$= \sum_{y \in Y} \max_{a \in A} \sum_{s \in y_{\eta'}} U(s,a)\,\phi(s)$$

$$= \sum_{y \in Y} \max_{a \in A} \sum_{\substack{\text{all } y \text{ such} \\ \text{that } y_\eta \subset y_{\eta'}}} \sum_{s \in y_\eta} U(s,a)\,\phi(s)$$

$$\leq \sum_{y \in Y} \sum_{\substack{\text{all } y \text{ such} \\ \text{that } y_\eta \subset y_{\eta'}}} \max_{a \in A} \sum_{s \in y_\eta} U(s,a)\,\phi(s) = E(U|\eta),$$

where η as fine as η' ensures a subset of Y with $y_{\eta'}$ equal to the union of y_η in that subset. Thus noiselessness, costlessness, and fineness combine to ensure that everything available under η' is also available under η.

To establish necessity, we proceed by contradiction. Suppose η and η' are not comparable with respect to fineness but $E(u|\eta) \geq E(u|\eta')$ universally holds. η not as fine as η' implies existence of s_1 and $s_2 \in S$ for which $\eta(s_1) = \eta(s_2)$ but $\eta'(s_1) \neq \eta'(s_2)$ (i.e., something distinguished under η' is not distinguished under η).

Similarly, the reverse implies existence of s_3 and $s_4 \in S$ for which $\eta'(s_3) = \eta'(s^4)$ but $\eta(s_3) \neq \eta(s_4)$. The two pairs could have *one* state in common or be distinct.

Case 1: Four distinct states. With $U(\cdot,\cdot)$, A and $\phi(\cdot)$ unrestricted, consider the two binary choice games:

		s_1	s_2	s_3	s_4	s_5	s_6	. . . .
Game 1	a_1	0	0	1	0	0	0	. . . .
	a_2	0	0	0	1	0	0	. . . .
Game 2	a_1	1	0	0	0	0	0	. . . .
	a_2	0	1	0	0	0	0	. . . .

For $U(\cdot)$ nonsatiating, η is strictly preferred in Game 1 and η' is strictly preferred in Game 2 (assuming $\phi(s_1)$, $\phi(s_2)$, $\phi(s_3)$, $\phi(s_4)$ > 0).

Case 2: Three distinct states. Let $s_1 = s_4$. η distinguishes s_3 while η' distinguishes s_2. The following two games provide our contradiction:

		s_1	s_2	s_3	s_4	s_5	. . . .
Game 1	a_1	0	0	1	0	0	. . . .
	a_2	1	1	0	1	1	. . . .
Game 2	a_1	0	1	0	0	0	. . . .
	a_2	1	0	1	1	1	. . . .

It ought to be clear why the restriction to costless structures is important here. (Alternatively, with risk neutrality we could separate "gross value" and "cost" . . .) Also note that fineness is an *incomplete* binary relation; hence we do *not* have a measure of the quality or quantity of information in general. So accounting standards or entropy won't surrogate for $E(U|\eta)$ as long as we focus on the properties of η *per se.* Similarly, we will have to be quite careful later on when we try to construct the demand curve for information.

Finally, two *very* important assumptions should be noted. First, this is based on "optimal" use of the information. What does this imply about the applicability of the theorem to a setting in which someone else uses the information? (For example, suppose central headquarters provides planning forecasts to division managers.) Second, the opportunity set, A, is assumed independent of the signal.

(What does this imply about applying the theorem in a public information setting?)

If you consider this comparison question a little more closely it should become apparent that additional comparisons may be possible. For example, you may not care about fineness comparability if it fails only on events that you "don't care" about distinguishing. To illustrate, consider a case where we have four states and the two structures listed below:

	s_1	s_2	s_3	s_4
η	y_1	y_2	y_3	y_3
η'	y'_1	y'_1	y'_2	y'_3

Fineness, of course, does not hold. But suppose your outcome structure is such that you don't care about distinguishing between s_3 and s_4:

	s_1	s_2	s_3	s_4
a_1	10	0	40	40
a_2	0	10	20	20
a_3	0	0	50	50

Clearly η is preferred to η' here (assuming they are both costless).

The point, of course, is that Theorem 3 addresses *all* choice problems in the S environment. Instead, we might consider $Z = \{z_1, z_2, z_3, z_4\}$ as some partitions of S and restrict ourselves to all choice problems for which Z is *payoff* adequate. This brings us to the "real" Blackwell Theorem, which I will briefly state using the notation in Marschak and Miyasawa [1968]:[3]

Symbol	Probability Matrix	Dimension
r	$[p(z_i)]$	$m \times 1$
q	$[p(y_j)]$	$n \times 1$
q'	$[p(y'_k)]$	$n' \times 1$
P	$[p(z_i, y_j)] = [p_{ij}]$	$m \times n$
P'	$[p(z_i, y_k)]$	$m \times n'$
π	$[p(z_i \mid y_j)] = [\pi_{ij}]$	$m \times n$
π'	$[p(z_i \mid y_k)] = [\pi_{ik}]$	$m \times n'$
Λ	$[p(y_j \mid z_i)] = [\lambda_{ij}]$	$m \times n$
Λ'	$[p(y_k \mid z_i)] = [\lambda_{ik}]$	$m \times n'$

Assume columns are independent, consistent with $r = \pi q$, etc. $r_i > 0$, $q_j > 0$, $q_k > 0$. Also, let Ω_Z be the set of all problems (U,p) in this environment for which Z is payoff adequate.

We now make a series of definitions:

(1) We say $P > P'$ if, for given P, P', $E(U|\eta) \geq E(U|\eta')$ for *all* problems in Ω_Z.
(2) We say $\Lambda > \Lambda'$ if, for given Λ, Λ', $E(U|\eta) \geq E(U|\eta')$ for all problems in Ω_Z and for all r.
(3) We say $\pi > \pi'$ if, for given π, π', $E(U|\eta) \geq E(U|\eta')$ for all problems in Ω_Z and all q, q' such that $\pi q = \pi' q'$.
(4) We say $\Lambda \mathscr{B} \Lambda'$ if there exists a matrix $B = [b_{jk}]$ such that $\Lambda' = \Lambda B$ and

$$\sum_{k=1}^{n'} b_{jk} = 1 \quad \text{for all } j, \quad \text{and} \quad b_{jk} \geq 0 \quad \text{for all } j, k.$$

(5) We say $(\pi, q) \; \Theta \; (\pi', q')$ if there exists a matrix $\theta = [\theta_{jk}]$ such that $\pi' = \pi\theta$, $q = \theta q'$, and

$$\sum_{j=1}^{n} \theta_{jk} = 1 \quad \text{for all } k \text{ and} \quad \theta_{jk} \geq 0 \quad \text{for all } j,k.$$

(6) We say $(\pi, q) \; \xi \; (\pi', q')$ if

$\sum_{j=1}^{n} q_j f(\pi_j) \geq \sum_{k=1}^{n'} q'_k f(\pi'_k)$ holds for any convex function on the m-dimensional simplex. Example:

$$f(\pi_j) = \max_{a \in A} \sum_{i=1}^{m} U(z_i, a) p(z_i y_j).$$

(7) The *payoff opportunity set* $B(U,\eta)$ is the convex hull of $\{W(\alpha, \eta) | \alpha : Y \rightarrow A\}$ where

$$W(\alpha, \eta) = [W_1(\alpha, \eta), \ldots, W_m(\alpha, \eta)] \quad \text{and}$$

$$W_i(\alpha, \eta) = \sum_{y \in Y} U(z_i, \alpha(y)) \, \phi(y | z_i, \eta).$$

THEOREM 4 (BLACKWELL). *In the assumed finite setting, all of the following conditions are equivalent:*

(1) $E(U|\eta) \geq E(U|\eta')$ for all choice problems for which Z is payoff adequate;
(2) $P > P'$;
(3) $\Lambda > \Lambda'$;
(4) $\Lambda \mathscr{B} \Lambda'$;

(5) $(\pi, q) \, \Theta \, (\pi', q')$;

(6) $\pi > \pi'$;

(7) $(\pi, q) \, \xi \, (\pi', q')$;

(8) $B(U, \eta') \cap B(U, \eta)$.

Hopefully, this provides some indication of the "roots" of our only general result on comparing information structures. The proof is somewhat long. I suggest you work through Marschak and Miyasawa [1968] first, then McGuire's paper in McGuire and Radner [1972], and then the original Blackwell papers [Blackwell and Girshick, 1954].

The "Cost and Value" Euphemism

Turning to the question of analyzing costly information alternatives, we often refer to the problem in terms of the "cost and value" of the information. The typical special order analysis is probably a good analogy. The only difficulty is that *cost* and *value* are ambiguous terms; and, when made precise, they are cumbersome at best to work with.

To begin, consider a familiar expression for value of information: "the most you could pay and be as well off with the information as without" [Demski and Feltham, 1976, p. 25]. Surely you would never pay a fixed price in excess of such an amount. But can you say more; does value defined in this way "correctly" rank information alternatives?

Consider the following example:

Outcome structure:

	s_1	s_2	s_3
a_1	\$50	\$50	0
a_2	0	0	\$60

Preferences and beliefs:

$$U(x) = ln(100 + x)$$

$$\phi(s_i) = 1/3, i = 1, 2, 3.$$

Information:

	State Partition	Cost
η^0:	$\{s_1, s_2, s_3\}$	\$0
η^1:	$\{\{s_1, s_2\}, \{s_3\}\}$	5
η^2:	$\{\{s_1\}, \{s_2, s_3\}\}$	3

Expected utility analysis:

$$E(U|\eta^0) = 2/3\, ln(100 + 50) + 1/3\, ln(100) = 4.88$$

$$E(U|\eta^1) = 2/3\, ln(100 + 50 - 5) + 1/3\, ln(100 + 60 - 5) = 5.00$$

$$E(U|\eta^2) = 1/3\, ln(100 + 50 - 3) + 1/3\, ln(100 - 3) + 1/3\, ln(100 + 60 - 3) = 4.87$$

Buying prices ("value" as defined above):

$$ln(100) = 2/3\, ln(100 + 50 - \underline{\underline{30.26}}) + 1/3\, ln(100 - \underline{\underline{30.26}})$$

$$ln(100) = 2/3\, ln(100 + 50 - \underline{\underline{53.22}}) + 1/3\, ln(100 + 60 - \underline{\underline{53.22}})$$

$$ln(100) = 1/3\, ln(100 + 50 - \underline{\underline{32.86}}) + 1/3\, ln(100 - \underline{\underline{32.86}}) + 1/3\, ln(100 + 60 - \underline{\underline{32.86}})$$

Selling prices

$$ln(100 + \underline{\underline{31.04}}) = 4.88 = E(U|\eta^0)$$

$$ln(100 + \underline{\underline{48.26}}) = 5.00 = E(U|\eta^1)$$

$$ln(100 + \underline{\underline{30.82}}) = 4.87 = E(U|\eta^2)$$

Another example is in Marschak and Radner [1972, Chapter 2].

	s_1	s_2	s_3	s_4
a_1	1	0	−100	−100
a_2	−100	−100	1	0
a_3	.4	−100	.4	−100
a_4	−100	.4	−100	.4
a_5	0	0	0	0

With $\phi(s_i) = 1/4$ $(i = 1, \ldots, 4)$ and $U(x) = x$ for $x \leq 1/2$ or $[1/2 + .2(x - 1/2)]$ for $x > 1/2$, consider

$$\eta^0 : \{s_1, s_2, s_3, s_4\}$$

$$\eta^1 : \{\{s_1, s_2\}, \{s_3, s_4\}\}$$

$$\eta^2 : \{\{s_1, s_3\}, \{s_2, s_4\}\}$$

$$E(U|\eta^0) = 0$$

$$E(U|\eta^1) = .3$$

$$E(U|\eta^2) = .4$$

You can easily check that minimum selling prices are 0, .3, .4, respectively, while maximum buying prices are 0, .5, .4, respectively.

Note that some regularity issues are present here,[4] but the real question is the inconsistency in rankings. A little reflection ought to convince you that the selling price representation is correct (more "wealth" is better than less "wealth.") Hence the buying representation is incorrect. The difficulty is risk aversion. In fact, it can be shown that with *decreasing* risk aversion (selling price increases with increasing initial "wealth") and desirable lotteries, the buying price $\leq$ the selling price, while the buying price $\geq$ the selling price for increasing risk aversion (see LaValle [1968]). Of course, the two are equal with constant risk aversion (the extreme form of which is risk-neutral behavior).

Observe, now, that we may with some calculation provide a cost and value of information representation of $E(U|\eta)$. *Define* value-cost as the minimum selling price. Use the "actual cost" if it is fixed; if it is random, use its certainty equivalent. (Value is then the minimum selling price when initial "wealth" is reduced by the cost.)

The point is quite simple. We are accustomed to thinking in cost and value terms and even to defining value as buying price. We typically illustrate all of this with a risk-neutral example. While this is fine in any constant risk aversion case, in general it is incorrect. Indeed, placing the problem in cost and value terms appears to be an overly cumbersome way to do the analysis.

Moreover, the "cost" is often quite subtle because we often produce the information rather than purchase it from the local merchant. For example, we change our advertising to see what happens, hire new employees at entry level positions, and so on.

We close this general discussion with an example of "learning by doing" inspired by Grossman, Kihlstrom, and Mirman [1977]. Two periods are present and two commodities may be purchased with the opportunity set $(a, b) \in \{(2,0), (1,1), (0,2)\}$. The outcome in each period will be $x = 1.6b + s \cdot a + e$, where $s \in \{1,2\}$ and $e \in \{-1,1\}$. With the $(1,1)$ combination we have

	$e = -1$	1
$s = 1$	1.6	3.6
2	2.6	4.6

while with $(2,0)$ we have

	$e = -1$	1
$s = 1$	1	3
2	3	5

Also, the individual is risk-neutral and is indifferent between consumption in the two periods (i.e., no discounting). Also, $\phi(s) = \phi(e) = 1/2$; s is fixed but e varies each period and the two periods are independent.

First, suppose consumption in the second period *cannot* depend on the first period's outcome. By inspection, the optimal consumption is $a = 0$, $b = 2$ in each period with an expected utility of $[1.5(0) + 1.6(2)] + [1.5(0) + 1.6(2)] = 6.4$.

Second, suppose second-period consumption *can* depend on the first period's outcome. Also note that the (1, 1) consumption schedule will precisely identify $s \in \{1, 2\}$. The optimal consumption schedule here is $a = 1$, $b = 1$ in the *first* period. If $x = 1.6$ or 3.6 obtains, then use $a = 0$, $b = 2$ in the second period. Otherwise, use $a = 2$, $b = 0$. The expected utility is $[1.5(1) + 1.6(1)] + [1/2(2(2) + 1.6(0)) + 1/2(1(0) + 1.6(2))] = 6.7$.

How do you interpret this? You consume good a in the initial period in order to produce information. The information, in turn, is used in selecting a second-period consumption schedule. How do you interpret each term in brackets in the two expected utility expressions? Can you place a learning interpretation on these terms? Is it also clear that introducing the possibility of revising second-period plans will not lower your first-period consumption of the questionable commodity, a?

Finally, can you place a cost and value interpretation on the story? (Be careful because I have presented the example with a risk-neutral setting.) In any event, note that $a > 0$ in the first period plays a dual role: it provides consumption and it provides information. Decomposition (e.g., into only consumption aspects) is our first exercise in the next lecture.

Notes

1. See Blackwell and Girshick [1954], Marschak and Radner [1972], and McGuire [1972].
2. To illustrate one, merely *assign*

$$U(a^4) = 4$$

$$U(a^3) = \begin{cases} 4 \text{ if } a^4 \sim a^3 \\ 3 \text{ otherwise} \end{cases}$$

$$U(a^2) = \begin{cases} U(a^3) \text{ if } a^3 \sim a^2 \\ 2 \text{ otherwise} \end{cases}$$

$$U(a^1) = \begin{cases} U(a^2) \text{ if } a^2 \sim a^1 \\ 1 \text{ otherwise} \end{cases}$$

This satisfies the inequalities, as does any strictly increasing transformation.

3. See pp. 45–82, following.

4. For example, real valued outcome function, continuous and strictly increasing $U(\cdot)$, etc. See LaValle [1968] for additional discussion.

References

Anscombe, F., and Aumann, R. "A Definition of Subjective Probability." *Annals of Mathematical Statistics,* March 1963.

Blackwell, D., and Girshick, M. A. *Theory of Games and Statistical Decisions.* New York: John Wiley & Sons, 1954.

Demski, J., and Feltham, G. *Cost Determination: A Conceptual Approach.* Ames, Iowa: Iowa State University Press, 1976.

Grossman, S.; Kihlstrom, R.; and Mirman, L. "A Bayesian Approach to the Production of Information and Learning by Doing." *Review of Economic Studies,* Oct. 1977.

Krantz, D. H.; Luce, R. D.; Suppes, P.; and Tversky, A. *Foundations of Measurement.* New York: Academic Press, 1971.

LaValle, I. H. "On Cash Equivalents and Information Evaluation in Decisions under Uncertainty, Parts I, II, and III." *Journal of the American Statistical Association,* March 1968.

McGuire, C. B. "Comparisons of Information Structures." In *Decision and Organization,* ed. by C. B. McGuire and R. Radner. New York: American Elsevier, 1972.

———, and Radner, R. (eds.). *Decision and Organization.* New York: American Elsevier, 1972.

Marschak, J., and Miyasawa, K. "Economic Comparability of Information Systems." *International Economic Review,* June 1968.

Marschak, J., and Radner, R. *Economic Theory of Teams.* New Haven: Yale University Press, 1972.

Mock, T. J. *Measurement and Accounting Information Criteria,* Studies in Accounting Research #13. American Accounting Association, 1976.

Savage, L. J. *The Foundations of Statistics.* New York: John Wiley & Sons, 1954.

von Neumann, J., and Morgenstern, O. *Theory of Games and Economic Behavior.* Princeton, N.J: Princeton University Press, 1947.

INTERNATIONAL ECONOMIC REVIEW
Vol. 15, No. 1, February, 1974

A BAYESIAN MODEL OF DEMAND FOR INFORMATION ABOUT PRODUCT QUALITY*

BY RICHARD KIHLSTROM[1]

INTRODUCTION

WHENEVER THERE IS UNCERTAINTY about product quality a consumer may benefit from obtaining information about the performance of commodities; indeed the choice of what information to purchase becomes an essential part of the consumption decision. Consumers acquire information from a variety of sources. For some commodities it is possible to test small amounts of a product before making a large purchase; taking a test drive in a car is an example. In other cases information is gathered informally from acquaintances. In yet other instances, information is supplied by newspapers, magazines and consumer information organizations. Regardless of the method used to collect information, the acquisition process is usually costly, sometimes in terms of time and often in terms of money. When the consumer makes the decision to purchase information he weighs these costs against the benefits of being informed.

The purpose of this paper is to develop a theory which explains consumer expenditures for product quality information. The theory is related to the neoclassical consumer theory but differs from it in several critical respects. There are important reasons why the standard consumer theory is inappropriate for the study of information demand. The primary reason is that information is fundamentally different from other commodities, and the difference is crucial. Consumers demand most other commodities for the desirable attributes they possess, whereas information possesses none of these attributes. A consumer purchases information because it helps him to make "better" purchases. The demand for information is therefore a derived demand that only arises when product quality is uncertain. These special features of information may give rise to demand behavior quite different from that usually observed for commodities. Since the neoclassical theory cannot be interpreted to incorporate the special features of information it is unable to explain the unique properties of information demand.

The theory presented in this paper should also be constrasted to Stigler's early contribution [**10**] to the economic theory of information. Stigler investigated consumer demand for information about prices of products. He did not treat the demand for information about product quality. Nor is it possible to simply extend his analysis to explain consumer demand for product quality information. The demands for the two types of information arise for different reasons

* Manuscript received June 12, 1973; revised September 27, 1973.
[1] This research was supported by the National Science Foundation under grant GS-3046. The author is grateful for this support. He also wishes to thank Hugo Sonnenschein for his comments on an earlier draft of this paper.

and each requires a separate explanation.

The theory of information demand presented in this paper is based on a model of the consumer in which product quality is uncertain and information increases utility by making better purchases possible. The utility of information is captured by using the Bayesian "preposterior" analysis. Product quality uncertainty is introduced by using a generalized version of a framework suggested by Lancaster. Commodities are demanded by consumers because they possess desirable attributes, and uncertainty about product quality is introduced by assuming that the amount of an attribute possessed by a commodity is a random variable.

By making use of a special hypothesis about the utility function, the model can be used to answer several questions about the determinants of demand for information. The questions considered are of two types. First, we ask how a consumer's demand for information is affected by his income and by the price of information. Specifically, do wealthy consumers demand more information than low income consumers? Also, does information demand fall when the price of information rises? Thus we first investigate whether information is a Giffen good or an inferior good. These questions arise naturally when the demand for any commodity is being studied. There is another question which applies only to information demand. Namely, which commodities will consumers choose to demand information about? Intuition suggests that several factors are important. Included among these are the consumer's familiarity with the product and his expectations about quality. We should also expect commodity prices and the consumer's preferences to play important roles in determining information demand. The model enables us to answer several questions about the effects of these factors on the demand for information. For example, we are able to determine what effect familiarity with a product has on the demand for information. Intuitively a consumer should buy less information about a product that is familiar; the analysis of the model constructed here confirms this expectation. We are also able to use the model to investigate whether more information will be demanded about a high priced product than a less expensive one. In addition, the model can be applied to ask whether a consumer is more likely to expend resources investigating a commodity if he expects it to be of high quality. A number of other related questions are also considered.

Several important features of the model constructed in this paper are based on ideas found in the statistics literature. The papers of Blackwell [**1**] and [**2**] and the book by Raiffa and Schlaiffer [**8**] are sources that proved to be particularly suggestive.

The model is a special case of the general Bayesian decision model described in Raiffa and Schlaiffer. Their model can be applied to any decision maker who has the opportunity to receive statistical information. By restricting our investigation to consumers who demand product quality information, we are able to carry the analysis further than Raiffa and Schlaiffer. In particular, we are able to characterize the optimal information demand and use comparative static techniques to study the economic factors which determine information demand.

The treatment of information in the model was suggested by the papers of Blackwell that deal with the "comparison of experiments." The theorems proved by Blackwell have been discussed in the economics literature by Marschak and Miyasawa [**6**] and Marschak and Radner [**7**].

1. THE MODEL—AN INFORMAL INTRODUCTION

This section introduces a two commodity example that is used in the remainder of the paper to analyze the demand for product quality information. This simple example captures the essential features of the general situation in which product quality is uncertain and costly information is available to the consumer. Thus much of the present analysis is useful in more general contexts. By eliminating less important details, the example enables us to focus on the central questions without the necessity for concern about distracting and inessential complications.

Suppose the consumer in question consumes two commodities which are bought and sold in competitive markets. We will call these commodities meat and cereal and discuss a situation in which unreliable food processing techniques result in cereal of uncertain food value. A number of alternative interpretations are, of course, possible; none of the results proved here depend on the specific interpretation given.

For simplicity, we assume that each commodity possesses a specific attribute which is desired by the consumer; meat provides proteins, and cereal provides carbohydrates. Since meat processing techniques do not usually result in a loss of food value, it is reasonable to assume that each pound of meat consumed supplies a fixed amount of protein. In such a situation the consumer will know exactly how much protein he is getting when he buys a pound of meat. If the preparation of cereal for consumption involves an unreliable process, a random amount of food value may be lost in processing. In that case the quantity of carbohydrates supplied by a unit of cereal will vary from unit to unit and the consumer will be uncertain about the quality of the cereal he buys.

If cereal is a commodity that is unfamiliar to the consumer, he will lack a reliable estimate of its average quality. We assume that it is possible for the consumer to improve his estimate of average quality by consulting research laboratories. The research laboratories examine samples of cereal and measure the amount of carbohydrates supplied. A laboratory will examine samples of any size. If large samples are studied, the quality of the cereal can be closely estimated. With small samples the estimates are not so reliable. However, the cost of observing a large sample exceeds that of a small sample, and this is reflected in the price charged to the consumer for samples of varying size. To be precise, let one unit of information be defined as the observation of a sample containing exactly one unit of cereal. If the consumer chooses to acquire, say, θ units of information then he asks the laboratory to examine a sample containing θ units of cereal. The market for information is competitive in the sense that there is a competitively determined price for information and every unit of information traded is sold at that price.

If the information provided by a sample were costless, the more informed choices made possible by its acquisition would clearly make the consumer better off. The problem is that information is not free. It must be paid for with income that could otherwise be used to buy the commodities. Furthermore, the better information provided by a larger sample costs more. Thus the consumer will choose to acquire a certain amount of information if the utility of the gain (better consumption choices resulting from its acquisition) exceeds the utility of the cost (the decrease in income which would otherwise be available for consumption of commodities).

1.2. *The formal model.* In the example just described, the consumer gets utility by consuming two "attributes," protein and carbohydrates, which are obtained from two commodities, meat and cereal, respectively. Meat is a "certain" commodity in the sense that each unit of meat provides a unit of protein with certainty; i.e., if we let m be the amount of meat consumed and p the amount of protein, then $m = p$. Cereal, however, is an "uncertain" commodity; i.e., the amount of carbohydrates provided by a unit of cereal is a random variable. Let c be the amount of cereal consumed and t the amount of carbohydrates provided by the cereal. The variable t is random because the amount of carbohydrates provided by each unit of cereal bought is uncertain. If we let $\tilde{\tau}$ represent the random variable "carbohydrates per unit of cereal bought," then $\tilde{t} = c\tilde{\tau}$.[2] Since it is impossible to obtain negative amounts of carbohydrates, the random variable $\tilde{\tau}$ takes only nonnegative values. In fact, we assume that $\tilde{\tau} = e^{\tilde{\varepsilon}}$ where $\tilde{\varepsilon}$ is a normal random variable and interpret the probability distribution of $\tilde{\varepsilon}$ as an a priori distribution which describes the consumer's initial subjective beliefs about what the value of $\tilde{\varepsilon}$ is likely to be. The probability that $\tilde{\varepsilon}$ lies in an interval (a, b) is the subjective probability (degree of confidence) that the consumer assigns to the possibility that each unit of cereal he buys will provide an amount of carbohydrates which is larger than e^a but smaller than e^b. If we let μ_0 be the mean and $1/\phi$ be the variance of the a priori distribution of $\tilde{\varepsilon}$, the parameter μ_0 is a measure of how optimistic the consumer is about the quality of the product. Alternatively μ_0 can be interpreted as his estimate of ε. When μ_0 is large, he expects large values of $\tilde{\tau}$, since these have high probability. The parameter ϕ is a measure of how confident he is about his initial expectations. When ϕ is large the variance is small and the a priori probability that $\tilde{\tau}$ will be close to e^{μ_0} is high. This is interpreted to mean that the consumer is confident about his estimate. Since consumers are usually more confident about familiar products, ϕ can also be interpreted as a measure of the consumer's familiarity with the commodity cereal.

The consumer's preferences for various attribute bundles (p, t) are described by the utility function $u(p, t)$, and, if no information about ε is available, his utility function of (m, c) is the expected utility

[2] Throughout the paper random variables are denoted by a tilde, "~."

$$(1.1) \qquad U(m, c) = \int_{-\infty}^{+\infty} u(m, ce^{\varepsilon}) f\left(\varepsilon \mid \mu_0, \frac{1}{\phi}\right) d\varepsilon.^3$$

In this way the consumer's preferences over *commodity* bundles (m, c) are derived from

(i) the preferences, represented by u, over the attribute bundles and

(ii) his expectations about the amount of t that c will deliver. These expectations are represented by $f(\varepsilon \mid \mu_0, (1/\phi))$.

The consumer then chooses (m, c) to maximize (1. 1) subject to his budget constraint $p_m m + p_c c = I$. Denote the optimal choice by (m_0, c_0). If u is strictly concave, U is also and (m_0, c_0) is unique.

Information is available from a research laboratory. The information comes in the form of observations of the quantity of carbohydrates supplied by each unit of cereal in a sample of θ (an integer) units.[4] These observations provide direct information about ε, since the distribution of each observation is assumed to depend on ε. Specifically, let $\tilde{y}_i$ represent the log of the quantity of carbohydrates supplied by the i-th observed unit of cereal. The distribution of $\tilde{y}_i$ is assumed to be normal with mean ε and variance 1. The observations, $\tilde{y}_1, \ldots, \tilde{y}_\theta$ are assumed to be independent. The cost to the consumer of observing a sample of size θ is $q\theta$ where q is the competitively determined price of observing one unit of cereal.

The consumer's opportunities for acquiring information can be conveniently summarized by making use of the fact that the sample mean

$$\tilde{x}_\theta = \frac{1}{\theta} \sum_{i=1}^{\theta} \tilde{y}_i$$

is a sufficient statistic, for ε, of $\tilde{y}_1, \ldots, \tilde{y}_\theta$. This means that observing $\tilde{x}_\theta$ is equivalent to observing $\tilde{y}_1, \ldots, \tilde{y}_\theta$. Thus the consumer can, in essence, choose to observe any one of an infinite number of normal random variables $\{\tilde{x}_\theta\}_{\theta=1}^{\infty}$, where the mean of $\tilde{x}_\theta$ is ε and its variance is $1/\theta$. The cost of observing $\tilde{x}_\theta$ is $q\theta$. In this formulation, information is available only in discrete amounts. Since it is convenient to have a model in which information is available in continuously variable amounts, we will assume that the laboratory provides a richer class of samples. Formally, we suppose that the consumer can choose to observe any one of an infinite number of independent random variables $\{\tilde{x}_\theta\}_{\theta \epsilon (0, \infty)}$, where $\tilde{x}_\theta$ is normal with mean ε and variance $1/\theta$. We will refer to θ as the amount of information obtained by observing $\tilde{x}_\theta$. And we will assume that the cost of observing $\tilde{x}_\theta$ is $q\theta$ where q is the price of information.

We have referred to θ as the amount of information provided by the observation of $\tilde{x}_\theta$. A rigorous justification for this terminology requires the derivation of an expression for the utility of observing $\tilde{x}_\theta$. Using such an expression it is

[3] Throughout the paper $f(x \mid \mu, \sigma^2)$ is the normal density function with mean μ and variance σ^2.

[4] In the analysis of this paper we will assume that sequential sampling is impossible. In other words the sample size θ must be determined before any observations are made.

possible to prove that the utility of observing $\tilde{x}_\theta$ is an increasing function of θ.[5] At this point, however, we can give an intuitive indication of why θ is an appropriate measure of information. First, note that when θ and θ' are integers, if $\theta' > \theta$ then $\tilde{x}_{\theta'}$ is more informative than $\tilde{x}_\theta$ in the sense that observing $\tilde{x}_{\theta'}$ rather than $\tilde{x}_{\theta'}$ is equivalent to observing $\theta' - \theta$ additional independent $\tilde{y}_i$'s. Also, notice that as θ rises, the variance of $\tilde{x}_\theta$ decreases and there is an increase in the probability that the realization of $\tilde{x}_\theta$ will be close to ε. Thus if θ is large, the consumer can be confident, but not certain, that ε will be large when he observes a large value of x; i.e., observing x when θ is large is much like observing ε.

We can now derive the consumer's utility function of information and describe how the consumer decides which sample to observe. First though, consider the extreme case in which the consumer can have perfect information about ε; i.e., he is able to observe ε before making his choice of m and c. Because of the simplicity of this extreme case, it is instructive to derive the utility of perfect information before deriving the utility of imperfect information. In the derivation we will assume that the information is free. The first point to emphasize is that the consumer can and does acquire the right to observe ε (the value taken by $\tilde{\varepsilon}$) before ε is actually observed. Thus the utility of perfect information is more accurately described as the utility of the opportunity to observe ε. It is the consumer's expected utility once he has acquired the right to observe ε, but it is computed before he actually knows ε. The derivation of the utility of perfect information is therefore a two step procedure. The first step is to compute, for each possible ε, the consumer's utility if $\tilde{\varepsilon}$ is observed to equal ε. This is the consumer's *ex post* utility. The second step is to compute the consumer's *ex ante* expected utility of information. In computing this expected value the consumer's *ex post* utility of observing $\tilde{\varepsilon} = \varepsilon$ is weighted by the probability that $\tilde{\varepsilon}$ will equal ε. The resulting expectation is the *ex ante* utility of perfect information.

We can now carry out the computation. Let $v(\varepsilon)$ represent the consumer's utility if $\tilde{\varepsilon}$ is observed to equal ε. The first step is to compute $v(\varepsilon)$. Note that when $\tilde{\varepsilon}$ is observed to equal ε, the consumer will choose c and m to maximize $u(m, ce^\varepsilon)$ subject to his budget constraint. If $(c(\varepsilon), m(\varepsilon))$ is the optimal choice then

$$v(\varepsilon) = u(m(\varepsilon), c(\varepsilon)e^\varepsilon)\,.$$

Performing the second step in the derivation, the utility of perfect information is seen to equal

$$Ev(\varepsilon) = \int_{-\infty}^{+\infty} u(m(\varepsilon),\ c(\varepsilon)e^\varepsilon)f\left(\varepsilon \middle| \mu_0, \frac{1}{\phi}\right)d\varepsilon\,.^6$$

Returning to the case of imperfect information the situation is similar. In

[5] The proof is outlined in footnote 9 below.

[6] Using this expression for $Ev(\varepsilon)$ we can prove that the consumer is better off with free perfect information than with no information at all. To prove this note that, for each ε, $v(\varepsilon) \geqq u(m_0, c_0\, e^\varepsilon)$. Integrating on both sides of this inequality yields $Ev(\varepsilon) \geqq U(m_0, c_0)$.

this case the consumer acquires the right to observe x, the value taken by $\tilde{x}_\theta$, before making a choice of m and c. The utility of θ units of (imperfect) information is the consumer's expected utility once he has acquired this right, and it is computed before the value of x is actually observed. Again a two step procedure is followed. First for each possible x, the *ex post* utility of observing $\tilde{x}_\theta = x$ is computed. Second, the *ex ante* expected utility of owning the right to observe $\tilde{x}_\theta$ is computed by weighting the utility of observing that $\tilde{x}_\theta$ equals x by the probability that $\tilde{x}_\theta$ equals x.

To perform the first step assume that the consumer has chosen to buy θ units of information. If $\tilde{x}_\theta$ is observed to equal x, the consumer can use this observation to revise his expectations about ε and to adjust his choice of m and c accordingly. For example, if x is large, he will expect ε to be large and choose a consumption bundle (m, c) that is appropriate for a large value of ε. Since we are assuming that the consumer is a Bayesian decision maker, his revised expectations about ε will be in the form of a normal posterior probability distribution of $\tilde{\varepsilon}$ given x. This distribution will have mean $\mu_{x,\theta}$ and variance σ_θ^2 where

$$\mu_{x,\theta} = \frac{\theta}{\phi + \theta} x + \frac{\phi}{\phi + \theta} \mu_0,$$

and

(1. 2)
$$\sigma_\theta^2 = \frac{1}{\phi + \theta}.$$ [7]

The posterior mean $\mu_{x,\theta}$ can be interpreted as the revised estimate of ε.

The change in expectations results in a revised utility function of the commodities. After observing x, the utility of (m, c) is given by the a posteriori expected utility

$$U_{x,\theta}(m, c) = \int_{-\infty}^{+\infty} u(m, ce^{\varepsilon}) f\left(\varepsilon \,|\, \mu_{x,\theta}, \sigma_\theta^2\right) d\varepsilon .$$

The consumer's remaining income is $I - q\theta$ which can be used to buy m and c. Thus he chooses $c(x, \theta)$ and $m(x, \theta)$ to maximize his revised utility function $U_{x,\theta}(m, c)$ subject to his reduced budget constraint $p_c c + p_m m = I - q\theta$. The utility of observing x when θ units of information have been purchased, i.e., the utility of observing x as the realization of $\tilde{x}_\theta$, is $U_{x,\theta}(m(x, \theta), c(x, \theta))$.

This completes the first step in the derivation of the utility of θ units of information. The second step is required to complete the derivation. First note that the consumer's a priori expectations about the values of x that are likely to be observed are represented by the marginal probability distribution of $\tilde{x}_\theta$. This marginal distribution is easily derived from $f(x \,|\, \varepsilon, (1/\theta))$, the conditional density of $\tilde{x}_\theta$ given ε, and $f(\varepsilon \,|\, \mu_0, (1/\phi))$, the marginal density of ε. In fact, under the normality assumptions made so far, the marginal density of $\tilde{x}_\theta$ is

[7] See Raiffa and Schlaiffer, [8].

$$f\left(x\mu_0, \frac{1}{\theta} + \frac{1}{\phi}\right) = \int_{-\infty}^{+\infty} f\left(x \mid \varepsilon, \frac{1}{\theta}\right) f\left(\varepsilon \mid \mu_0, \frac{1}{\phi}\right) d\varepsilon .$$

Using the marginal distribution of $\tilde{x}_\theta$, the utility of θ units of information is given by the expected utility

$$\text{(1.4)} \qquad H(\theta) = \int_{-\infty}^{+\infty} U_{x,\theta}(m(x, \theta), c(x, \theta)) f\left(x \mid \mu_0, \frac{1}{\theta} + \frac{1}{\phi}\right) dx .$$ [8]

In this model, the consumer's demand for information is the value of θ which maximizes the utility function $H(\theta)$. Note that $H(\theta)$ is a function of the prices (q, p_c, p_m), income, I, and the parameters μ_0 and ϕ which determine the consumer's expectations about product quality. The utility function u is also a determinant of $H(\theta)$. As a result, the consumer's demand for information is a function of prices, income, expectations and his preferences for the attributes. The remainder of the paper investigates the functional relationship implied by the model, between these variables and information demand.

Before proceeding to the analysis of information demand we conclude this section with a brief comment on the opportunities for information consumption assumed in the model. Note that the consumer could spend $q\theta$ on information in a variety of ways; e.g., he could buy one observation $\tilde{x}_\theta$ or he could have any two independent observations $\tilde{x}_{\theta_1}$ and $\tilde{x}_{\theta_2}$ such that $\theta_1 + \theta_2 = \theta$. We have assumed that he will always buy $\tilde{x}_\theta$. If sequential sampling were possible; i.e., if the consumer could make the decision to observe $\tilde{x}_{\theta_2}$ after observing $\tilde{x}_{\theta_1}$; this assumption could fail to hold. In other words with sequential sampling a situation might arise in which the consumer preferred to observe $\tilde{x}_{\theta_1}$ and $\tilde{x}_{\theta_2}$ rather than $\tilde{x}_\theta$, When sequential sampling is ruled out (as it is here) this possibility is eliminated; there is no incentive for the consumer to buy $\tilde{x}_{\theta_1}$ and $\tilde{x}_{\theta_2}$ rather than $\tilde{x}_\theta$. This occurs because $\tilde{x}_\theta$ has the same distribution (conditional on ε) as

$$\tilde{x} = \frac{1}{\theta}(\theta_1 \tilde{x}_{\theta_1} + \theta_2 \tilde{x}_{\theta_2})$$

and $\tilde{x}$ is a sufficient statistic of $\tilde{x}_{\theta_1}$ and $\tilde{x}_{\theta_2}$.[9] As a result the utility of observing $\tilde{x}_\theta$ is equal to the utility of observing both $\tilde{x}_{\theta_1}$ and $\tilde{x}_{\theta_2}$.

2. THE DETERMINATION OF INFORMATION DEMAND—A SPECIAL CASE

In the neoclassical theory of the consumer, commodity demand has been studied at two levels of generality. On the one hand, Hicks [3] and Samuelson [9] obtained very general results which are stated in terms of the matrix of

[8] A straightforward extension of the argument outlined in footnote 6 can be used to prove that when $q = 0$, $H(\theta)$ exceeds $U(m_0, c_0)$. In other words when information is free the consumer is better off observing $\tilde{x}_\theta$ than he is with no information at all.

[9] The fact that $\tilde{x}_\theta$ is distributed as a sufficient satistic of $\tilde{x}_{\theta_1}$ and $\tilde{x}_{\theta_2}$ can also be used to prove that $H(\theta)$ is an increasing function of θ. The proof makes use of the fact that the consumer prefers to observe both $\tilde{x}_{\theta_1}$ and $\tilde{x}_{\theta_2}$ rather than just $\tilde{x}_{\theta_1}$. This obvious fact is proved formally by an argument similar to the one outlined in footnote 6.

Slutsky substitution terms. On the other hand, by making use of special assumptions about the consumer's utility function the neoclassical theory has also led to many fruitful specific hypotheses about commodity demand. In particular, the Cobb-Douglas and CES utility functions are often used in this way. The model of information demand just described can be investigated at two analogous levels of generality. The general theorems are derived in a separate paper [4]. The present paper proceeds at the less general level. A special assumption is made about the utility function of attributes and the implications of this assumption are developed. The advantage of the less general approach lies in the strength of the results obtained. In [4] the usual price is paid for generality; the general theorems obtained there are much weaker than the results proved in this paper.

We assume that the utility function is

$$u(p, t) = -\alpha\frac{1}{p} - \beta\frac{1}{t} \tag{2. 1}$$

where $\alpha, \beta > 0$, which is a CES utility function with elasticity of substitution one-half. This utility function has several virtues. First, it is sufficiently tractable to enable us to obtain reasonably specific hypotheses about the determinants of information demand. In addition, this class of utility functions is rich enough to allow for an interesting range of demand behavior.

Using (2. 1), the utility of information $H(\theta)$ is derived and the demand for information is characterized. It is then possible to use standard comparative static techniques to describe how income, prices, expectations and the parameters α, β of the utility function affect information demand.

With the utility function (2. 1),

$$U_{x,\theta}(m, c) = -\alpha\frac{1}{m} - \beta\left(e^{-\mu_{x,\theta}+(1/2)(1/(\phi+\theta))}\right)\frac{1}{c} \tag{2. 2}$$

and the consumer chooses

$$\begin{aligned} m(x, \theta) &= \frac{I - q\theta}{\left(p_c p_m \dfrac{\beta}{\alpha}\right)^{(1/2)}\left(e^{-(1/2)\mu_{x,\theta}+(1/4)(1/(\phi+\theta))}\right) + p_m} \\ c(x, \theta) &= \frac{I - q\theta}{\left(p_c p_m \dfrac{\alpha}{\beta}\right)^{(1/2)}\left(e^{(1/2)\mu_{x,\theta}-(1/4)(1/(\phi+\theta))}\right) + p_c}. \end{aligned} \tag{2. 3}$$

As in the general case, the utility of θ units of information is derived by substituting (2. 3) in (2. 2) and then taking the expected value by integrating over all possible x's. To perform this computation, we use

$$\int_{-\infty}^{+\infty} e^{-a\mu_{x,\theta}} f\left(x \,|\, \mu_0, \frac{1}{\theta} + \frac{1}{\phi}\right) dx = e^{-a\mu_0+(1/2)a^2(\phi^{-?}/(\phi^{-1}+\theta^{-1}))}.$$

Then

$$H(\theta) = -\frac{N(\theta)}{I - q\theta}, \tag{2.4}$$

where

$$N(\theta) = \alpha p_m + \beta p_c e^{-\mu_0 + (1/2)(1/\phi)} + 2(\alpha\beta p_c p_m)^{(1/2)} e^{-(1/2)\mu_0 + v(\theta,\phi)}$$

and

$$v(\theta, \phi) = \frac{1}{4}\,\frac{(1/2)\theta + \phi}{\phi(\theta + \phi)}.$$

The consumer's demand for information is the value of θ which maximizes the utility of information function $H(\theta)$.

Our first proposition sets the stage for later results. It states that, for the utility function (2. 1), the consumer's demand for information is unique. It also uses the first order maximum condition to derive an equation that characterizes the optimal information demand when that demand is positive. The propositions which follows use this equation to investigate the effect of income, prices and expectations on the information demands made by consumers, who actually purchase information. Later propositions investigate the circumstances in which consumers decide not to purchase information.

PROPOSITION 1. *If u is given by* (2. 1), *then* $H(\theta)$ *has a unique maximizer* $\hat{\theta}$ *in the interval* $[0, I/q]$. *If information demand is positive; i.e., if* $\hat{\theta} > 0$; *then*

$$\frac{I}{q} - \hat{\theta} = -\frac{N(\hat{\theta})}{\dfrac{\partial N(\hat{\theta})}{\partial \theta}}. \tag{2.5}$$

PROOF. The fact that H takes a maximum on the interval from $[0, I/q)$ is implied by the continuity of H and the fact that H approaches minus infinity as θ approaches (I/q).

To prove that the maximizing value $\hat{\theta}$ is unique, first differentiate H with respect to θ. The expression obtained is

$$\frac{\partial H}{\partial \theta} = -\frac{(I - q\theta)\dfrac{\partial N}{\partial \theta} + qN}{(I - q\theta)^2}$$

where $N(\theta)$ is defined above and

$$\frac{\partial N}{\partial \theta} = e^{-(1/2)\mu_0 + v(\theta,\phi)}\left(-\frac{1}{8}\,\frac{1}{(\theta + \phi)^2}\right) 2(p_c p_m \alpha\beta)^{(1/2)}.$$

Differentiating again

$$\frac{\partial^2 H}{\partial \theta^2} = -\frac{(I - q\theta)^3 \dfrac{\partial^2 N}{\partial \theta^2} + 2(I - q\theta)q\left[(I - q\theta)\dfrac{\partial N}{\partial \theta} + qN\right]}{(I - q\theta)^4},$$

where

$$\frac{\partial^2 N}{\partial\theta^2} = 2(p_c p_m \alpha\beta)^{(1/2)} e^{-(1/2)\mu_0 + v(\phi,\theta)} \left[\frac{1}{8}\left(\frac{1}{\theta+\phi}\right)^3\right]\left(2 + \frac{1}{8}\left(\frac{1}{\theta+\phi}\right)\right) > 0 .$$

Now suppose that $\hat{\theta}_1$ and $\hat{\theta}_2$ both maximize H, and that $\hat{\theta}_1 \neq \hat{\theta}_2$. In that case a local interior minimizer, θ^*, of H must exist somewhere between $\hat{\theta}_1$ and $\hat{\theta}_2$. The necessary conditions for a local minimizer imply

$$\frac{\partial H(\theta^*)}{\partial\theta} = 0$$

and

$$\frac{\partial^2 H(\theta^*)}{\partial\theta^2} \geq 0 .$$

But using the expressions just derived for $(\partial H/\partial\theta)$ and $(\partial^2 H/\partial\theta^2)$ it is easy to show that $(\partial H(\theta^*)/\partial\theta) = 0$ implies $(\partial^2 H(\theta^*)/\partial\theta^2) < 0$, a contradiction. So θ^* must fail to exist and $\hat{\theta}_1$ must equal $\hat{\theta}_2$. This proves the uniqueness of $\hat{\theta}$.

To prove that (2. 5) holds at $\hat{\theta}$ set the expression for $(\partial H/\partial\theta) = 0$ and re-arrange.||

Equation (2. 5) provides the basis for a comparative static investigation into the effects of prices, income and expectations on information demand. The effects of price and income are considered first. Proposition 2 demonstrates that information is neither a Giffen nor an inferior good.[10] That is it obeys the "law of demand" and wealthy consumers demand more information than less affluent consumers with the same preferences.

PROPOSITION 2. *Assume that the utility function is* (2. 1). *If* $\hat{\theta} > 0$ *then* $(\partial\hat{\theta}/\partial I) > 0$ *and* $(\partial\hat{\theta}/\partial q) < 0$; *i.e., information demand increases with income and falls when the price of information rises.*

PROOF. Implicitly differentiate (2. 5) and use the inequality

$$\frac{\partial}{\partial\theta}\left[\frac{N(\hat{\theta})}{\frac{\partial N(\hat{\theta})}{\partial\theta}}\right] < 0 .\|$$

We can now describe the effect of the consumer's a priori expectations on information demand. Recall that the consumer's expectations about product quality are represented by a normal probability distribution with mean μ_0 and variance ϕ. The parameter μ_0 has been interpreted as the consumer's estimate of product quality. When μ_0 is large, the consumer has high expectations about the quality of the uncertain product. The parameter ϕ measures the consumer's

[10] Since the model of information demand constructed in this paper differs from the neo-classical model of consumer demand, it is not immediately clear that a Slutsky equation applies to information demand. Therefore, it is at least conceivable that information may be a Giffen good but not an inferior good. That this cannot happen is proved in another paper [4].

confidence in his estimate of product quality. Large values of ϕ mean that the consumer is familiar with the uncertain product and confident in his a priori expectations about its quality. The next proposition makes use of these interpretations of μ_0 and ϕ. It asserts that the products which a consumer investigates most thoroughly are those which he expects to be of intermediate quality. In other words, it does not pay for the consumer to become well informed about products which he expects to be either very good or very bad. The proposition also demonstrates that consumers demand more information about unfamiliar products. The remarks which follow the statement of the proposition discuss the intuitive plausibility of these results.

PROPOSITION 3. *Suppose the utility function is* (2.1), $\hat{\theta} > 0$. *Then, other things equal, information demand is highest for commodities for which the expected quality level is neither very high nor very low; more precisely*

$$\frac{\partial \hat{\theta}}{\partial \mu_0} \geq 0 \quad \text{if} \quad \mu_0 - \frac{1}{2}\phi^{-1} \leqq \log \frac{\beta p_c}{\alpha p_m}$$
$$\leq 0 \quad \text{if} \quad \mu_0 - \frac{1}{2}\phi^{-1} \geqq \log \frac{\beta p_c}{\alpha p_m}.$$

In addition, the amount of information demanded about an uncertain product is a decreasing function of the consumer's confidence in his a priori expectations; formally

$$\frac{\partial \hat{\theta}}{\partial \phi} < 0.$$

REMARKS. That consumers buy more information about unfamiliar products is not surprising; but the result that either very high or very low expectations will lead to low information demand is less intuitive. To understand why this result is plausible consider the relationship between the consumer's commodity choices and the message x provided by the information acquired. By differentiating equation (2. 3) with respect to x, it is relatively easy to show that $\partial c/\partial x$ is approximately zero when e^{μ_0} is either very large or near zero. This means that the consumer's commodity choices are essentially independent of the observation x when the consumer has either very high or very low expectations. But if the consumer's decisions are independent of the observation x, the information obtained by observing x is of little value to the consumer. When the value of information is low the demand for information should be low.

PROOF. Implicitly differentiating the equation $\partial H(\hat{\theta})/\partial\theta = 0$ we obtain

$$\frac{\partial \hat{\theta}}{\partial \mu_0} = -\frac{\dfrac{\partial^2 H}{\partial \mu_0 \partial \theta}}{\dfrac{\partial^2 H}{\partial \theta^2}} = -\frac{(I - q\theta)\dfrac{\partial^2 N}{\partial \mu_0 \partial \theta} + q\dfrac{\partial N}{\partial \mu_0}}{(I - q\theta)^2 \dfrac{\partial^2 H}{\partial \theta^2}}.$$

It was shown in the proof of Proposition 1 that the denominator in this expression is negative. Now

$$\frac{\partial^2 N}{\partial \mu_0 \partial \theta} = -\frac{1}{2}\frac{\partial N}{\partial \theta} > 0\,, \text{ and}$$

$$\begin{aligned}\frac{\partial N}{\partial \mu_0} &= -\beta p_c e^{-\mu_0+1/2\phi} - (\alpha\beta p_c p_m)^{1/2} e^{-\mu_0/2+v(\theta,\phi)} \\ &= -N + \alpha p_m - 4(\theta+\phi)^2 \frac{\partial N}{\partial \theta}\,.\end{aligned}$$

Thus

$$\begin{aligned}&(I - q\theta)\frac{\partial^2 N}{\partial \mu_0 \partial \theta} + q\frac{\partial N}{\partial \mu_0} \\ &= -(I-q\theta)\frac{1}{2}\frac{\partial N}{\partial \theta} - q\left\{N - \alpha p_m + 4(\theta+\phi)^2\frac{\partial N}{\partial \theta}\right\} \\ &= q\frac{1}{2}\frac{\partial N}{\partial \theta}\left\{-\left(\frac{I}{q}-\theta\right) - 2\frac{N}{\frac{\partial N}{\partial \theta}} + \frac{2\alpha p_m}{\frac{\partial N}{\partial \theta}} - 8(\theta+\phi)^2\right\} \\ &= q\frac{1}{2}\frac{\partial N}{\partial \theta}\left\{-\frac{N}{\frac{\partial N}{\partial \theta}} + \frac{2\alpha p_m}{\frac{\partial N}{\partial \theta}} - 8(\theta+\phi)^2\right\}.\end{aligned}$$

This last equality follows from the first order condition (2. 5). Substituting

$$-2(p_c p_m \alpha\beta)^{(1/2)} e^{-(\mu_0/2)+v(\theta,\phi)}\left(\frac{1}{8}\,\frac{1}{(\theta+\phi)^2}\right)$$

for $\partial N/\partial \theta$ yields

$$\begin{aligned}&(I - q\theta)\frac{\partial^2 N}{\partial \mu_0 \partial \theta} + q\frac{\partial N}{\partial \mu_0} \\ &= q\frac{1}{2}\frac{\partial N}{\partial \theta}[8(\theta+\phi)^2]\left(\frac{N - 2\alpha p_m}{2(p_c p_m \alpha\beta)^{(1/2)} e^{-(\mu_0/2)+v(\theta,\phi)}} - 1\right) \\ &= q\frac{1}{2}\frac{\partial N}{\partial \theta}[8(\theta+\phi)^2] \times \\ &\quad \left(\frac{2(\alpha\beta p_m p_c)^{(1/2)} e^{-(\mu_0/2)+v(\theta,\phi)} + \beta p_c e^{-\mu_0+(1/2)\phi^{-1}} - \alpha p_m}{2(p_c p_m \alpha\beta)^{(1/2)} e^{-(\mu_0/2)+v(\theta,\phi)}} - 1\right) \\ &= q\frac{1}{2}\frac{\partial N}{\partial \theta}[8(\theta+\phi)^2]\left(\frac{\beta p_c e^{-\mu_0+(1/2)\phi^{-1}} - \alpha p_m}{2(p_c p_m \alpha\beta)^{(1/2)} e^{-(\mu_0/2)+v(\theta,\phi)}}\right).\end{aligned}$$

So

$$(I - q\theta)\frac{\partial^2 N}{\partial \mu_0 \partial \theta} + q\frac{\partial N}{\partial \mu_0} \geq 0$$

$$\text{iff } e^{-\mu_0+(1/2)\phi^{-1}} \geq \frac{\alpha p_m}{\beta p_c}$$

and

$$\frac{\partial\hat{\theta}}{\partial\mu_0} \geq 0 \quad \text{iff} \quad \mu_0 - \frac{1}{2}\phi^{-1} \leq \log\left(\frac{\beta p_c}{\alpha p_m}\right).$$

To prove $(\partial\hat{\theta}/\partial\phi) < 0$, again implicitly differentiate $\partial H(\hat{\theta})/\partial\theta = 0$ to obtain

$$\frac{\partial\hat{\theta}}{\partial\phi} = -\frac{\dfrac{\partial^2 H}{\partial\phi\partial\theta}}{\dfrac{\partial^2 H}{\partial\theta^2}}.$$

Recall that at $\hat{\theta}$, $\partial^2 H/\partial\theta^2 < 0$; this was shown in Proposition 1. Now

$$\frac{\partial^2 H}{\partial\phi\partial\theta} = \frac{-1}{(I-q\theta)^2}\left[\frac{\partial^2 N}{\partial\phi\partial\theta}(I-q\theta) - q\frac{\partial N}{\partial\phi}\right],$$

and

$$\frac{\partial N}{\partial\phi} = 2(\alpha\beta p_m p_c)^{(1/2)} e^{(-\mu_0/2)+v(\theta,\phi)}\frac{\partial v}{\partial\phi} - \frac{1}{2}\phi^{-2}\beta p_c e^{-\mu_0+(1/2)\phi^{-1}}$$

where

$$\frac{\partial v}{\partial\phi} = -\frac{1}{8}\left[\frac{1}{\dfrac{\phi^2}{\theta}+\phi}\right]^2\left(\frac{2\phi}{\theta}+1\right) - \frac{1}{4}\frac{1}{(\theta+\phi)^2} < 0.$$

Thus

$$\frac{\partial N}{\partial\phi} < 0.$$

Also

$$\frac{\partial^2 N}{\partial\phi\partial\theta} = -2(\alpha\beta p_c p_m)^{(1/2)} e^{-(\mu_0/2)+v(\theta,\phi)}\left(\frac{1}{8}(\theta+\phi)^{-2}\right)\frac{\partial v}{\partial\phi} + 2(\alpha\beta p_c p_m)^{(1/2)} e^{-(\mu_0/2)+v(\theta,\phi)}\left(\frac{1}{4}\frac{1}{(\theta+\phi)^3}\right) > 0.$$

Thus

$$\frac{\partial^2 H}{\partial\phi\partial\theta} < 0 \quad \text{and} \quad \frac{\partial\hat{\theta}}{\partial\phi} < 0.$$

Up to this point the discussion has concentrated on the cases in which consumers demand some information. There are, of course, many circumstances in which a consumer may choose not to purchase information. In the model that we have constructed, these circumstance can be completely characterized by a single condition involving income, prices, expectations and preferences. Proposition 4 describes this necessary and sufficient condition for zero information demand.[11] Although the condition appears complicated, the configurations of income, prices, expectations and preferences which satisfy it can be described relatively easily. This is done in the three corollaries that follow Proposition 4. The first corollary states that a consumer will decide not to purchase information if he has a low income relative to both the price of information and the parameter ϕ which represents his degree of familiarity with the uncertain product. The commodity price ratio as well as the consumer's preferences and expectations are the factors which determine exactly how low income must be for zero information demand to arise. This is demonstrated in the third corollary to Proposition 4. The third corollary shows how it may happen that very wealthy consumers demand no information even when the price of information is low; this will occur if any of the important factors just mentioned are so extreme that the consumer's commodity choices are essentially determined independent of the information he is likely to receive from those samples which he can afford to purchase. The second corollary provides the step which enables us to prove the results in Corollary 3.

PROPOSITION 4. *If u is given by* (2. 1), *then* $\hat{\theta} = 0$ *if and only if*

$$\frac{I}{q} \leq \gamma \tag{2. 6}$$

where

$$\gamma = 8\phi^2\left\{\frac{1}{2}\left[\xi + \frac{1}{\xi}\right] + 1\right\}$$

and

$$\xi = \left(\frac{\alpha p_m}{\beta p_c}\right)^{(1/2)} e^{(1/2)\mu_0 - (1/4)\phi^{-1}}.$$

PROOF. Suppose (2. 6) holds. Using the equations

$$v(0, \phi) = \frac{1}{4}\phi^{-1},$$

$$\frac{\partial N(0)}{\partial \theta} = (e^{-(1/2)\mu_0 + (1/4)\phi^{-1}})\left(-\frac{1}{8}\phi^{-2}\right)2(p_c p_m \alpha\beta)^{(1/2)},$$

[11] Equation (1. 4) defines $H(\theta)$ only when $\theta > 0$. When $\theta = 0$, $H(\theta)$ is defined to be $H(0) = U(m_0, c_0)$. When we use this model to study the conditions under which no information is demanded, it is important to know that $H(\theta)$ is continuous at zero. This result has not yet been proven in general, but it has been shown to hold for the special utility function (2. 1). The proof is omitted.

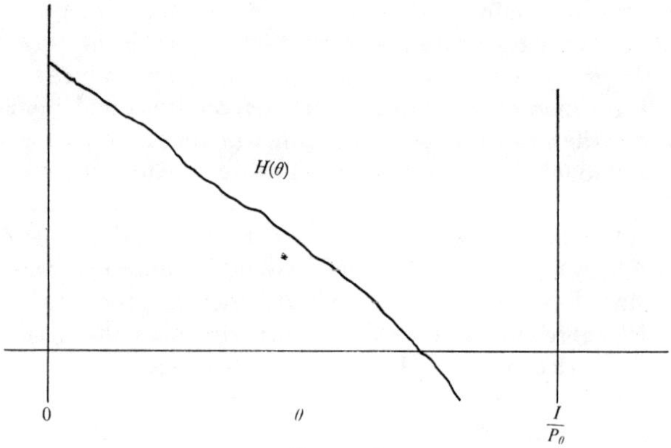

FIGURE 1

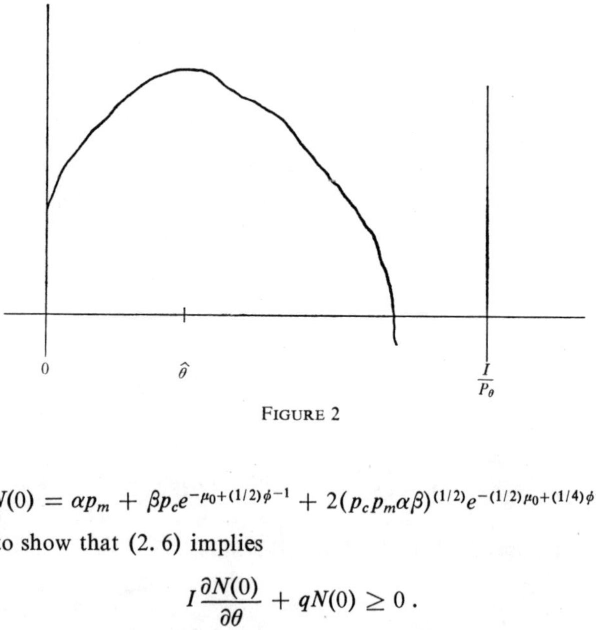

FIGURE 2

and

$$N(0) = \alpha p_m + \beta p_c e^{-\mu_0 + (1/2)\phi^{-1}} + 2(p_c p_m \alpha\beta)^{(1/2)} e^{-(1/2)\mu_0 + (1/4)\phi^{-1}}$$

it is easy to show that (2. 6) implies

$$I\frac{\partial N(0)}{\partial \theta} + qN(0) \geq 0 .$$

Using the expression for $(\partial H/\partial \theta)$ obtained in Proposition 1, this inequality implies

$$\frac{\partial H(0)}{\partial \theta} \leq 0 .$$

Therefore $\hat{\theta} = 0$ is the unique maximizer of H. In this case H is as shown in Figure 1.

If (2.6) fails, $(\partial H(0)/\partial\theta) > 0$ and $\hat{\theta} > 0$. In this case H is as shown in Figure 2.||

Proposition 4 asserts that a consumer will not buy information if his income is low relative to both the price of information and the value of γ (γ is defined in (2.6)). This implies that low income consumers may decide not to buy information in the same circumstances in which more affluent consumers demand information. But when information is expensive even affluent consumers may find that the benefits of information are outweighed by the costs and choose not to make the purchase. The other situations in which information demand is not observed occur when γ is large. The corollaries which follow investigate the circumstances that may give rise to a large value for γ. The first corollary shows that high ϕ values will make γ large enough to imply that no information is demanded. Keeping the interpretation of ϕ in mind, this means that a consumer will buy information about a familiar product only if the information is very inexpensive or he is very wealthy.

COROLLARY 1. *If the utility function is* (2.1), *the consumer will demand no information about cereal if*

$$\frac{1}{16}\frac{I}{q} \leqq \phi^2 . \tag{2.7}$$

PROOF. If $\xi > 0$, as it is in (2.6), the minimum of the function

$$g(\xi) = \frac{1}{2}\left[\frac{1}{\xi} + \xi\right] + 1$$

occurs at $\xi = 1$. So for $\xi > 0$,

$$\frac{1}{2}\left[\frac{1}{\xi} + \xi\right] + 1 \geqq 2 = g(1) .$$

Using this inequality

$$\frac{1}{16}\frac{I}{q} \leqq \phi^2$$

implies

$$\frac{I}{q} \leqq 2 \cdot 8\phi^2 \leqq 8\phi^2\left\{\frac{1}{2}\left[\frac{1}{\xi} + \xi\right] + 1\right\},$$

and Proposition 4 then implies $\hat{\theta} = 0$.||

While Corollary 1 agrees with our intuition, it has an empirical implication which our intuition could not have predicted. Because of Corollary 1, we know that if a consumer is observed to buy information the inequality (2.7) must fail to hold; i.e., ϕ must be less than $(1/4)\sqrt{(I/q)}$. Therefore, if a consumer is observed to purchase information we can use (2.7) and the observable data I and q to compute an upper bound on the parameter ϕ of his a priori probability distribution.

The second corollary is the basis for understanding how the commodity price ratio (p_m/p_c) in addition to the consumer's expectations (represented by μ_0) and preferences (represented by α/β) influences his decision to purchase information. A brief investigation of the condition (2. 6) shows that these factors operate by determining the value of γ through their influence on ξ. We have already seen that consumers will choose not to demand information if γ is large. The pertinent question to ask, then, is what values of (p_m/p_c), μ_0 and (α/β) will result in ξ values which make γ large. Corollary 2 provides part of the answer by showing that consumers demand no information when ξ is either very high or very low relative to I, q, and ϕ. To complete the answer we have to know how p_m/p_c, μ_0 and α/β affect ξ. The relationship between these factors and ξ is described in Corollary 3.

COROLLARY 2. For each I, q and ϕ, there exist two numbers $\delta_1(I, q, \phi)$ and $\delta_2(I, q, \phi)$ such that $\hat{\theta} = 0$ if and only if $\xi \leqq \delta_1$ or $\xi \geqq \delta_2$.

PROOF. Since

$$\lim_{\xi \to 0} \left\{ \frac{1}{2} \left[\xi + \frac{1}{\xi} \right] + 1 \right\} = \lim_{\xi \to +\infty} \left\{ \frac{1}{2} \left[\xi + \frac{1}{\xi} \right] + 1 \right\} = +\infty ,$$

there exists $\delta_1(I, q, \phi)$ and $\delta_2(I, q, \phi)$ such that $\xi \leq \delta_1$ or $\xi \geq \delta_2$ implies

$$\frac{1}{8} \frac{I}{q\phi^2} \leqq \left\{ \frac{1}{2} \left[\xi + \frac{1}{\xi} \right] + 1 \right\} . \tag{2. 6'}$$

Inequality (2. 6′) is equivalent to (2. 6). Therefore Proposition 4 implies that $\hat{\theta} = 0$, if and only if $\xi \leqq \delta_1$ or $\xi \geqq \delta_2$.‖

Corollary 2 asserts that consumers do not demand information when ξ is either extremely high or extremely low relative to I, q and ϕ. We can now describe, in Corollary 3, the economic circumstances which lead to extreme ξ values and zero information demand.

COROLLARY 3. (i) For any fixed values of α/β, μ_0 and ϕ there exist two numbers ν_1 and ν_2 such that $\hat{\theta} = 0$ if $p_m/p_c \leqq \nu_1$ or $p_m/p_c \geqq \nu_2$. This means that, other things equal, consumers will not purchase information about an uncertain product which is either very inexpensive or very high in price relative to other products.

(ii) For any fixed values of p_m/p_c, μ_0, and ϕ there exist two numbers ρ_1 and ρ_2 such that $\hat{\theta} = 0$ if $\alpha/\beta \leqq \rho_1$ or $\alpha/\beta \geqq \rho_2$. This result can be interpreted to imply that a consumer whose preferences are strongly skewed in favor of one commodity or the other will not find it worthwhile to demand information about product quality. (See the comments which follow the proof.)

(iii) For any fixed values of p_m/p_c, α/β and ϕ there exist two numbers ζ_1 and ζ_2 such that $\hat{\theta} = 0$ if $e^{\mu_0} \leqq \zeta_1$ or $e^{\mu_0} \geqq \zeta_2$. This implies that, other things equal, a consumer will choose not to purchase information if the uncertain product promises to be of especially high quality; but very low expectations for product quality will also eliminate the incentive for the consumer to demand information.

PROOF OF I. (the proofs of (ii) and (iii) are similar)
The equation for ξ in (2. 6) implies that

$$\lim_{p_m/p_c \to 0} \xi = 0 \quad \text{and} \quad \lim_{p_m/p_c \to \infty} \xi = \infty .$$

We can therefore choose ν_1 such that $p_m/p_c \leqq \nu_1$ implies $\xi \leqq \delta_1$ where δ_1 is defined in Corollary 2; ν_2 can be chosen similarly.||

The interpretation of conclusions (i) and (iii) are straightforward. To interpret conclusion (ii), note that if the attributes protein and carbohydrate could be purchased directly, carbohydrate consumption would be low when α/β is large. In other words, a consumer with the utility function (2. 1) will exhibit a strong preference for carbohydrates when α/β is near zero and a weak preference for carbohydrates when α/β is large. Therefore when α/β is near zero the consumer's preferences will be skewed in favor of cereal, and conclusion (ii) implies that information demand is zero. If α/β is large the consumer's preferences are now skewed in favor of meat, but again conclusion (ii) implies that no information is demanded.

The conclusions of Corollary 3 are all intuitively plausible. Information demand was shown to be zero when one commodity is expensive relative to the other, when one commodity is strongly preferred over the other and when initial expectations are either extremely optimistic or pessimistic. In each of these cases the benefits derived from information are low because the consumer's commodity choices are determined independent of the message provided by the information. To show this formally, differentiate the equation for $c(x, \theta)$ with respect to x. When p_m/p_c, α/β or e^{μ_0} are either large or near zero then $\partial c/\partial x$ is approximately zero, indicating that the consumer's commodity choices are essentially independent of the observation.

SUMMARY

By making a special hypothesis about the utility function in the model constructed in Section 1, we have been able to describe the economic circumstances which lead to information demand. All of the results have strong intuitive appeal. A good example is the conclusion of Proposition 3 which asserts that consumers demand more information about unfamiliar products. Another example is Corollary 3 which implies that consumers will not buy information about very expensive or very inexpensive commodities. Another conclusion of Corollary 3 is that consumers will not buy information about products which they expect to be of extremely low quality or about products which are expected to be of extremely high quality. Corollary 3 also asserts that a consumer whose preferences are strongly skewed in favor of one commodity is not likely to demand information. The plausibility of these results is demonstrated by showing that all of the circumstances in which Corollary 3 asserts information demand fails to arise are the same circumstances in which the consumer's commodity choices are unresponsive to new information.

Another result proved in the paper asserts that information is neither an inferior nor a Giffen good.

While this paper has not focused on the empirical applications of the model, Corollary 1 does have an interesting empirical implication. If a consumer buys information about a product, Corollary 1 can be used, in conjunction with price-income data, to obtain an upper bound on the parameter which measures the degree of familiarity with that product.

University of Massachusetts, Amherst, and State University of New York, Stony Brook, U.S.A.

REFERENCES

[1] BLACKWELL, D., "Comparison of Experiments," *Proceedings of the Second Berkeley Symposium on Mathematical Statistics and Probability* (Berkeley: University of California Press, 1951), 93–102.

[2] ———, "Equivalent Comparisons of Experiments," *Annals of Mathematical Statistics*, XXIV (June, 1953), 265–272.

[3] HICKS, J. R., *Value and Capital*, 2d edition (Oxford: Oxford University Press, 1939).

[4] KIHLSTROM, R. E., "A General Theory of Demand for Information about Product Quality", forthcoming in *Journal of Economic Theory*.

[5] LANCASTER, KELVIN, "A New Approach to Consumer Theory," *Journal of Political Economy*, LXXIV (April, 1966), 132–157.

[6] MARSCHAK, JACOB AND KOICHI MIYASAWA, "Economic Comparability of Information Systems," *International Economic Review*, IX (June, 1968), 137–174.

[7] ——— AND R. RADNER, *Economic Theory of Teams* (New Haven: Yale University Press, 1972).

[8] RAIFFA, H. AND R. SCHLAIFFER, *Applied Statistical Decision Theory* (Boston: Division of Research, Harvard Business School, 1961).

[9] SAMUELSON, PAUL A., *Foundations of Economic Analysis* (Cambridge: Harvard University Press, 1945).

[10] STIGLER, GEORGE J., "The Economics of Information," *Journal of Political Economy*, XIX (June, 1961), 213–225.

DISCUSSION SUMMARY

This paper develops a model which describes the economic conditions which lead to the demand for information. More specifically, the paper explains consumer expenditures on information about product quality.

Information is basically different from other goods. It is not a commodity with intrinsically desirable attributes. Individuals use information to make "better" decisions about uncertain events, e.g., product quality. The demand for information is not direct; it is a derived demand.

A two-commodity example is used to analyze the demand for product quality information. The two commodities, meat and cereal, are bought and sold in competitive markets. Each commodity has a single attribute which is desired by the consumer: meat has protein, cereal has carbohydrates. The consumer is certain about the amount of protein in a unit of meat and uncertain about the carbohydrate content of a unit of cereal. The consumer can purchase information in order to improve his estimate of the average quality (amount of carbohydrates) of the cereal.

The market for information is competitive. Each unit of information is sold at the equilibrium price prevailing in the market.

The paper then goes on to develop a general expression for the expected utility of information (equation 1.4). A very important assumption made in the development of this function is that sequential sampling is ruled out.

Most of the interesting results that are derived in this paper are made possible by assuming a constant elasticity of supply (CES) utility function (equation 2.1). Although the use of this specific form of utility function detracts from the generality of the analysis, it enables the author to obtain reasonably specific hypotheses about the determinants of demand for information. Standard comparative static techniques are then used to describe how prices, income, expectations, and the parameters of the utility function affect information demand.

Using the CES utility function, a specific expected utility of information function is derived (equation 2.4). The consumer will demand information such that his expected utility will be maximized.

The first-order conditions for maximization of the expected utility of information are used as the basis for the development of four propositions that are presented in the paper.

Proposition 1 states that the consumer's demand for information is unique. Proposition 2 shows that information is a normal good; that is, if two consumers have the same preferences, the wealthier consumer will demand more information. Proposition 3 demonstrates that a consumer's demand for information will be low for products which he expects to be either of very high quality or of very poor quality. It also shows that a consumer will demand more information about a product with which he is unfamiliar.

Proposition 4 describes a necessary and sufficient condition for consumers to demand zero information. It examines the configurations of income, prices, preferences, and expectations which will result in no information being demanded. A consumer will demand no information if his income is low relative to the price of information and his degree of familiarity with the product. Very wealthy consumers may demand no information even when the price of information is low. This will occur if any of the factors just mentioned are so extreme that the consumer's commodity choices are determined essentially independent of the information that he is likely to receive from those samples which he can afford to purchase.

INTERNATIONAL
ECONOMIC
REVIEW

June, 1968
Vol. 9, No. 2

ECONOMIC COMPARABILITY OF INFORMATION SYSTEMS*

BY JACOB MARSCHAK AND KOICHI MIYASAWA[1]

1. INTRODUCTION

AN INFORMATION SYSTEM is a set of potential messages to be received by the decision maker. It is characterized by the statistical relation of the messages to the payoff-relevant events, and also by the message cost.[2] Neglecting this cost, the (gross) value of an information system for a given user is the (gross) payoff that he would obtain, on the average, if he would respond to each message by the most appropriate decision. Thus (gross) information value depends not only on the statistical relation between messages and events but also on the payoff function. The latter expresses the user's "tastes" and "technology." The ordering of statistically defined information systems by their values is therefore at most a partial one. This contrasts with the complete ordering of information systems (channels) by their equivocation (a statistical parameter used in the classical information theory that disregards variation of payoff functions from user to user).

Indeed, if "noise" is defined to increase with equivocation[3] a "noisy" information system may be more valuable to a given user than a noiseless one: the betting sports fan may have reason to prefer the sports page of a newspaper to its society page even though both pages have the same number of English words and the sports page has misprints, the society page none.

The partial ordering of information systems by their (gross) values will be studied. In particular, conditions, sufficient or necessary, will be stated under which two systems are comparable, so that one of them is "more in-

* Manuscript received February 28, 1966.

[1] This work was supported partly by the office of Naval Research under Task 047-041 and partly by the Western Management Science Institute under a grant from the Ford Foundation. Reproduction in whole or in part is permitted for any purpose of the United States Government. During 1964/5, Koichi Miyasawa, Professor of Statistics at the University of Tokyo, was post-doctoral Fellow under a Ford Foundation Grant to the University of California.

The article is the product of very close collaboration although a few of the sections are predominantly the results of the work of one of the two authors (e.g., Sections 1-7 in the case of Marschak [10, (12-4)]; and Theorem 8.2 in the case of Miyasawa). We owe thanks to Dr. Leif Appelgren, Stockholm, for the constructive criticism and to Professor Arthur Geoffrion of the Western Management Science Institute for many corrections and improvements.

[2] This cost will be assumed additive. We shall thus treat a special case only: see Section 4.

[3] See footnote 7 on the textbook terminology regarding "noiselessness" and "equivocation."

formative" than the other in the following sense: one of them can never have smaller value than the other for any payoff function defined on a given set of events. The ordering of information systems according to their informativeness has applications in the economics of information and organization; and also, as shown by D. Blackwell, in statistics (where messages and events correspond, respectively, to observations and hypotheses).[4]

Sections 1-5 will define concepts useful for the statement of our problem of finding conditions for the comparability of information systems. The remaining sections seek to solve this problem and to prove inclusion relations between the various conditions studied.

2. EVENTS AND DECISIONS

For a given actor (decision-maker), we define a set X of *states* x of the environment (not controlled by the actor[5]), a set C of *Consequence* c. Each function from X to C is called an act by Savage [**16**]. However, not all acts thus defined are feasible. Define the set A consisting of all feasible acts, a. These we shall call actions.[6] The set A can be thought of as the resources or technology available to the particular actor. Each action a maps X into C

$$a(x) = c \ .$$

This is, in general, a many-to-one mapping, for each state x may describe the environment in unlimited detail, and some of this detail may be irrelevant in the following sense. Two distinct states, x and x' may be such that $a(x) = a(x')$ for every a in A. We shall then say that x and x' are equivalent with respect to A. We can partition X into equivalence sets of the form

$$z_x^A \equiv \{x' \in X: a(x') = a(x), \text{ all } a \in A\} \ . \quad (2.1.\text{A})$$

Denote this partition by Z^A. Each equivalence set z^A in Z^A may be called an event, relevant with respect to technology A; or, briefly, an A-relevant event.

Example. Suppose X is an n-tuple of variables, some of them continuous, with n arbitrarily large; the consequences of any action of yours are not affected by many of these variables (political situation in Uganda) or by minor variations of the remaining ones (seconds of daily sunshine).

The set of states of the environment can be "coarsened" still further if we pay attention, not only to the actor's technology but also to his tastes. It would suffice for this purpose, to replace in (2.1.A) the equality sign between $a(x')$ and $a(x)$ by some symbol representing the actor's indifference between

[4] Blackwell [**2**], Blackwell and Girschick [**4**], also McGuire [**13**].

[5] Thus, in the case of sequential decisions, a state x would describe the time-seqence of external conditions. The sequence of states in the language of systems theory and dynamic programming corresponds (with the exception of the initial state) to a consequence in our terminology.

[6] In an earlier paper (Marschak [**11**]) the existence and uniqueness of the sets of payoff-relevant actions and events was proved, using a set of physically distinct feasible actions. We take this opportunity for a *correction* (due to K. Miyasawa): Theorem 3 of [**11**] is not valid, nor is its validity necessary for the proof of the main existence and uniqueness theorem.

these two consequences. There is no need to use numerical utilities. But since the numerical utility concept will be needed soon anyway, denote by u the actor's utility function, a function from C to the set of the reals, and write

$$\omega(x, a) \equiv u(a(x)) \equiv u(c) ; \tag{2.2}$$

the function ω from $X \times A$ to the reals is called the *payoff function.* New partition X into equivalence sets of the form

$$z_x^\omega \equiv \{x' \in X: \omega(x', a) = \omega(x, a), \text{ all } a \in A\} . \tag{2.1.ω}$$

This partition, denoted by Z^ω, is clearly coarser than Z^A (i.e., Z^A is a sub-partition of Z^ω). We shall call z^ω, a typical equivalence set in Z^ω, an *event, relevant with respect to the payoff function* ω; or briefly, an ω-relevant event.

Example. Suppose each consequence of any of your actions is a triple (c_1, c_2, c_3) where c_1 and c_2 are your profits of this and of the next year, measured in cents; and c_3 is the amount of air pollution created by your plant. Suppose you are indifferent between $c \equiv (c_1, c_2, c_3)$ and $c' \equiv (c_1', c_2', c_3')$ because you are not concerned with differences less than \$1, or because you are willing to trade off a part of this year's profit for a profit increase in the next year, or because air pollution results only in other people's discomfort. Then $u(c) = u(c')$; and if, for all actions a in A, $a(x) = c$ and $a(x') = c'$, then the states x and x' belong to the same payoff-relevant event z^ω.

Considerations of "taste" induce also a coarsening of the set of actions. It may happen that, for two distinct actions a and a', and for all x in X,

$$u(a(x)) = u(a'(x)); \text{ that is, } \omega(x, a) = \omega(x, a') .$$

Let us, then, define a partition D^ω of A into equivalence sets of the form

$$d_a^\omega \equiv \{a' \in A: \omega(x, a') = \omega(x, a), \text{ all } x \in X\} . \tag{2.3}$$

For convenience we shall call D^ω the set of *ω-relevant decisions*; its typical element d^ω will sometimes be denoted briefly as d.

Example. Let each consequence be a triple (c_1, c_2, c_3) defined in the previous example; suppose you are indifferent to air pollution and that two methods of production, a and a', always yield (i.e., for every x) the same profits but different amounts of air pollution. Then a and a' belong to the same ω-relevant decision d^ω.

Observing that ω is constant on $z^\omega \times d^\omega$, we may write without ambiguity $\omega(z^\omega, d^\omega)$ where ω is defined over the domain $Z^\omega \times D^\omega$ instead of $X \times A$.

In what follows we shall be interested in varying the payoff function ω subject to a constraint depending on an arbitrarily fixed partition Z of X into *events* z. Given a payoff function ω, Z is called *ω-adequate* if it is a sub-partition of the *ω-relevant* partition Z^ω, see Marschak-Radner [12, (chapter 2)]; for example, Z^A (relevant with respect to technology but not necessary with respect to tastes) is ω-adequate. Then every $z \in Z$ is a subset of exactly one $z^\omega \in Z^\omega$ and we can write, without danger of ambiguity, $\omega(z, d^\omega)$, where the function ω is defined over the domain $Z \times D^\omega$. Now let Ω_Z be the set of all payoff functions ω for which Z is ω-adequate. Given a fixed set Z of events we shall vary the payoff function ω over the set Ω_Z.

It has been shown—see Savage [**16**]—that certain plausible, quasi-logical postulates imply for a consistent decision-maker: (a) the existence of a numerical function u on the set C of consequences; hence a numerical function ω on $Z \times D^{\omega}$; and (b) the existence of a probability measure $\mathcal{P}$ on X; hence of a probability function $p(z)$ on Z, with the following property: given two decisions d and d' in D^{ω}, a consistent actor will not prefer d' to d if (assuming Z finite for simplicity)

$$\sum_{z \in Z} \omega(z, d)p(z) \geqq \sum_{z \in Z} \omega(z, d')p(z) . \tag{2.4}$$

The two compared averages are called the (expected) utilities of the decisions d and d', respectively. The proposition just stated is called the expected utility theorem. Roughly, it says that an actor conforming with certain consistency postulates (and with the rules of ordinary logic) maximizes the expected utility of decision.

We stated above that the set $A = \{a\}$ of actions (i.e., feasible acts) represents the actor's technology, and that the utility function u on the set C represents his tastes; hence the payoff function $\omega(x, a) \equiv u(a(x))$ reflects both. We can now add his beliefs, represented by the probability measure $\mathcal{P}$ on X. In what follows we shall consider $\mathcal{P}$ and Z fixed; and we shall permit ω to vary over the set Ω_Z for which Z is ω-adequate. This will enable us to discuss the "informativeness" of information systems for an arbitrary set of their users: see *Example* in Section 5.

3. INFORMATION SYSTEMS

An *information system* Y is a set consisting of (potential) *messages* y. We shall regard Y as another partition of the set X of states x. Unlike partition Z of X into payoff-adequate events z, the partition Y of X into messages y is not associated with the feasibility of actions and the indifference among their results. Instead, Y is associated with some object—an instrument—that produces messages. See Figures 1a–1c. *Example*: The state x may be such that (a) my barometer shows low pressure: this message y; and that (b) the visibility at the airport is low, thus affecting the success of a decision to fly: this is event z.

In the language of information theory, a set Z of events would be called "source" and a set Y of messages, a "channel." In the language of statistical inference, Z represents a set of alternative hypotheses, and Y represents the set of outcomes of an experiment and is itself called an experiment.

If a probability measure $\mathcal{P}$ is defined on X, the joint probability function on $Z \times Y$ is determined. In fact, given a set $(Y, Y', Y'', \cdots)$ of *available information systems*, the multivariate distribution on $Z \times Y \times Y' \times Y'' \times \cdots$ is defined. We shall write, using the same symbol $p(\ )$ for probability functions over different domains, yet without risk of ambiguity:

probability of event,

$$\Pr(x \in z) \equiv p(z) ;$$

probability of message,

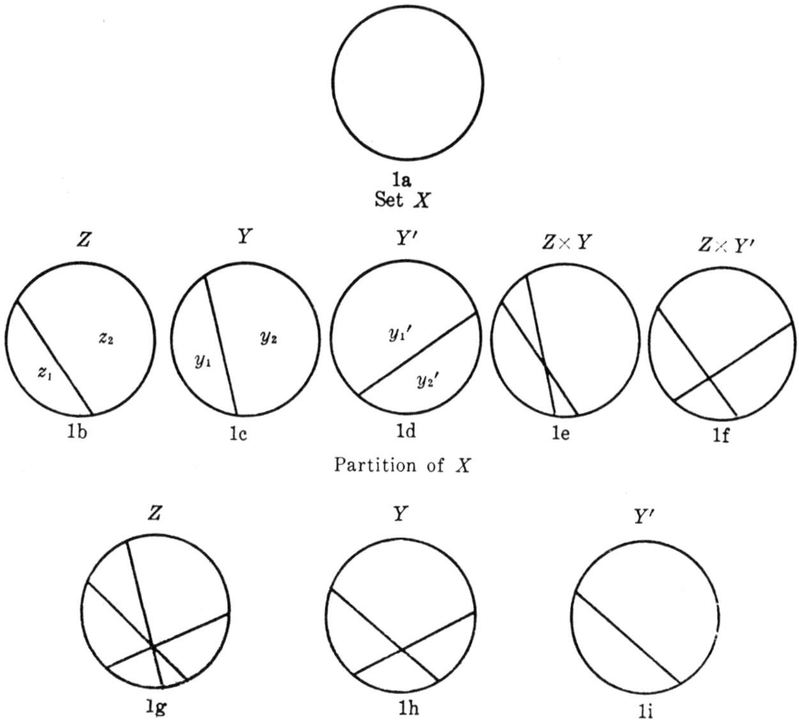

Noiseless Cases ($Z \, s \, Y$, $Z \, s \, Y'$), with $Y s Y'$

FIGURE 1

SET X AND ITS PARTITIONS

$$\Pr(x \in y) \equiv p(y) ,$$

($p(z)$ and $p(y)$ are all positive since z and y are non-empty);

joint probability of event and message,

$$\Pr(x \in z \cap y) \equiv p(z, y) ;$$

posterior probability of event, given the message,

$$p(z, y)/p(y) \equiv p(z \mid y) ;$$

likelihood of message, given the event,

$$p(z, y)/p(z) \equiv p(y \mid z) .$$

When comparing two information systems Y and Y' we shall also use expressions like the following:

probability of joint occurrence of message $y \in Y$ and $y' \in Y'$,

$$\Pr(x \in y \cap y') = p(y, y') ;$$

probability of joint occurrence of event z and messages y, y',

$$\Pr(x \in z \cap y \cap y') = p(z, y, y') ;$$

probability of y', given y,

$$p(y, y')/p(y) \equiv p(y' \mid y) ;$$

posterior probability of event z, given messages y, y',

$$p(z, y, y')/p(y, y') \equiv p(z \mid y, y') ;$$

and so on.

For simplicity of reasoning, we have assumed the set Z of events and the sets $Y, Y', \cdots$, of messages *finite*. (No such assumption will be made about X, the set of states, except in Theorem 11.4.) Specifically,

$$Z \equiv (z_1, \cdots, z_m); \quad Y \equiv (y_1, \cdots, y_n); \quad Y' \equiv (y'_1, \cdots, y'_{n'}); \quad m, n, n', \cdots \geqq 2 .$$

The generic elements z of Z, y of Y, y' of Y', $\cdots$, can be regarded as random variables taking, respectively, the values

$$z_i (i = 1, \cdots, m); \quad y_j (j = 1, \cdots, n); \quad y'_k (k = 1, \cdots, n'); \cdots .$$

In most of our discussion Z will be fixed, and the effects of varying Y (i.e., of replacing it by Y', say) will be studied—see Figures 1b-1f—using for the three marginal probabilities the following vectors (the various alternative notations will be used according to convenience):

$$\begin{aligned} &\text{the } (m \times 1)\text{-vector } [p(z)] \equiv [p(z_i)] \equiv [r_z] \equiv [r_i] \equiv r \\ &\text{the } (n \times 1)\text{-vector } [p(y)] \equiv [p(y_j)] \equiv [q_j] \equiv q^Y \equiv q \\ &\text{the } (n' \times 1)\text{-vector } [p(y')] \equiv [p(y'_k)] \equiv [q'_k] \equiv q^{Y'} \equiv q' . \end{aligned}$$

For the joint probabilities of events and messages; the posterior probabilities of events (given the message in Y); and the likelihoods of those messages (given the events in Z), we use the $(m \times n)$-matrices

$$\begin{aligned} [p(z, y)] &\equiv [p(z_i, y_j)] \equiv [p_{zy}] \equiv [p_{ij}] \equiv P^Y \equiv P \\ [p(z \mid y)] &\equiv [p(z_i \mid y_j)] \equiv [\pi_{zy}] \equiv [\pi_{ij}] \equiv \Pi^Y \equiv \Pi \\ [p(y \mid z)] &\equiv [p(y_j \mid z_i)] \equiv [\lambda_{zy}] \equiv [\lambda_{ij}] \equiv \Lambda^Y \equiv \Lambda \end{aligned}$$

and the corresponding $(m \times n')$-matrices for Y'

$$P^{Y'} \equiv P'; \quad \Pi^{Y'} \equiv \Pi'; \quad \Lambda^{Y'} \equiv \Lambda' .$$

By definition (writing henceforth $\sum_y, \sum_z$ for summation over sets Y, Z)

(3.1.1) $$\sum_z p_{zy} = q_y > 0, \quad \sum_y p_{zy} = r_z > 0, \quad \pi_{zy} \geqq 0, \quad \lambda_{zy} \geqq 0$$

(3.1.2) $$p_{zy} = \lambda_{zy} r_z = \pi_{zy} q_y \geqq 0$$

(3.1.3) $$1 = \sum_y q_y = \sum_z r_z = \sum_y \lambda_{zy} = \sum_z \pi_{zy} = \sum_y \sum_z p_{zy} .$$

Moreover, with Z fixed, r is fixed and we have for any Y, Y'

(3.2) $$\Pi q = r = \Pi' q' .$$

We shall also use the $(n \times n')$-matrix

$$[p(y' \mid y)] \equiv [p(y'_k \mid y_j)] \equiv [\gamma_{yy'}] \equiv [\gamma_{jk}] \equiv \Gamma \,. \tag{3.3}$$

Clearly,

$$\gamma_{yy'} \geqq 0; \quad \sum_{y'} \gamma_{yy'} = 1\,; \tag{3.4}$$

$$q' = \Gamma_{(\tau)} q\,, \tag{3.5}$$

where $\Gamma_{(\tau)}$ is the transpose of Γ. Similarly, we define the $(n' \times n)$-matrix

$$[p(y \mid y')] \equiv [p(y_j \mid y'_k)] \equiv [\gamma'_{yy'}] \equiv [\gamma'_{jk}] \equiv \Gamma'\,, \tag{3.3'}$$

$$\gamma'_{yy'} \geqq 0; \quad \sum \gamma'_{yy'} = 1\,, \tag{3.4'}$$

$$q = \Gamma' q'\,. \tag{3.5'}$$

Let T and T' be two partitions of X. T is said to be a *subpartition* of (or *finer than*) T' (or, equivalently, T' is coarser than T),

$$T \,\mathrm{s}\, T' \tag{3.6}$$

if each t in T is contained in one of the t' in T'; or equivalently, there is a many-to-one correspondence $T \to T'$. Condition (3.6) implies—and, in case of X finite, is equivalent to—the following: for any $t \in T, t' \in T'$,

$$p(t' \mid t) = \begin{cases} 1 & \text{if } t \subset t' \\ 0 & \text{otherwise}\,. \end{cases} \tag{3.7}$$

In particular, if the set Z of events is finer than the information system Y, (see Figures 1g, 1h)

$$Z \,\mathrm{s}\, Y\,, \tag{3.8}$$

we shall say that Y is *noiseless* (with respect to Z). In this case there is a *many-to-one correspondence* $Z \to Y$; and it will follow that

$$p(y \mid z) \equiv \lambda_{zy} = \begin{cases} 1 & \text{if } z \subset y \\ 0 & \text{otherwise}\,. \end{cases} \tag{3.9}$$

Thus each row of Λ^Y consists of one 1 and $n-1$ zeros if Y is noiseless.[7]

In Section 11, we shall consider the case when the two compared informa-

[7] This agrees with the terminology of Feinstein [7, (23)]; but Abramson [1, (11-2)] calls the case (3.10) a "deterministic channel," and reserves the adjective "noiseless" for the case when the correspondence $Z \to Y$ is one-to-many, hence in our notation,

$$p(z \mid y) = \Pi_{zy} = \begin{cases} 1 & \text{if } y \subset z \\ 0 & \text{otherwise}\,, \end{cases}$$

so that each column of Π^Y consists of 1 one and $m-1$ zeros. In this case, however, it should be easy (i.e., costless) for the user to consider all messages corresponding to the same event, as one and the same message; this establishes a *one-to-one* correspondence between the set of messages (thus redefined) and the set of events. This is sometimes called perfect information. Then Π and Λ are the same (permutation) matrix:

$$\lambda_{zy} = \pi_{zy} = \begin{cases} 1 & \text{if } z = y \\ 0 & \text{otherwise}\,. \end{cases}$$

It seems to us therefore that the case called "noiseless" by Abramson is of little interest: it collapses into the case of perfect information which is a specical case of noiseless information, in Feinstein's and our sense.

tion systems, Y and Y' are both *noiseless* (see Figures 1g, 1h, 1i):
Condition (N): $Z \text{ s } Y, Z \text{ s } Y'$.

If two information systems Y and Y' (noiseless or not) are such that Y is finer than Y', and thus Y' *coarser* than Y we write
Condition (C): $Y \text{ s } Y'$.

In this case we can also say that Y' is obtained from Y by *collapsing*, or *condensing*, several messages in Y into a single message in Y'. Under condition (C) there is a many-to-one correspondence $Y \to Y'$, and (C) will imply, as in (3.7) that

$$p(y' \mid y) \equiv \gamma_{yy'} = \begin{cases} 1 & \text{if } y \subset y' \\ 0 & \text{otherwise} . \end{cases} \tag{3.10}$$

4. INFORMATION VALUES: GROSS AND NET

The actor associates each message in Y with some decision in D^ω. This mapping will be called a *decision* rule, δ^ω, an element of a set Δ^ω. Without danger of ambiguity we shall often omit the superscript ω. Thus

$$\begin{aligned} d &= \delta(y) , \\ \omega(z, d) &= \omega(z, \delta(y)); \qquad z \in Z, y \in Y, d \in D, \delta \in \Delta . \end{aligned} \tag{4.1}$$

Thus, given the payoff function ω, the utility of the result depends on the event z, the message y and the decision rule δ.

The utility amount $\omega(z, \delta(y))$ may be interpreted by expressing the economic effect (i.e., the effect upon the utility to the decision-maker), not only of decision $\delta(y)$, given event z, but also of the decision rule δ itself. For example, a simple (e.g., linear) decision rule is less costly to apply than a complicated one. Moreover, a decision rule from Y to D, where D consists of feasible decisions (actions), may itself be non-feasible—for example, if it is so complicated as to exceed the decision-making capabilities of available men or machines. Strictly speaking, we should define a feasible subset Δ_φ of Δ, for use in any further economic discussion of information systems. For the sake of simplicity we shall neglect in most of the following both the cost and the possible non-feasibility of decision rules and assume $\Delta_\varphi = \Delta$.

An optimal decision rule δ^* in Δ maximizes the utility averaged over all messages y in Y. The maximum expected utility thus achieved will be denoted by $U(P^Y; \omega)$ for it will depend on the joint probability P^Y of y and z (with Z fixed) and on the payoff function ω:

$$\begin{aligned} U(P^Y; \omega) &\equiv \sum_y \sum_z \omega(z, \delta^*(y)) p_{zy} \\ &\geqq \sum_y \sum_z \omega(z, \delta(y)) p_{zy} \end{aligned} \tag{4.2}$$

for all δ in Δ. Then, since $p_{zy} = q_y \pi_{zy}$, we have

$$\begin{aligned} U(P^Y; \omega) &\equiv \max_{\delta \in \Delta} \sum_y q_y \sum_z \pi_{zy} \omega(z, \delta(y)) \\ &\equiv \sum_y q_y \max_{d \in D} \sum_z \pi_{zy} \omega(z, d) \\ &\equiv \sum_y q_y \sum_z \pi_{zy} \omega(z, d_y) \equiv \sum_y \sum_z p_{zy} \omega(z, d_y) , \end{aligned} \tag{4.3}$$

thus defining $d_y \equiv \delta^*(y)$ as the optimal decision in response to message y:

$$\sum_z \pi_{zy}\omega(z, d_y) \geqq \sum_z \pi_{zy}\omega(z, d), \quad \text{all } d \in D. \tag{4.4}$$

In order to guarantee the achievement of a maximum in (4.3), (4.4), we shall henceforth assume that the set of real numbers $\omega(z, d)$, $d \in D^\omega$, is bounded from above and closed and that ω is continuous.

A more appropriate and precise name for the quantity $U(P^Y; \omega)$ would be *gross* value of Y, in contrast to its *net* value. So far, we have neglected those economic effects of an information instrument that are due not to decision based on messages received through the instrument but to its other properties, roughly called "cost of information." For example, one of two compared instruments may be more expensive, or it may send messages that while related to events by the same probability distribution are more time-consuming. Strictly speaking, these two instruments produce two different partitions of X: for the occurrence of a particular message belongs to the detailed description of a state x; and the consequence may depend, not only on decision d and event z but also on the manner in which the message received through a particular instrument affects the user's resources and well-being, through the expenditure of time, money and effort involved in the process of receiving the message. Equation (3.2) should be replaced by a more general one

$$u(c) \equiv u(d(z), y) \equiv \omega_Y(z, d, y) \tag{4.5}$$

say, where y belongs to a set Y of messages associated with a particular instrument. The new function ω_Y may be called the *net payoff function*. In a simple but important case

$$\omega_Y(z, d, y) = \omega(z, d) - \kappa(y), \tag{4.6}$$

where, for example, $\kappa(y)$ is the monetary cost associated with message y, $\omega(z, d)$ is the ("gross") monetary profit from decision d when event z occurs, and utility is linear in money: see Raiffa and Schlaifer [15, (section 4)]. In general the net value of an information system Y can be written as

$$U_Y(Y) \equiv \max_{\delta \in \Delta} \sum_z \sum_y \omega_Y(z, \delta(y), y)p_{zy} \tag{4.7}$$

so that in the special, additive case (4.6) we have,

$$U_Y(Y) = U(P^Y; \omega) - \sum_y \kappa(y)p(y). \tag{4.8}$$

In what follows we shall indeed assume (4.6), hence (4.8). This will permit us to study the economic effect of statistical properties of an information system, separated from the system's cost properties. But remember that in the general case (4.5), (4.7), the net value of an information system cannot be decomposed into gross payoff and cost as additive components.

5. COMPARISON OF (GROSS) INFORMATION VALUES

We shall compare the (gross) values of two information systems, Y and Y', having fixed the set Z of events and thus the vector $r = [r_z]$ of marginal probabilities of events and the set Ω_Z of considered payoff functions.

Example. To expand further the flight passenger's case of Section 2: We can ask whether a barometer or a hygrometer (with messages referring to humidity) is preferable to a user who has a ranch, an airplane, or both. The uses considered will define the set Z of payoff-adequate weather descriptions which will permit the necessary comparison.

In the ("Bayesian") spirit of the expected utility theorem, the two joint distributions P^Y and $P^{Y'}$ (also denoted as P and P') are known to the decision maker. He knows therefore also the pairs

$$(\Pi_*, q_*) \text{ and } (\Pi'_*, q'_*),$$
$$(\Lambda_*, r_*) \text{ and } (\Lambda'_*, r_*),$$

indicating by the star subscript (as it will be sometimes useful to do) that those matrices and vectors are known. Such knowledge is usually assumed in operations research problems—including the most general ones of sequential decision making, in which one starts with an initial distribution of states seen as time sequences and conditional upon the sequence of decisions: see Miyasawa [14]. The knowledge of r_* is also often assumed in information theory: for each channel Y, the joint distribution $p(z, y)$ is known, permitting one to compute, for a given source Z, the equivocation characterizing the channel Y[8]

$$H(Z \mid Y) = -\sum_y p(y) \sum_z p(z \mid y) \log p(z \mid y). \tag{5.1}$$

(Compare this with (4.3)!)

Also, $U(P^Y; \omega)$ and $U(P^{Y'}; \omega)$ can sometimes be ordered, for all ω considered without the knowledge of the distributions P^Y aed $P^{Y'}$ and only knowing the process that produces Y and Y' and imposes certain general restrictions on the trivariate distribution of z, y, y'. Such will be, in fact, the content of Sections 6 and 7.

It is also useful to consider where the comparison between information values of Y and Y' is made by someone who uses the knowledge of $\Pi = \Pi_*$ and $\Pi' = \Pi'_*$ (ignoring or being ignorant of q, q'); or who uses the knowledge of $\Lambda = \Lambda_*$ and $\Lambda' = \Lambda'_*$ (ignoring or being ignorant of the value of r). Such cases of limited knowledge will be considered because they may simplify the procedure of comparing information values. In addition, an actor may have knowledge of posterior probabilities of π_{zy} associated with each message y, but have trouble ascertaining the probability q_y of each message: this makes the comparison of Π with Π' interesting. (Note, however, that the probability vectors q, q', r even though ignored or not known are constrained by identity (3.2).)

[8] The equivocation $H(Z \mid Y) = 0$ if and only if all $p(z \mid y) \equiv \pi_{zy} = 1$ or 0, i.e., if and only if Y is noiseless in the sense of Abramson and not in the sense used by Feinstein and ourselves. On the other hand, Y is noiseless in the latter sense, i.e., all $p(y \mid z) \equiv \lambda_{zy} = 1$ or 0, if and only if the expression

$$H(Y \mid Z) \equiv -\sum_z p(z) \sum_y p(y \mid z) \log p(y \mid z) = 0.$$

Following Abramson, the latter expression might be called equivocation of Y with respect to Z.

Finally the ignorance of the (prior) distribution of hypotheses is maintained in non-Bayesian statistics, making it impossible to use other than the likelihood matrices $\Lambda = \Lambda_*$ and $\Lambda' = \Lambda'_*$.

Whenever P^Y, $P^{Y'}$ are known (hence $r, \Lambda, \Lambda', \Pi, \Pi'$ have known values r_*, Λ_*, etc.) and are such that

$$U(P^Y; \omega) \geqq U(P^{Y'}; \omega)\,, \qquad \text{all } \omega \text{ in } \Omega_Z\,, \tag{5.2}$$

we shall write

Condition (P): $P^Y > P^{Y'}$ (or briefly: $P > P'$),

and say: "Y is more informative[9] than Y' as revealed by their joint distributions P, P' with Z" or simply "P *is more informative than* P'." Note that (5.2) can be rewritten thus

$$U(\Pi_*, q_*; \omega) \geqq U(\Pi'_*, q'_*; \omega), \text{ all } \omega \text{ in } \Omega_Z; \text{ or } (\Pi_*, q_*) > (\Pi'_*, q'_*)\,, \tag{5.2.1}$$

or

$$U(\Lambda_*, r_*; \omega) \geqq U(\Lambda'_*, r_*; \omega), \text{ all } \omega \text{ in } \Omega_Z; \text{ or } (\Lambda_*, r_*) > (\Lambda'_*, r_*)\,. \tag{5.2.2}$$

If r is ignored or not known, we may ask whether

$$U(\Lambda_*, r; \omega) \geqq U(\Lambda'_*, r; \omega)\,, \qquad \text{all } \omega \text{ in } \Omega_Z \text{ and all } r\,; \tag{5.3}$$

and, if so, write (omitting the stars for brevity)

Condition (Λ): $\Lambda > \Lambda'$

and say: "Y is more informative than Y' as revealed by the likelihood matrices Λ and Λ'," or simply: "Λ *is more informative than* Λ'."

Finally, it may also be of interest to ask whether or not

$$U(\Pi_*, q; \omega) \geqq U(\Pi'_*, q'; \omega) \text{ for all } \omega \text{ in } \Omega_Z \text{ and all } q, q' \text{ such that } \Pi_* q = \Pi'_* q'\,. \tag{5.4}$$

This question arises naturally when the marginal probabilities q, q', r are ignored or not known. Since Z, hence r, is the same for both information systems, $\Pi_* q = \Pi'_* q'$ by (3.2). When (5.4) is satisfied we shall say (omitting stars for brevity) that "Y is more informative than Y' as revealed by the posterior probabilities Π, Π'"; or briefly "Π *is more informative than* Π'," and write

Condition (Π): $\Pi > \Pi'$.

The binary relation "$>$" defined above on the set of all matrices P, or all matrices Π, or all matrices Λ, as the case may be, induces in all cases at most a partial ordering on the P (or the Π or the Λ), hence on any set of available information systems. For, in general, there will be some pairs (P, P') or (Π, Π') or (Λ, Λ') for which there exist two payoff functions, ω and ω' in Ω_Z, such that the inequality in (5.2) or (5.3) or (5.4) is valid for ω but not for ω'. In contrast, the equivocation (5.1) used in information theory does not depend on the payoff function and thus induces complete (and weak)

[9] Strictly speaking, the term "not less informative" would be more appropriate. We have chosen terms that will be shown to harmonize with those of Blackwell: see Section 13.

ordering. It will be shown that lower equivocation is necessary but not sufficient for higher informativeness: see Section 12.

Since q, q' and r are all fixed (at starred values) in condition (P) but not in condition (Λ) nor in condition (Π), condition (P) is weaker than either of the other two, and we have

THEOREM 5.1. $(\Lambda) \Rightarrow (P); (\Pi) \Rightarrow (P)$.

We shall now prove that (Λ) and (P) are equivalent.

THEOREM 5.2. $(P) \Rightarrow (\Lambda)$.

PROOF. By Theorem 5.1, it will be enough to prove $(P) \Rightarrow (\Lambda)$. Let $P^Y \equiv (\Lambda, r)$, $P^{Y'} \equiv (\Lambda', r)$ and assume that, as in (5.2.2) but with stars omitted for brevity, condition (P) holds. From (3.1.2) and (4.3), for any payoff function $\omega \in \Omega_Z$ from $D^\omega \times Z$ to the reals,

$$U(P^Y; \omega) \equiv U(\Lambda, r; \omega) \equiv \sum_y \max_{d \in D^\omega} \sum_z r_z \lambda_{zy} \omega(z, d) . \tag{5.5}$$

For any given $r = \bar{r}$ define a new payoff function $\bar{\omega}$ in Ω_Z by

$$\bar{\omega}(z, d) = \frac{\bar{r}_z}{r_z} \omega(z, d); D^{\bar{\omega}} = D^\omega . \tag{5.6}$$

Then, replacing ω by $\bar{\omega}$ in (5.5),

$$U(P^Y; \bar{\omega}) = \sum_y \max_{d \in D^\omega} \sum_z \bar{r}_z \lambda_{zy} \omega(z, d) = U(\Lambda, \bar{r}; \omega) . \tag{5.7}$$

By similar reasoning,

$$U(P^{Y'}; \bar{\omega}) = U(\Lambda', \bar{r}; \omega) . \tag{5.7'}$$

From condition (P), we know

$$U(P^Y; \bar{\omega}) \geqq U(P^{Y'}; \bar{\omega}) . \tag{5.8}$$

Therefore by (5.7), (5.7′) and (5.8),

$$U(\Lambda, \bar{r}; \omega) \geqq U(\Lambda', \bar{r}; \omega) , \tag{5.9}$$

where $\bar{r}$ and ω are arbitrary, so that (5.3) is satisfied. Thus (P) implies (Λ).

It follows from Theorem 5.2 that, if one system is more informative than another as revealed by their respective likelihood matrices, no further knowledge is added by knowing the prior probabilities of events. On the other hand, we shall show in Section 9, Theorem 9.3 that (P) implies (Π) only under certain conditions. Anticipating this result we state a summarizing

THEOREM 5.3. $(\Pi) \Rightarrow (P) \Leftrightarrow (\Lambda)$,

using here and henceforth the symbol $\Rightarrow$ for "implies but is not implied by."

We conclude this section by remarking that it is not possible to apply the relation "more informative than" to net rather than gross information values. Modifying the notation of (4.7) in an obvious way, suppose that the net payoff functions ω_Y and $\omega_{Y'}$ defined respectively on $Z \times D \times Y$ and $Z \times D \times Y'$ are such that for some positive number k

(5.10) $$k > U_Y(Y; \omega_Y) - U_{Y'}(Y'; \omega_{Y'}) \geqq 0 ;$$

then there exists another pair of net payoff functions, $\bar{\omega}_Y$ and $\bar{\omega}_{Y'}$, such that

$$U_Y(Y; \bar{\omega}_Y) - U_{Y'}(Y'; \omega_{Y'}) < 0 :$$

for example, let

$$\bar{\omega}_Y(z, d, y) = \omega_Y(z, d, y) - \frac{1}{2}k ; \qquad \bar{\omega}_{Y'}(z, d, y') = \omega_{Y'}(z, d, y') + \frac{1}{2}k .$$

In particular, when the net payoffs can be decomposed into gross payoffs and information costs as in (4.6), it is always possible to imagine information cost functions $\kappa(y)$, $\kappa'(y')$ that would reverse the second inequality in (5.10).

6. GARBLED INFORMATION

For any joint distribution of three variables z, y, y' the following identities hold:

(6.1) $$\frac{p(y' \mid y, z)}{p(y' \mid y)} \equiv \frac{p(z \mid y, y')}{p(z \mid y)} \equiv \frac{p(y, y' \mid z)}{p(y \mid z) \cdot p(y' \mid y)} ,$$

since each of these three ratios is equal to

$$\frac{p(z, y, y') \cdot p(y)}{p(z, y) \cdot p(y, y')} .$$

We shall say that, for a given set Z of events, the information system Y in *garbled* into Y' when, for all $z \in Z, y \in Y, y' \in Y$ the following condition holds:

Condition (*G*): *Each of the three ratios in* (6.1) *is equal to* 1.

(G) can therefore be written in three equivalent forms. Each seems to agree with the ordinary usage of the term garbling.[10]

(G_1) $$p(y' \mid y, z) = p(y' \mid y) ,$$

i.e., given message y of the original information system Y, the conditional probability of message y' of the garbled system Y' does not depend on event z.

(G_2) $$p(z \mid y, y') = p(z \mid y) ,$$

i.e., the posterior probability of event z given the original message y, does not depend on the garbled message y'.

(G_3) $$p(y, y' \mid z) = p(y \mid z) \cdot p(y' \mid y) :$$

this describes the generation of the pair of messages, y and y': while in general $p(y, y' \mid z) = p(y \mid z) \cdot p(y' \mid y, z)$, this identity becomes in the garbling case, (G_3), because of (G_1).

The following condition that is implied, but does not imply[11] condition (G), is obtained by summing (G_3) over y

[10] This is called "cascade" in information theory; e.g., Abramson [1, (section 5.9)].

[11] A rigorous proof will be given in Section 9.

$$p(y' \mid z) \equiv \sum_y p(y, y' \mid z) = \sum_y p(y \mid z) p(y' \mid y), \qquad \text{all } z \in Z, y' \in Y';$$

or, in the notation of Section 2,

$$\lambda'_{zy'} = \sum_y \lambda_{zy} \gamma_{yy'} . \tag{6.2}$$

Using matrix notation we rewrite this as

Condition (Γ): $\Lambda' = \Lambda\Gamma$,
and obtain

THEOREM 6.1. $(G) \mapsto (\Gamma)$.

A row-stochastic, or Markov, matrix is one with non-negative elements only, and with all row-sums=1. Denote the class of all Markov matrices of order $n \times n'$ by $\mathscr{M}$, and the class of their transposes, i.e., of all "column-stochastic" matrices of order $n' \times n$, by $\mathscr{M}_{(\tau)}$. Then obviously

$$\Gamma \in \mathscr{M}, \Gamma' \in \mathscr{M}_{(\tau)} . \tag{6.3}$$

In honor of David Blackwell, we have called the following condition

Condition (B): There exists a matrix $B = [\beta_{jk}]$ such that

$$\begin{array}{ll} (\mathrm{B}_0) & B \in \mathscr{M} \\ (\mathrm{B}_1) & \Lambda' = \Lambda B . \end{array} \tag{6.4}$$

Condition (B) is implied by the garbling condition (G), but not conversely; for we can prove

THEOREM 6.2. $(G) \mapsto (\Gamma) \mapsto (B)$.

PROOF. By (6.3), (Γ) implies (B). The converse is not necessarily true (see Section 9). Hence our theorem follows from Theorem 6.1. We shall now prove the important

THEOREM 6.3. $(B) \Rightarrow (\Lambda)$.

PROOF. For any $(\Lambda, r) \equiv (\Pi, q)$ and ω, define for every message y_j the optimal decision d_j; that is, by (4.4),

$$\sum_{i=1}^{m} \pi_{ij}\omega(z_i, d_j) \geqq \sum_{i=1}^{m} \pi_{ij}\omega(z_i, d) , \qquad \text{all } d \in D^\omega; \tag{6.5}$$

or, omitting the summation limits for brevity and writing

$$\omega(z_i, d_j) \equiv u_{ij} ,$$

$$\sum_i \pi_{ij} u_{ij} \geqq \sum_i \pi_{ij}\omega(z_i, d) , \qquad \text{all } d \in D^\omega , \tag{6.6}$$

$$\sum_i r_i \lambda_{ij} u_{ij} \geqq \sum_i r_i \lambda_{ij} \omega(z_i, d) , \qquad \text{all } d \in D^\omega , \tag{6.7}$$

by (3.1.2). Then by (4.3)

$$\begin{aligned} U(P; \omega) &\equiv U(\Lambda, r; \omega) \equiv U(\Pi, q; \omega) \\ &= \sum_{i,j} q_j \pi_{ij} u_{ij} = \sum_{i,j} r_i \lambda_{ij} u_{ij} . \end{aligned} \tag{6.8}$$

Similarly, for $(\Lambda', r) \equiv (\Pi', q')$, we define $d'_k \in D^\omega$ and $u'_{ik} \equiv \omega(z_i, d_k)$ so that

$$(6.6') \qquad \sum_i \pi'_{ik} u'_{ik} \geqq \sum_i \pi'_{ik} \omega(z_i, d)\,, \qquad \text{all } d \in D^\omega\,,$$

$$(6.7') \qquad \sum_i r_i \lambda'_{ik} u'_{ik} \geqq \sum_i r_i \lambda'_{ik} \omega(z_i, d)\,, \qquad \text{all } d \in D^\omega\,,$$

and we have

$$(6.8') \qquad \begin{aligned} U(P'; \omega) &\equiv U(\Lambda', r; \omega) \equiv U(\Pi', q'; \omega) \\ &= \sum_{i,k} q'_k \pi'_{ik} u'_{ik} = \sum_{i,k} r_i \lambda'_{ik} u'_{ik}\,. \end{aligned}$$

Suppose (B) holds. Then by (6.8′), (6.7), (6.8) we have, for any r, ω,

$$\begin{aligned} U(\Lambda; r; \omega) &= \sum_{j,k} \beta_{jk} \sum_i r_i \lambda_{ij} u'_{ik} \\ &\leqq \sum_{j,k} \beta_{jk} \sum_i r_i \lambda_{ij} u_{ij} = \sum_{i,j} r_i \lambda_{ij} u_{ij} \\ &= U(\Lambda, r; \omega)\,. \end{aligned}$$

This proves that (B) implies (Λ). In Section 8 we shall prove the converse, so that (B) ⇔ (Λ).

From Theorems 6.1, 6.2 and 6.3 we immediately obtain

THEOREM 6.4. *If Y is garbled into Y' then Y is more informative than Y' as revealed by their likelihood matrices Λ and Λ'.*

The following theorem summarizes the inclusion relations stated in this and the preceding section:

THEOREM 6.5. $(G) \mapsto (\Gamma) \mapsto (B) \Leftrightarrow (\Lambda) \Leftrightarrow (P) \Leftarrow\!\dashv (\Pi)\,.$

The proof of this theorem will be complete when, as mentioned before, it is shown that (Λ) implies (B) (Section 8) and that (B) does not imply (Γ) nor does (Γ) imply (G) (Section 9). Pending these proofs we have proved so far only the weaker

THEOREM 6.6. $(G) \Rightarrow (\Gamma) \Rightarrow (B) \Rightarrow (\Lambda) \Leftrightarrow (P)\,.$

7. COLLAPSING INFORMATION AND JOINING INFORMATION

The case in which Y' is condensed from Y was defined at the end of Section 3 as

$$(C) \qquad Y \,\mathrm{s}\, Y'\,,$$

i.e., each y in Y is contained in one y' in Y'. Hence by (2.7)

$$\begin{array}{lll} \text{either} & y \subset y', & p(y' \mid y) = 1, \quad p(y, y' \mid z) = p(y \mid z) \\ \text{or} & y \not\subset y', & p(y' \mid y) = 0, \quad p(y, y' \mid z) = 0\,. \end{array}$$

In either case, (G_1) is satisfied. Hence (C) implies (G); but the converse is obviously not true. Collapsing information is thus a special case of garbling. We state this as

THEOREM 7.1. $(C) \mapsto (G)\,.$

Let every message in Y be obtained by *joining* a message in Y' with a message belonging to a third information system, T. Then,[12] since Y, Y', T

[12] See, e.g., Halmos [8].

are partitions of X,

Condition (J): $Y = Y' \times T = \{(y' \cap t)\}$, $y' \in Y', t \in T$.
Clearly Y is finer than Y', so that (J) implies (C); but the converse is, of course, not true, and we have

THEOREM 7.2. $(J) \models\!\Rightarrow (C)$.

We can combine these results with those of Sections 5 and 6 into

THEOREM 7.3. $(J) \models\!\Rightarrow (C) \models\!\Rightarrow (G) \models\!\Rightarrow (\Gamma) \models\!\Rightarrow (B) \Rightarrow (\Lambda) \Leftrightarrow (P)$.

Thus Y' is less informative than Y when Y' is garbled or condensed from Y; or when Y is formed by joining Y' with a message from a third information system. Garbling and condensing information occurs when an intermediate node is inserted in a communication network—as, for example, when reports are processed into commands. Joining information occurs when information is centralized. It follows that inserting an intermediate node never increases, and centralizing information never decreases, the gross expected payoff. But the *net* payoffs may be ordered differently. For example, the cost of centralizing information may offset its advantages (see remarks at the end of Section 5) or such centralization may call for rules that are not feasible (cf. Section 4).

8. EQUIVALENCE OF CONDITIONS (B), (Λ), (P) AND (θ)

THEOREM 8.1. $(B) \Leftrightarrow (P) \Leftrightarrow (\Lambda)$.

PROOF. Because of Theorem 5.2 and 6.3, it will suffice to prove (P) ⇒ (B). We shall first prove the following:

LEMMA. If (P) holds, then for any real $(n' \times m)$-matrix $V = [v_{ki}]$ there exists a matrix $M = [m_{kj}] \in \mathscr{M}_{(\tau)}$ such that

$$\sum_{i,k,j} m_{kj} r_i \lambda_{ij} v_{ik} \geqq \sum_{i,k} r_i \lambda'_{ki} v_{ki} \,. \tag{8.1}$$

To prove the lemma let us define, for a given matrix $V = [v_{ki}]$ the payoff function ω as follows: $D^\omega = \{d_1, \cdots, d_{n'}\}$, and

$$\omega(z_i, d_k) = v_{ki} \,, \qquad i = 1, \cdots, m; k = 1, \cdots, n' \,. \tag{8.2}$$

Now define, for each message y_j in Y, the optimal decision $d_{k(j)} \in D^\omega$ by

$$\sum_i r_i \lambda_{ij} \omega(z_i, d_{k(j)}) \geqq \sum_i r_i \lambda_{ij} v_{ki} \,, \qquad k = 1, \cdots, n'; j = 1, \cdots, n \,; \tag{8.3}$$

then by (4.3), (2.1.2)

$$U(P^Y; \omega) = \sum_{i,j} r_i \lambda_{ij} v_{k(j)i} \,. \tag{8.4}$$

Now, for any matrix $T = [t_{kj}] \in \mathscr{M}_{(\tau)}$, we have by (8.3)

$$\sum_{i,j,k} t_{kj} r_i \lambda_{ij} v_{k(j)i} = \sum_{i,j} r_i \lambda_{ij} v_{k(j)i} \geqq \sum_{i,j,k} t_{kj} r_i \lambda_{ij} v_{ki} \,, \tag{8.5}$$

since $t_{kj} \geqq 0, \sum_k t_{kj} = 1$. That is

$$U(P^Y; \omega) \geqq \sum_{i,j,k} t_{kj} r_i \lambda_{ij} v_{ki} . \tag{8.6}$$

Now by definition,

$$U(P^{Y'}; \omega) \geqq \sum_{i,k} r_i \lambda'_{ik} \omega(z_i, d_k) , \qquad \text{all } d_k \in D^\omega, \text{ i.e.,} \tag{8.7}$$

$$U(P^{Y'}; \omega) \geqq \sum_{i,k} r_i \lambda'_{ik} v_{ki} . \tag{8.8}$$

If condition (P) holds then,

$$U(P^Y; \omega) \geqq U(P^{Y'}; \omega) . \tag{8.9}$$

Let our matrix T be such that

$$t_{kj} = \begin{cases} 1 & \text{if } k = k(j) \\ 0 & \text{otherwise.} \end{cases}$$

Then (8.6) becomes an equality. Therefore by (8.8) and (8.9) T has the properties of the matrix M required in the lemma.

To complete the proof of the theorem, let $\mathscr{V}$ be the set of all $(n' \times m)$-matrices $V = [v_{ki}]$ such that $0 \leqq v_{ki} \leqq 1$; as before, let $M = [m_{kj}]$ belong to $\mathscr{M}_{(\tau)}$; and define a function $\Psi(M, V)$ on $\mathscr{M}_{(\tau)} \times \mathscr{V}$ by

$$\Psi(M, V) = \sum_{i,j,k} m_{kj} r_i \lambda_{ij} v_{ki} - \sum_{i,k} r_i \lambda'_{ik} v_{ki} . \tag{8.10}$$

Then Ψ is a bilinear function of M and V; and the factors $\mathscr{M}_{(\tau)}$ and $\mathscr{V}$ of its domain are both closed, bounded and convex sets in $(n' \times n)$- and $(n' \times m)$-spaces, respectively. Therefore, by a saddle point theorem—see, e.g., Karlin [9, (II, theorem 1.51)], there exists a pair $[m^0_{kj}] \equiv M^0 \in \mathscr{M}_{(\tau)}$ and $V^0 \in \mathscr{V}$ such that

$$\Psi(M, V^0) \leqq \Psi(M^0, V^0) \leqq \Psi(M^0, V) , \tag{8.11}$$

for all $M \in \mathscr{M}_{(\tau)}$ and $V \in \mathscr{V}$.

Suppose (P) holds. Applying our lemma to $V = V^0$, we see that there exists a matrix $M \in \mathscr{M}_{(\tau)}$ such that $\Psi(M, V^0) \geqq 0$. Therefore by (8.11) $\Psi(M^0, V^0) \geqq 0$ and thus

$$\Psi(M^0, V) \geqq 0 , \qquad \text{all } V \in \mathscr{V} . \tag{8.12}$$

Define $V^{(ki)} \in \mathscr{V}$ as a matrix whose (k, i)-th element is 1 and all other elements are 0. Then by (8.10), (8.12)

$$\Psi(M^0, V^{(ki)}) = \sum_j m^0_{kj} r_i \lambda_{ij} - r_i \lambda'_{ik} \geqq 0 ,$$

and since all $r_i > 0$ by (3.1.1), we have

$$\sum_i m^0_{kj} \lambda_{ij} \geqq \lambda'_{ik} , \qquad i = 1, \cdots, m; k = 1, \cdots, n' . \tag{8.13}$$

If in (8.13) at least one of the inequalities is strict, we obtain a contradiction

$$\sum_{i,j,k} m^0_{kj} \lambda_{ij} = \sum_{i,j} \lambda_{ij} = m > \sum_{i,k} \lambda'_{ik} = m , \tag{8.14}$$

since $\sum_k m^0_{kj} = \sum_j \lambda_{ij} = \sum_k \lambda'_{ik} = 1$. Therefore

(8.15) $$\sum_j m^0_{kj}\lambda_{ij} = \lambda'_{ik}\,, \qquad i = 1, \cdots, m;\ k = 1, \cdots, n', \text{ i.e.,}$$

(8.16) $$\Lambda' = \Lambda M^0_{(\tau)}$$

where $M^0_{(\tau)}$ is the transposed matrix of M^0, hence

(8.17) $$M^0_{(\tau)} \in \mathcal{M}\,.$$

Now put $B = M^0_{(\tau)}$. Then B fulfills the conditions (6.4). This proves that (P) $\Rightarrow$ (B) and completes the proof of our theorem.

We shall now show that the following condition (which will prove useful in Section 9) is equivalent to (B) and thus to (P) and (Λ):

Condition (θ): There exists a matrix $\theta \equiv [\theta_{jk}]$ such that

$$(\theta_0):\ \theta \in \mathcal{M}_{(\tau)}$$
$$(\theta_1):\ \Pi' = \Pi\theta \text{ and}$$
$$(\theta_2):\ q = \theta q'\,.$$

Note that (θ) is a property of the joint distributions P, P', while (B) is a property of the likelihoods Λ, Λ' only.

THEOREM 8.2. *(B)* $\Leftrightarrow$ (θ).

PROOF. By definition (see Section 3),

(8.19) $$q_j = \sum_i r_i\lambda_{ij} > 0, \quad q'_k = \sum_i r_i\lambda'_{ik} > 0$$

(8.20) $$q_j\pi_{ij} = r_i\lambda_{ij} \geqq 0, \quad q'_k\pi'_{ik} = r_i\lambda'_{ik} \geqq 0\,.$$

Suppose (B) is true: that is, there exists $B \equiv [\beta_{jk}]$ such that

(8.21) $$\lambda'_{ik} = \sum_j \lambda_{ij}\beta_{jk}; \quad \beta_{jk} \geqq 0, \quad \sum_k \beta_{jk} = 1\,.$$

Then by (8.19)

(8.22) $$q'_k = \sum_{i,j} r_i\lambda_{ij}\beta_{jk} = \sum_j q_j\beta_{jk}\,.$$

Given the matrix B define a matrix $[\theta_{jk}] \equiv \theta$ by the following equations:

(8.23) $$\theta_{jk}q'_k = \beta_{jk}q_j\,, \qquad \text{all } j, k\,.$$

It is easily verified that θ is in $\mathcal{M}_{(\tau)}$ (using (8.22)); that $q = \theta q'$ (using (8.4) and (8.23)); and that $\Pi' = \Pi\theta$ (using (8.20), (8.21), (8.23)). Hence (B) $\Rightarrow$ (θ). To prove the converse, note that condition (θ_1) implies, by (8.20)

$$\pi'_{ik} = \frac{r_i\lambda'_{ik}}{q'_k} = \sum_j \pi_{ij}\theta_{jk} = \sum_j \frac{r_i\lambda_{ij}}{q_j}\theta_{jk}\,,$$

(8.24) $$\lambda'_{ik} = q'_k \sum_j \frac{\theta_{ik}}{q_j}\lambda_{ij}\,.$$

Define $B \equiv [\beta_{jk}]$ by (8.23). Then by (θ_2)

$$\sum_k \beta_{jk} = \frac{1}{q_j}\sum_k \theta_{jk}q'_k = \frac{q_j}{q_j} = 1; \quad \beta_{jk} \geqq 0\,,$$

hence $B \in \mathscr{M}$; moreover by (θ_1) and (8.23), $\Lambda' = \Lambda B$. Thus B satisfies both conditions in (6.4), and we have proved that $(\theta) \Rightarrow$ (B). This completes the proof.

Combining Theorems 8.1 and 8.2, we have

THEOREM 8.3. $(P) \Leftrightarrow (\Lambda) \Leftrightarrow (B) \Leftrightarrow (\theta)$.

Using the matrix $\Gamma' \equiv [p(y \mid y')]$ defined in (3.3′) we introduce

Condition (Γ'): $\Pi' = \Pi\Gamma'$.

Then we have

THEOREM 8.4. $(G) \Rightarrow (\Gamma') \Rightarrow (\theta)$.

PROOF. Consider the identities

$$p(y, z \mid y') = p(y, y', z)/p(y') = p(z \mid y, y') \cdot p(y, y')/p(y')$$
$$p(y, z \mid y') = p(z \mid y, y') \cdot p(y \mid y') ;$$

summing over y

$$p(z \mid y') = \sum_y p(z \mid y, y') \cdot p(y \mid y') .$$

This becomes, if (G_2) holds,

$$p(z \mid y') = \sum_y p(z \mid y) \cdot p(y \mid y')$$

$$\Pi' = \Pi\Gamma' .$$

This proves $(G) \Rightarrow (\Gamma')$. It is clear that if (Γ') holds, then (θ) is satisfied with $\theta = \Gamma'$. This completes the proof.

If a matrix B, and therefore also matrix θ, exists, it is possible to interpret the information systems Y and Y' *as if* Y were garbled into Y', although it is not known whether or not the trivariate distribution on $Z \times Y \times Y'$ satisfies condition (G).

Example. As in Section 2, let z be the visibility at the airport. Let y be the true atmospheric pressure, and y' be the reading on a barometer. Then presumably condition (G) is satisfied, and by the proof of Theorems 6.5 and 8.4, conditions (B) and (θ) are satisfied by matrices $B = \Gamma$ and $\theta = \Gamma'$ (and possibly also other matrices). If, on the other hand, we interpret y', not as a reading on a barometer, but as, say, the true level of humidity, then we have no reason to suppose that Y is garbled into Y' (or conversely). If the bivariate distributions on $Z \times Y$ and $Z \times Y'$, respectively, happen to satisfy condition (B), hence (θ), it may be useful to interpret the matrix θ *as if* it were identical with Γ' (and B with Γ). That is, we can conceive of the messages y_j as follows: given y'_k, the message y_j will be produced, using a random device, with probability $p(y_j \mid y'_k) = \theta_{jk}$, $j = 1, \cdots, n$.

9. COMPARATIVE INFORMATIVENESS REVEALED BY POSTERIOR PROBABILITIES ONLY: THE CASE OF INDEPENDENT Π MATRIX

Let π_j and π'_k be the j-th column of Π and the k-th column of Π' respectively. Now, π_j and π'_k can be interpreted as m-dimensional vectors or points in m-dimensional space. Accordingly Π and Π' can be interpreted—whenever it is convenient—as two sets of vectors: $\Pi \equiv \{\pi_1, \cdots, \pi_n\}$, $\Pi' \equiv \{\pi'_1, \cdots, \pi'_{n'}\}$. Let S^{m-1} be the simplex defined by the set of all points $v = (v_1, \cdots, v_m)$ such that $v_i \geqq 0, \sum v_i = 1$. Clearly both Π and Π' are subsets of S^{m-1}.

Define the following condition: the set Π' is contained in the convex hull $K(\Pi)$ of the set Π:

Condition (K): $\Pi' \subset K(\Pi)$.

This is represented by Figures 2a, 3a, 3b, 4, but not by Figures 2b, 3d. Clearly (K) is equivalent to the following condition: there exists a matrix M such that

$$M \in \mathscr{M}_{(\tau)};\ \Pi' = \Pi M : \tag{9.1}$$

(9.1) is identical with conditions (θ_0) and (θ_1) of Section 8. Hence (θ) which requires, in addition, (θ_2), implies but is not implied by (K). We have thus

THEOREM 9.1. $(\theta) \mapsto (K)$.

In this section we shall consider the case when the columns of the matrix Π (but not necessarily of Π') are linearly independent, that is:

Condition (I_π): (rank of Π) $= n$.

This condition will be later shown to apply in two important cases: the binomial case ($n = 2$) of Section 10 and the noiseless case of Section 11.

Similarly we introduce

Condition (I_Λ): (rank of Λ) $= n$.

Noting that the r_i and q_j are all > 0 it is easy to prove

THEOREM 9.2. $(I_\pi) \Leftrightarrow (I_\Lambda)$.

Now we shall prove

THEOREM 9.3. *If conditions* (I_π) *and* (θ) *(hence also condition* (B)*) are true, then* (B) *and* (θ) *are satisfied by a unique pair of matrices* B, θ *related by the equations*

$$\theta_{jk} q'_k = \beta_{jk} q_j\,, \qquad \text{all } j, k\,. \tag{8.23}$$

PROOF. By the hypothesis, we have

$$(\theta_1)\colon \Pi' = \Pi\theta, \quad (B_1)\colon \Lambda' = \Lambda B\,,$$

and Π consists of linearly independent columns. Then by Theorem 9.2, Λ also consists of linearly independent columns. Therefore, in the above relations (θ_1) and (B_1), θ and B are unique. Now in proving Theorem 8.2 we have shown that if a matrix B satisfying condition (B) exists then a matrix θ defined by equations (8.23) will satisfy condition (θ); and conversely. Hence the unique pair B, θ satisfying $(B), (\theta)$ respectively must also satisfy equations (8.23). Stronger than Theorem 9.3 is

THEOREM 9.4. $[(I_\Lambda)$ *and* $(B)] \Leftrightarrow [(B)$ *with unique* $B] \Leftrightarrow [(\theta)$ *with unique* $\theta]$.

PROOF. By Theorems 9.2 and 9.3, it is sufficient to prove that, when (B)

FIGURES 2, 3, 4

SIMPLEX REPRESENTATION OF POSTERIOR PROBABILITIES

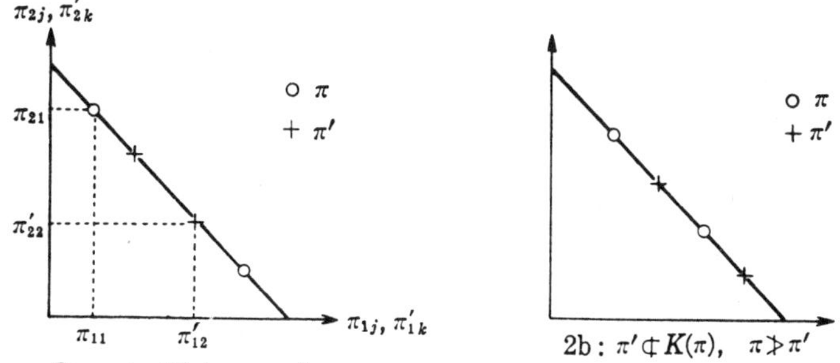

2a: $\pi' \subset K(\pi)$, $\pi > \pi'$ 2b: $\pi' \not\subset K(\pi)$, $\pi \not> \pi'$

FIGURE 2

$m = 2$

Y, Y' BINARY: $m = 2 = n = n'$

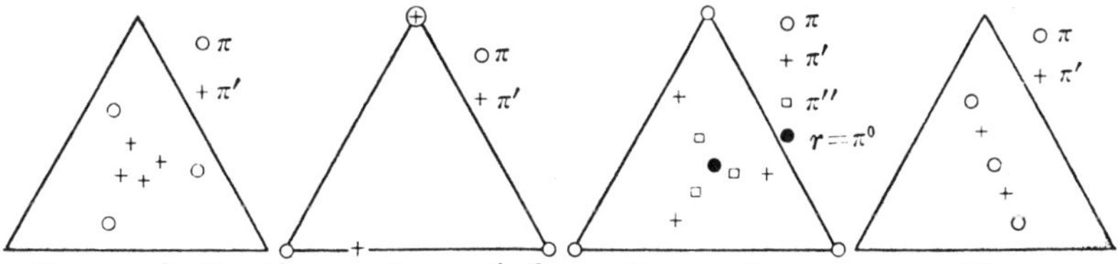

3a: $m=3=n$ $\pi' \subset K(\pi)$, $\pi > \pi'$ 3b: $m=3=n$, $n'=2$ Y, Y' noiseless 3c: $m=3$ $\pi > \pi' > \pi'' > \pi^0$ 3d

FIGURE 3

$m = 3$

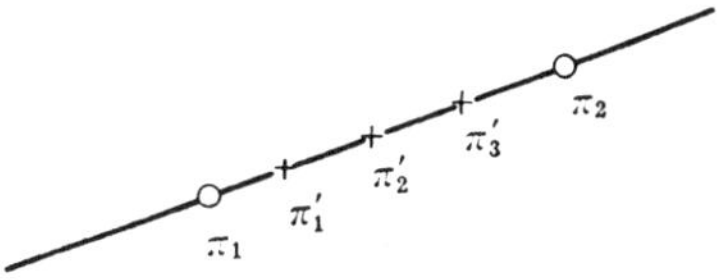

FIGURE 4

$m \geqq 2$

Y BINOMIAL: $n = 2$

holds and B is unique, then (I_Λ) holds. Suppose (B) holds, with unique $B \equiv [\beta_{jk}]$ but (I_Λ) does not hold. Let $g < n$ and let $\lambda_1, \cdots, \lambda_g$ be linearly independent, while $\lambda_{g+1}, \cdots, \lambda_n$ are linearly dependent on $\{\lambda_1, \cdots, \lambda_g\}$. That is

$$\lambda_h = \sum_{l=1}^{g} a_{hl}\lambda_l\,, \qquad h = g+1, \cdots, n\,. \tag{9.2}$$

By condition (B) and (9.2)

(9.3) $$\lambda'_k = \sum_{j=1}^{n} \beta_{jk}\lambda_j = \sum_{l=1}^{g} \left(\beta_{lk} + \sum_{h=g+1}^{n} a_{hl}\beta_{hk}\right)\lambda_l\,, \qquad k = 1, \cdots, n'\,.$$

Let us define a matrix $\Delta \equiv [\delta_{jk}]$ as follows:

(9.4) $$\delta_{j1} = \beta_{j1} + \varepsilon_j$$

(9.5) $$\delta_{js} = \beta_{js} - \frac{1}{n'-1}\varepsilon_j\,, \qquad s = 2, \cdots, n';\ j = 1, \cdots, n\,,$$

where ε_j, $j = 1, \cdots, n$ are numbers such that

(9.6) $$\varepsilon_l + \sum_{h=g+1}^{n} a_{hl}\varepsilon_h = 0\,, \qquad l = 1, \cdots, g\,.$$

We shall prove our theorem for the case in which all $\beta_{jk} > 0$. Clearly it is possible to choose all ε_j, $j = 1, \cdots, n$ which satisfy (9.6) and have arbitrarily small absolute values. Then, for $\beta_{jk} > 0$ and $|\varepsilon_j|$ sufficiently small, we have by (9.4), (9.5)

(9.7) $$\delta_{jk} \geqq 0, \qquad \sum_k \delta_{jk} = \sum_k \beta_{jk} = 1\,.$$

By (9.4), (9.5), (9.6),

(9.8) $$\delta_{lk} + \sum_h a_{hl}\delta_{hk} = \beta_{lk} + \sum_h a_{hl}\beta_{hk}\,.$$

Therefore by (9.2), (9.3), (9.8),

(9.9) $$\lambda'_k = \sum_{l=1}^{g}\left(\delta_{lk} + \sum_h a_{hl}\delta_{hk}\right)\lambda_l = \sum_{j=1}^{n}\delta_{jk}\lambda_j\,.$$

Then it follows from (9.7) and (9.8) that $\Delta \in \mathscr{M}$, $\Delta \neq B$, and $\Lambda' = \Lambda\Delta$. The part of the theorem involving θ is proved similarly.

We shall now show that, under condition (I_π), if Y' is obtained by garbling Y—see Section 6—then the matrices B and θ are identical, respectively, with the matrices $\Gamma \equiv [\gamma_{jk}]$ and $\Gamma' \equiv [\gamma'_{jk}]$ defined in Section 3:

$$\gamma_{jk} \equiv p(y'_k \mid y_j); \qquad \gamma'_{jk} \equiv p(y_j \mid y'_k)\,.$$

THEOREM 9.5. $[(I_\pi)$ *and* $(G)] \Rightarrow (B = \Gamma, \theta = \Gamma')$.

PROOF. By Theorem 6.5 and 8.2, condition (G) implies that

$$\Lambda' = \Lambda\Gamma, \quad \Lambda' = \Lambda B, \quad \Pi' = \Pi\theta\,.$$

Hence $\Lambda(\Gamma - B) = 0$. Let (I_π) hold. Then by Theorem 9.2, Λ consists of independent columns, and therefore $\Gamma = B$, i.e.:

$$\gamma_{jk} \equiv p(y'_k \mid y_j) = \beta_{jk}\,, \qquad \text{all } j, k\,.$$

By Theorem 9.3, θ is uniquely defined by

$$\theta_{jk} = \beta_{jk}q_j/q'_k = p(y'_k \mid y_j)p(y_j)/p(y'_k)$$
$$= p(y_j \mid y'_k)\,;$$

hence

$$[\theta_{jk}] = [\gamma'_{jk}], \qquad \theta = \Gamma'\,.$$

We shall now prove that (Γ) does not imply (G), nor does (B) imply (Γ). Condition (P) means

(9.10) $$p(y' \mid z) = \sum_y p(y \mid z) p(y' \mid y) .$$

On the other hand we have identically

(9.11) $$p(y' \mid z) = \sum_y p(y, y' \mid z) = \sum_y p(y \mid z) p(y' \mid z, y) .$$

If Π is linearly dependent, then by Theorem 9.4, equations (9.10), (9.11) are consistent with the inequality

$$p(y' \mid y) \neq p(y' \mid z, y) ,$$

as contrasted with (G_1). Hence (G) does not necessarily follow from (Γ). Similarly we can prove that (B) does not imply (Γ).

We shall now show that the independence condition (I_π) is both sufficient and necessary for the equivalence of the conditions (P), (Π) and (K). We shall start with

THEOREM 9.6. $(I_\pi) \Rightarrow ((K) \Leftrightarrow (P))$.

PROOF. By Theorems 8.3 and 9.1, we always have (P) ⇒ (K). Therefore we need only prove that (K) ⇒ (P) if the linear independence condition (I_π) holds; i.e., that

(9.12) $$(\mathrm{I}_\pi) \Rightarrow ((\mathrm{K}) \Rightarrow (\mathrm{P})) .$$

Let Y and Y' be two information systems with known $P^Y \equiv (\Pi_*, q_*)$ and $P^{Y'} \equiv (\Pi'_*, q'_*)$ respectively, where by (3.2)

(9.13) $$\Pi_* q_* = \Pi'_* q'_* .$$

Suppose (K) holds; that is, there exists a matrix M satisfying (9.1) with $\Pi = \Pi_*$, $\Pi' = \Pi'_*$. Then by (9.13)

(9.14) $$\Pi_*(q_* - M q'_*) = 0 .$$

If (I_π) holds for Π_*, then, the linear independence of its columns implies

(9.15) $$q_* = M q'_* ,$$

so that, by (9.1), all three components of condition (θ) hold. Hence by Theorem 8.3, (P) holds. This proves that

(9.16) $$(\mathrm{I}_\pi) \Rightarrow ((\mathrm{K}) \Rightarrow (\mathrm{P})) .$$

We shall now prove

THEOREM 9.7. $(I_\pi) \Rightarrow ((P) \Leftrightarrow (\Pi))$.

PROOF. Since by Theorem 5.1, (Π) always implies (P), we need only to prove that (P) implies (Π) if (I_π) holds; i.e., that

(9.17) $$(I_\pi) \Rightarrow ((P) \Rightarrow (\Pi)) .$$

First note that since (P) is equivalent to (θ) by Theorem 8.3, condition (Π) is by definition equivalent to the following: for any q, q' such that

(9.18) $$\Pi_* q = \Pi'_* q'$$

there exists a matrix θ such that

$$\theta \in \mathscr{M}_{(\tau)} ,$$

(9.19) $$\Pi'_* = \Pi_* \theta ,$$

$$q = \theta q' .$$

The last three conditions correspond to the three components of condition (θ), applied here to all q, q' consistent with (9.18), and not only (as in (9.13)) to a particular q_*, q'_*.

Suppose (P), or equivalently (θ), holds for the known (starred) distributions; that is, there exists a matrix θ_* (say) such that

(9.20.0) $$\theta_* \in \mathscr{M}_{(\tau)} ,$$

(9.20.1) $$\Pi'_* = \Pi_* \theta_* ,$$

(9.20.2) $$q_* = \theta_* q'_* .$$

Thus, under condition (P), there exists at least one triple (q, q', θ) which satisfied (9.19), viz., the triple (q_*, q'_*, θ_*). Now let q, q' be undetermined except for the constraint (9.18). Then by (9.20.1),

(9.21) $$\Pi_*(q - \theta_* q') = 0 .$$

If the columns of Π_* are linearly independent then (9.21) implies $q = \theta_* q'$; i.e., (P) then implies (Π) with $\theta = \theta_*$. Therefore

(9.22) $$(I_\pi) \Rightarrow ((P) \Rightarrow (\Pi)) .$$

This completes the proof.

Combining Theorems 9.6 and 9.7, we have

THEOREM 9.8. $(I_\pi) \Rightarrow ((K) \Rightarrow (P) \Rightarrow (\Pi))$.

Example. Let $m = n = n' = 3$. Figure 3c shows a sequence of triangles (with vertices representing the matrices Π, Π', Π'', Π^0), nestling in each other and containing the point r; the largest triangle coincides with the simplex itself, and the sequence shrinks to the point r as its lower bound. The vertices of any of these triangles represent the set $\Pi = \{\pi_1, \pi_2, \pi_3\}$ of some information system Y, and the triangle itself is $K(\Pi)$. If the triangle corresponding to Y' is nestled in the triangle corresponding to Y, then $\Pi' \subset K(\Pi)$; and since the vertices are not colinear, condition (I_π) is satisfied. Hence by Theorem 9.2, $\Pi > \Pi'$: the system Y is more informative than Y', as revealed by the posterior probabilities alone. Note that the vertices of the largest triangle in the sequence, i.e. of the simplex itself, give perfect information; while the lower bound represented by point r is just as informative as "null information," i.e. the knowledge of the prior probabilities alone, without any messages. The sequence is ordered according to informativeness, and so is any other sequence of nestling triangles. The set of all triangles is a lattice, partially ordered by the relation "more informative than," with "complete information" as the maximum element, and "null information" as the infimum.

10. BINOMIAL AND BINARY INFORMATION SYSTEMS

The numbers m, n, n' are always $\geqq 2$. Following Blackwell and Girshick [4] the case $m = 2$ will be called *dichotomy*. If information system Y consists of 2 messages, $n = 2$, it is called *binomial*; and when $m = n = 2$, the information—theoretical literature—e.g., Feinstein [7]—calls the channel (the information system) Y, *binary*. We shall denote these conditions thus:

$$(\text{d}): \quad m = 2; \qquad (\text{b}): \quad n = 2; \qquad (\text{b}'): \quad n' = 2\,.$$

Thus a binary channel is defined by (b) and (d).

Since always $m \geqq 2$, condition (b) implies that the columns of the matrix Π are linearly independent. Thus (b) implies (I_π), but of course, not conversely. Hence by Theorem 9.8

THEOREM 10.1. $(b) \mapsto ((K) \Leftrightarrow (\Pi) \mapsto (P))$.

The case is illustrated on Figure 4, where the points π_1, π_2 representing Y, and the points π_1', π_2', π_3' representing Y' are all arranged on a straight line in a space of m dimensions (arbitrary $m \geqq 2$), and all π_k' lie *between* π_1 and π_2.

The more special case $n = n' = m = 2$—i.e. (b), (b′) and (d)—occurs in the testing of simple hypotheses and in comparing "binary channels." After labelling the two events z_1 and z_2 arbitrarily, let us label the two messages in Y so that

$$\pi_{11} \geqq \pi_{12}\,. \tag{10.1}$$

Then condition (K) takes the form

$$\begin{aligned} \pi_{11} &\geqq \pi_{11}' \geqq \pi_{12}\,, \\ \pi_{11} &\geqq \pi_{12}' \geqq \pi_{12}\,, \end{aligned} \tag{10.2}$$

and by Theorem 10.1, we have

THEOREM 10.2. *Let Y and Y' be two binary channels (i.e., let $m = n = n' = 2$); then Y is more informative than Y' if and only if the posterior probabilities satisfy the relation* (10.2); *provided the two messages in Y are labelled so as to make $\pi_{11} \geqq \pi_{12}$.*

This criterion (usable only when the posterior probabilities are known) is simpler than the one provided by Blackwell-Girshick [4, (section 12.5)] and based on the likelihood matrix Λ.

11. COMPARISON OF NOISELESS INFORMATION SYSTEMS

Let Y be a noiseless information system, i.e. $Z \,\text{s}\, Y$ (see Section 2). Then $\lambda_{ij} \equiv p(y_j \mid z_i) = 1$ or 0, all i, j. In general, $\sum_j \lambda_{ij} = 1$ and $\sum_i \gamma_i \lambda_{ij} = q_j > 0$. Therefore, if Y is noiseless, then each row of its Λ matrix contains one and only one non-zero ($= 1$) element and each column contains at least one non-zero ($= 1$) element. Now $\pi_{ij} = r_i \lambda_{ij} / q_j$. Hence, whenever $\lambda_{ij} = 1$ or 0, then $\pi_{ij} = r_i / q_j$ (> 0) or 0, respectively. Therefore;

(11.1) *If Y is noiseless, then each row of its Π matrix contains one and only one non-zero (> 0) element and each column contains at least one non-zero (> 0) element.*

Using (11.1) we shall prove the following property of condition (N) defined in Section 3:

THEOREM 11.1. *(N)* $\models\Rightarrow$ *((I_π) and $(I_{\pi'})$)*.

PROOF. Suppose Y is noiseless and let

$$\sum_{j=1}^{n} g_j \pi_{ij} = 0 , \qquad \text{all } i = 1, \cdots, m , \tag{11.2}$$

for some real numbers $g_1, \cdots, g_n$. We shall then show that $g_j = 0$, for all j, i.e., the columns of Π are linearly independent. We note that by (11.1), for any fixed j, say $j = j_1$, there is at least one i, say $i = i_1$, such that $\pi_{i_1 j_1} > 0$. Then by (11.1), $\pi_{i_1 j} = 0$, for all $j \neq j_1$. Therefore, for $i = i_1$, (11.2) becomes $g_{j_1}\pi_{i_1 j_1} = 0$. Since $\pi_{i_1 j_1} > 0$, we have

$$g_{j_1} = 0 , \qquad j_1 = 1, \cdots, n ; \tag{11.3}$$

that is, (I_π) holds. Similarly, for Y' noiseless, we have $(I_{\pi'})$. The converse obviously does not hold.

Using Theorems 9.7 and 11.1, we have

THEOREM 11.2. $(N) \models\Rightarrow ((P) \Leftrightarrow (\Pi) \Leftrightarrow (K))$.

In Section 2, we defined condition (C); and by Theorem 7.3, (C) $\models\Rightarrow$ (P). Hence by Theorem 11.2, we have

THEOREM 11.3. $(N) \models\Rightarrow ((C) \Rightarrow (\Pi) \Leftrightarrow (P) \Leftrightarrow (K))$.

Thus, if both Y and Y' are noiseless, and Y is finer than Y', then Y is more informative than Y', as revealed by posterior probabilities of events

$$\Pi' = \Pi M, \; M \equiv [\mu_{jk}] \in \mathscr{M}_{(\tau)} , \tag{11.4}$$

which is, of course, our condition (K).

Remark 1. The matrix $M \equiv [\mu_{jk}]$ in (11.4), with $ZsYsY'$, $\Pi' = \Pi M$, has the following interpretation:

$$M = \Gamma' \equiv [\gamma'_{jk}] \equiv [p(y_j \mid y'_k)] ,$$

since by Theorems 11.1, 11.3, 7.1, 9.5, we have $\theta = \Gamma' = M$.

Example. Let $ZsYsY'$, so that by Theorem 11.3 and Remark 1, $\Pi' = \Pi M$, $\mu_{jk} = p(y_j \mid y'_k)$; let the posterior probability matrices be as follows (with $0 < \pi'_{11} = 1 - \pi'_{21} < 1$);

$$\Pi = \begin{pmatrix} 1 & 0 & 0 \\ 0 & 1 & 0 \\ 0 & 0 & 1 \end{pmatrix} \qquad \Pi' = \begin{pmatrix} \pi'_{11} & 0 \\ \pi'_{21} & 0 \\ 0 & 1 \end{pmatrix} .$$

Then $y'_1 = y_1 \cup y_2$, $y'_2 = y_3$. Since Π is the identity matrix I, we have $\Pi' = \Pi M = IM = M = \Gamma'$. The case is illustrated in Figure 3b, where the point π'_1 divides the base of the triangle in proportion $\pi'_{21} : \pi'_{11} = p(y_2 | y'_1) : p(y_1 | y'_1)$.

Now we shall prove the following

THEOREM 11.4. *$(N) \models ((C) \Leftrightarrow (K) \Leftrightarrow (\Pi) \Leftrightarrow (P))$, when X is finite.*

PROOF. By Theorems 11.2 and 11.3, it will suffice to prove that

$$(N) \models ((K) \Rightarrow (C)), \text{ when } X \text{ is finite.}$$

Let us assume (N) and (K): that is, $Z s Y$, $Z s Y'$ and (11.4) holds, so that

$$\pi'_{ik} = \sum_j \pi_{ij}\mu_{jk}, \qquad \text{all } j, k. \tag{11.5}$$

For any fixed k, say $k = k_1$, let $z_{i_1} \in Z$ be contained in y'_k (remember that Z is a sub-partition of the noiseless information system Y'.) Then $\lambda'_{i_1 k_1} = 1$, and

$$\pi'_{i_1 k_1} > 0. \tag{11.6}$$

Since Y is noiseless, by (11.1) the i_1-th row of Π contains one and only one non-zero element, say $\pi_{i_1 j_1} > 0$. Then

$$\pi_{i_1 j_1} > 0, \qquad \pi_{i_1 j} = 0, \qquad \text{for all } j \neq j_1. \tag{11.7}$$

In (11.5), let $i = i_1$ and $k = k_1$; then by (11.7),

$$\pi'_{i_1 k_1} = \pi_{i_1 j_1}\mu_{j_1 k_1}; \tag{11.8}$$

hence

$$\mu_{j_1 k_1} > 0, \tag{11.9}$$

by (11.6), (11.7), (11.8). Suppose X is finite. Then $\pi_{i_1 j_1} > 0$, (i.e., $\lambda_{i_1 j_1} = 1$) implies $z_{i_1} \subset y_{j_1}$; therefore, (11.7) admits of the following interpretation:

(11.10) *For any fixed $k = k_1$, and any $z_{i_1} \subset y'_{k_1}$, there exists at least one y_{j_1} such that $z_{i_1} \subset y_{j_1}$.*

Now, for this y_{j_1}, let $z_{i'} \in Z$ be contained in y_{j_1}. Then $\lambda_{i' j_1} = 1$ and

$$\pi_{i' j_1} > 0, \qquad \pi_{i' j} = 0, \qquad \text{for all } j \neq j_1, \tag{11.11}$$

by (11.1). Then, for $i = i'$ and $k = k_1$ (11.5) becomes

$$\pi_{i' k_1} = \pi_{i' j_1}\mu_{j_1 k_1}, \tag{11.12}$$

so that by (11.9), (11.11) and (11.12), $\pi_{i' k_1} > 0$, $\mu_{i' k_1} = 1$. When X is finite this implies $z_{i'} \subset y'_{k_1}$. This proves that

(11.13) *For any y_{j_1} such that $y_{j_1} \cap y'_{k_1} \neq \varnothing$ $\;y_{j_1} \subset y'_{k_1}$.*

From (11.10) and (11.13), we conclude that, if (N) and (K) hold and X is finite, then any y'_k is a union of disjoint y's, i.e., $Y s Y'$, viz., (C) holds. This completes the proof.

Remark 2. Let Y be noiseless: If the columns of Π' are linear combinations of Π, that is, if there exists a $n \times n'$ matrix $A = [\alpha_{jk}]$ such that $\Pi' = \Pi A$, i.e.,

$$\pi'_{ik} = \sum_j \pi_{ij}\alpha_{jk}, \qquad \text{all } i, k, \tag{11.14}$$

then $A \in \mathscr{M}^{(c)}_{n \times n'}$; hence (K) holds.

To prove, sum both sides of (11.14) with respect to i; then $\sum_j \alpha_{jk} = 1$, all k (since $\sum_i \pi'_{ik} = \sum_i \pi_{ij} = 1$). It remains to prove that $\alpha_{jk} \geqq 0$ for all j, k. Fix $j = j_1$, $k = k_1$, and let $i = i_1$ be such that $\pi_{i_1 j_1} > 0$. Since Y is noiseless, we have by (11.1), (11.14)

$$\pi'_{i_1 k_1} = \pi_{i_1 j_1} \alpha_{j_1 k_1} .$$

Since $\pi_{i_1 j_1} > 0$, if $\pi'_{i_1 k_1} > 0$ we have $\alpha_{j_1 k_1} > 0$; and if $\pi'_{i_1 k_1} = 0$, then $\alpha_{j_1 k_1} = 0$. Hence $\alpha_{jk} \geqq 0$, all j, k, completing the proof.

12. CONVEX OPERATORS ON POSTERIOR PROBABILITIES: THE EQUIVOCATION PARAMETER

For any payoff function ω, we shall define a function υ_ω on the simplex S^{m-1} (i.e., on the set of all vectors $\xi \equiv (\xi_1, \cdots, \xi_m)$ such that $\xi_i \geqq 0$, $\xi_i = 1$) as follows:

$$\upsilon(\xi) \equiv \max_{d \in D^\omega} \sum_{i=1}^{m} \omega(z_i, d)\xi_i . \tag{12.1}$$

Then by (4.3), we have

$$U(P; \omega) \equiv \sum_{j=1}^{n} q_j \upsilon_\omega(\pi_j) , \tag{12.2}$$

where π_j is the j-th column of Π. Consider a pair of probability distributions (Π, q), (Π', q') with the following property:[13]
Condition (φ): For any convex function φ on S^{m-1}

$$\sum_{k=1}^{n} q_j \varphi(\pi_j) \geqq \sum_{k=1}^{n'} q_k \varphi(\pi'_k) . \tag{12.3}$$

We shall prove[14]

THEOREM 12.1. $(P) \Leftrightarrow (\varphi)$.

PROOF. First we shall prove $(\varphi) \Rightarrow (\mathrm{P})$. We have by (12.1), for any two vectors $\xi_1 \equiv (\xi_{11}, \cdots, \xi_{m1})$, $\xi_2 \equiv (\xi_{12}, \cdots, \xi_{m2})$, both in S^{m-1}, and letting $0 \leqq \alpha \leqq 1$,

$$\begin{aligned} \upsilon_\omega(\alpha\xi_1 + (1-\alpha)\xi_2) &\leqq \alpha \max_{d \in D^\omega} \sum_i \omega(z_i, d)\xi_{i1} + (1-\alpha) \max_{d \in D^\omega} \sum_i \omega(z_i, d)\xi_{i2} \\ &= \alpha\upsilon_\omega(\xi_1) + (1-\alpha)\upsilon_\omega(\varphi_2) . \end{aligned} \tag{12.4}$$

That is, υ_ω is a convex function on S^{m-1}. Therefore, using expression (12.2) for $U(P; \omega)$ and a similar one for $U(P'; \omega)$, condition (φ) is seen to imply that $U(P; \omega) \geqq U(P'; \omega)$, all ω, i.e., condition (P).

[13] In DeGroot's [6] definition of an information amount $I[Y; r; \phi]$ it is reasonable to require that $I[Y, r; \phi] \geq 0$ for all Y and r. He proves that an (uncertainty) function ϕ is concave on S^{m-1} is a necessary and sufficient condition for that.

[14] Compare also Blackwell-Girshick [4]. While that book is restricted to finite sets of messages and of events, earlier work of Blackwell [2, 3] extends also to cases when the set of messages are continuous. Accordingly our conditions (B), (W), (φ), all equivalent to (P), are generalized into $(\tilde{\mathrm{B}})$, $(\tilde{\mathrm{W}})$, $(\tilde{\varphi})$, say. Blackwell [3] proved that $(\tilde{\mathrm{B}}) \Rightarrow (\tilde{\mathrm{W}})$ and also $(\tilde{\mathrm{B}}) \Rightarrow (\tilde{\varphi})$; compare also DeGroot [6]. We do not know whether, conversely, corresponding to our theorems for finite information systems, one also has $(\tilde{\mathrm{W}}) \Rightarrow (\tilde{\mathrm{B}})$ and $(\tilde{\varphi}) \Rightarrow (\tilde{\mathrm{B}})$.

Next we shall prove (P) $\Rightarrow$ (φ). By Theorem 8.3, (P) $\Leftrightarrow$ (θ). Therefore, if (P) holds, then there exists

$$\theta = [\theta_{jk}]$$

such that

(12.5.0) $$\theta_{jk} \geqq 0, \qquad \sum_j \theta_{jk} = 1\,,$$

(12.5.1) $$\pi'_k = \sum_j \pi_j \theta_{jk}\,, \qquad \text{all } k\,,$$

(12.5.2) $$q_j = \sum_k \theta_{jk}\, q'_k\,, \qquad \text{all } j\,.$$

Hence for any convex function φ on S^{m-1}, we have

(12.6) $$\begin{aligned} \sum_j q_j \varphi(\pi_j) &= \sum_k q'_k \sum_j \theta_{jk} \varphi(\pi_j) \\ &\geqq \sum_k q'_k \varphi\Big(\sum_j \theta_{jk}\pi_j\Big) = \sum_k q'_k \varphi(\pi'_k)\,; \end{aligned}$$

hence (P) $\Rightarrow$ (φ), completing the proof of the theorem.

Let φ^* be a particular convex function on S^{m-1}, and suppose

Condition (φ^*): $\sum_{j=1}^{n} q_j \varphi^*(\pi_j) \geqq \sum_{k=1}^{n'} q'_k \varphi^*(\pi'_k)\,.$

Clearly (φ^*) cannot be a sufficient condition for (P) to be satisfied: for (P) induces only a partial ordering on the set of information systems while (φ^*) induces a complete ordering. At the same time, by Theorem 12.1, (φ^*) is a necessary condition for (P). Thus

THEOREM 12.2. *(P)* $\Leftrightarrow$ (φ) $\mapsto$ (φ^*).

An important special case is that of the equivocation parameter $H(Z \mid Y)$ of classical information theory, defined in (5.1) or, in another notation, by

(12.7) $$H(Z \mid Y) \equiv -\sum_j q_j \sum_i \pi_{ij} \log \pi_{ij}\,.$$

The function

$$H(\xi) \equiv \sum_i \xi_i \log \xi_i\,,$$

where $\xi \equiv (\xi_1, \cdots, \xi_m) \in S^{m-1}$, is well known to be convex.[15] Therefore, if we introduce

Condition (H): $H(Z \mid Y) \leqq H(Z \mid Y')$.

we can replace, Theorem 12.2, (φ^*) by (H) and obtain

THEOREM 12.3. *(P)* $\mapsto$ *(H)*:

i.e., lower equivocation is necessary but not sufficient for higher informativeness.

13. SOME RELATIONS WITH BLACKWELL'S RESULTS

Using our terminology and notation we can say that in Blackwell [2], an information system Y is defined by its likelihood matrix Λ without referring

[15] Since $d^2(\xi_i \log \xi_i)/d\xi_i^2 = 1/\xi_i > 0$ for non-negative ξ_i, the matrix of second derivatives of $H(\xi)$, which is diagonal, is positive definite—a suffient condition for convexity.

to the probability distribution on Z. Given an information system Y and a payoff function ω, we shall define a set W_Y^ω in m-dimensional space as follows. Let D^ω be the set of decisions related to ω and let Δ_Y^ω be the set of all decision rules δ from Y to D^ω. Corresponding to each $\delta \in \Delta_Y^\omega$, define a point

(13.1) $$\omega(\delta) \equiv (\omega_1(\delta), \cdots, \omega_m(\delta))$$

in m-dimensional space by

(13.2) $$\omega_i(\delta) \equiv \sum_y \omega(z_i, \delta(y))p(y \mid z_i) , \qquad i = 1, \cdots, m .$$

Then the set W_Y^ω is defined as follows

(13.3) $$W_Y^\omega \equiv \{w(\delta); \delta \in \Delta_Y^\omega\} .$$

The set $W_{Y'}^\omega$ is defined similarly. Assume that both W_Y^ω and $W_{Y'}^\omega$ are closed sets. In Blackwell's definition,[16] Y is said to be more informative than Y', if the convex hull of W_Y^ω, $K(W_Y^\omega)$, contains $W_{Y'}^\omega$ for all ω. We shall call *Condition* (W): $K(W_Y^\omega) \supset W_{Y'}^\omega$, for all ω.

Blackwell [3] and Blackwell-Girshick [4] have proved

THEOREM 13.1. $(W) \Leftrightarrow (B)$.

From this theorem and our Theorem 8.3, we immedicately obtain

THEOREM 13.2. $(P) \Leftrightarrow (\Lambda) \Leftrightarrow (W) \Leftrightarrow (B) \Leftrightarrow (\theta)$.

Here we shall give a direct proof of the equivalence of three conditions (P), (Λ) and (W) without going through condition (B)

(13.4) $$(\mathrm{P}) \Leftrightarrow (\Lambda) \Leftrightarrow (\mathrm{W}) .$$

First note that $U(P; \omega)$ can be expressed by means of the set W_Y^ω defined in (13.3)

$$U(P; \omega) \equiv U(\Lambda_*, r_*; \omega) = \max_{\delta \in \Delta_Y^\omega} \sum_i r_{*i} \sum_y \omega(z_i, \delta(y))p(y \mid z_i)$$

$$= \max_{\delta \in \Delta_Y^\omega} \sum_i r_{*i} w_i(\delta) , \qquad \text{where } P \equiv (\Lambda_*, r_*) ,$$

(13.5) $$U(P; \omega) \equiv U(\Lambda_*, r_*; \omega) = \max_{w \in W_Y^\omega} \sum_i r_{*i} w_i , \qquad \text{where } w = (w_1, \cdots, w_m) .$$

Similarly, we have

(13.6) $$U(P'; \omega) \equiv U(\Lambda'_*, r_*; \omega) = \max_{w \in W_{Y'}^\omega} \sum_i r_{*i} w_i , \qquad \text{where } P' \equiv (\Lambda'_*, r_*) .$$

Suppose (W) holds, i.e., $K(W_Y^\omega) \supset W_{Y'}^\omega$, for all ω. Then for any r,

(13.7) $$\max_{w \in W_Y^\omega} \sum_i r_i w_i \geqq \max_{w \in W_{Y'}^\omega} \sum_i r_i w_i , \qquad \text{for all } \omega .$$

By (13.5) and (13.6), the relation (13.7) is equivalent to

(13.8) $$U(\Lambda_*, r; \omega) \geqq U(\Lambda'_*, r; \omega) , \qquad \text{for all } r, \omega .$$

Hence (W) implies (Λ). And since clearly $(\Lambda) \Rightarrow (\mathrm{P})$, we have proved that

[16] A definition of more informativeness by condition (W) was originally proposed by Bohnenblust, Shapley and Sherman [5].

(W) ⇒ (Λ) ⇒ (P).

Next, we shall prove that (P) implies (W); that is, if

(13.9) $$u(\Lambda_* r_*; \omega) \geqq u(\Lambda'_*, r_*; \omega)\,, \qquad \text{for all } \omega\,,$$

then (W) holds. (The proof is similar to that of Theorem 8.1.) Let $(g_1, \cdots, g_m)$ be an arbitrary set of m real numbers; define

(13.10) $$h_i \equiv g_1/r_{*i} \qquad i = 1, \cdots, m\,.$$

For any payoff function ω, we define a payoff function $\bar{\omega}$ by $D^{\bar{\omega}} = D^{\omega}$ and

(13.11) $$\bar{\omega}(z_i, d) = h_i \omega(z_i, d), \qquad d \in D^{\omega},\ i = 1, \cdots, m\,.$$

Then it is clear that

(13.12) $$\bar{w}_i(\delta) \equiv \sum_y \bar{\omega}(z_i, \delta(y))p(y \mid z_i) = h_i w_i(\delta)\,, \qquad i = 1, \cdots, m\,,$$

where $\delta \in \Delta_Y^{\omega} \equiv \Delta_Y^{\bar{\omega}}$, and $w_i(\delta)$ is defined by (13.2).

Let us define a linear transformation T from m-space to m-space by $Tw \equiv T(w_1, \cdots, w_m) = (h_1 w_1, \cdots, h_m w_m)$. Then from (13.12) we have $\bar{w}(\delta) \equiv (\bar{w}_1(\delta), \cdots, \bar{w}_m(\delta)) = Tw(\delta)$, for all $\delta \in \Delta_Y^{\omega} \equiv \Delta_Y^{\bar{\omega}}$. Therefore W_Y^{ω} defined by (13.3) and $W_Y^{\bar{\omega}}$ defined similarly with respect to $\bar{\omega}$ are related by

(13.3) $$W_Y^{\bar{\omega}} = TW_Y^{\omega}\,.$$

From (13.5) and (13.13), we have

(13.14) $$\begin{aligned} U(\Lambda_*, r_*; \bar{\omega}) &= \max_{w \in W_Y^{\bar{\omega}}} \sum r_{*i} w_i \\ &= \max_{w \in W_Y^{\omega}} \sum r_{*i} (Tw)_i \end{aligned}$$

where $(Tw)_i$ is the i-th coordinate of the point Tw, that is, from the definition of T and (13.10),

(13.15) $$(Tw)_i = h_i w_i = \frac{g_i}{r_{*i}} w_i\,, \qquad i = 1, \cdots, m\,.$$

Therefore, from (13.14) and (13.15), we have

(13.16) $$U(\Lambda_*, r_*; \bar{\omega}) = \max_{w \in W_Y^{\omega}} \sum_i g_i w_i\,.$$

Similarly

(13.16′) $$U(\Lambda'_*, r_*; \bar{\omega}) = \max_{w \in W_{Y'}^{\omega}} \sum_i g_i w_i\,.$$

From (13.9), (13.16) and (13.16′) we have

(13.17) $$\max_{w \in W_Y^{\omega}} \sum_i g_i w_i \geqq \max_{w \in W_{Y}^{\omega}} \sum_i g_i w_i\,,$$

where $(g_1, \cdots, g_m)$ and ω is any set of m real numbers and ω is any payoff function. Therefore (13.17) implies

$$K(W_Y^{\omega}) \supset W_Y^{\omega}\,, \qquad \text{for all } \omega\,,$$

that is, (W). Accordingly (P) ⇒ (W) is proved. This completes a proof of the equivalence relation (13.4) which includes Theorem 5.2 as a part of it.

14. DICHOTOMIES: $m = 2$

In the dichotomy case, Z consists of two events z_1 and z_2: $m = 2$. As in (9.19), let

(14.1) $$\Pi_* q = \Pi'_* q' (= r) ,$$

where Π_*, Π'_*, but not q, q', r are fixed. Henceforth we shall omit the asterisk without ambiguity.

With respect to an information system Y, define two functions $G_Y(t)$ and $F_Y(t)$ on $[0, 1]$ as follows:[17]

(14.2) $$G_Y(t) \equiv \sum_{\pi_{1j} \leqq t} q_j ,$$

(14.3) $$F_Y(t) \equiv \int_0^t G_Y(u) du .$$

$G_{Y'}(t)$ and $F_{Y'}(t)$ are defined similarly with respect to Y'. Clearly $G_Y(t)$ is a monotone non-decreasing step function with a jump of q_j at $t = \pi_{1j}$, $j = 1, \cdots, n$.

From the consistency condition (14.1),

$$F_Y(1) = \int_0^1 G_Y(t) dt = 1 - \sum_j q_j \pi_{1j} = 1 - r_1 = r_2 ,$$

$$F_{Y'}(t) = \int_0^1 G_{Y'}(t) dt = 1 - \sum_k q'_k \pi'_{1k} = 1 - r_1 = r_2 .$$

Therefore

(14.4) $$F_Y(1) = F_{Y'}(1) = r_2 .$$

It will become clear that the relation (14.4) is a key point in our proof of Theorem 14.3 below. Now we shall introduce

Condition (F): $F_Y(t) \geqq F_{Y'}(t)$, all t, $0 \leqq t \leqq 1$.

Then, following a reasoning similar to that of Blackwell-Girshick [4, (theorem 12.4.1)], it is easy to prove[18]

[17] Compare $G_Y(t)$ and $F_Y(t)$ with $F_P(t)$ and $C_P(t)$ in Blackwell-Girshick [4, (theorem 12.4.1)]. If $r_1 = r_2 = 1/2$, then our $G_Y(t), F_Y(t)$ become equal to Blackwell-Girshick's $F_P(t), C_P(t)$ respectively.

[18] We shall show that Theorem 14.1 can be proved by almost the same device as given by Blackwell-Girshick [4] in their proof of their Theorem 12.4.1. When $m = 2$, condition (φ) is equivalent to the following condition: For any convex function φ on $[0, 1]$,

$$\sum_{j=1}^{n} q_j \varphi(\pi_{1i}) \geqq \sum_{k=1}^{n'} q_{k'} \varphi(\pi_{1k}) .$$

Defining a function $f_t(u)$ on $[0, 1]$ for each $t, 0 \leqq t \leqq 1$, by

$$f_t(u) = \begin{cases} t - u, & \text{for } 0 \leqq u \leqq t \\ 0, & \text{for } 0 \leqq u \leqq 1 , \end{cases}$$

any (continuous) convex function φ on $[0, 1]$ can be uniformly approximated by a function of the form (*Continued on next page*)

THEOREM 14.1. *When $m = 2$, $(\varphi) \Leftrightarrow (F)$.*

Then by Theorems 12.1 and 14.1, we have

THEOREM 14.2. *When $m = 2$, $(\Pi) \Leftrightarrow (F)$.*

Referring to the definition of points π_j, π'_k in S^{m-1}, we shall introduce the following condition for $m = 2$.

Condition (c): *All points π'_k of Π' lie between two consecutive points of Π.* (See Figure 5a).

On Figure 6a, the graphs of the functions $G_Y(t)$ and $G_{Y'}(t)$ are drawn on the same interval [0, 1]. The interval [0, 1] is partitioned into sub-intervals by points $\pi_{11}, \cdots, \pi_{1n}$ and $\pi'_{11}, \cdots, \pi'_{1n'}$. Among these sub-intervals, the ones where

$$G_Y(t) > G_{Y'}(t) \tag{14.5}$$

shall be denoted by $I_+^{(1)}, I_+^{(2)}, \cdots$, and the ones where

$$G_Y(t) < G_{Y'}(t) \tag{14.6}$$

shall be denoted by $I_-^{(1)}, I_-^{(2)}, \cdots$. (Note that $G_Y(t) - G_{Y'}(t)$ and $G_{Y'}(t) - G_Y(t)$ are constant positive numbers on $I_+^{(\alpha)}$ and $I_-^{(\beta)}$ respectively.) The length of those intervals will also be denoted by $I_+^{(\alpha)}, I_-^{(\beta)}$, respectively.

Define the positive real numbers $A^{(1)}, A^{(2)}, \cdots$ and $B^{(1)}, B^{(2)}, \cdots$ by

$$A^{(\alpha)} \equiv I_+^{(\alpha)}(G_Y(t) - G_{Y'}(t)), \quad t \in I_+^{(\alpha)}, \tag{14.7}$$

$$B^{(\beta)} \equiv I_-^{(\beta)}(G_{Y'}(t) - G_Y(t)), \quad t \in I_-^{(\beta)}. \tag{14.8}$$

Then by (14.4),

$$A^{(1)} + A^{(2)} + \cdots = B^{(1)} + B^{(2)} + \cdots. \tag{14.9}$$

The following theorem gives a simpler characterization of "greater informativeness" than Blackwell-Girshick's Theorem 12.4.1 [4].

THEOREM 14.3. *When $m = 2$, $(\Pi) \Rightarrow (c)$.*

PROOF. Without loss of generality, let $\pi_{11} < \pi_{12} < \cdots < \pi_{1n}$ and $\pi'_{11} < \pi'_{12} <$

$$g(u) = \sum_s c_s f_{t_s}(u) + au + b,$$

where $c_s \geqq 0$. Now without loss of generality, we assume that

$$\pi_{11} < \pi_{12} < \cdots < \pi_{1n} \quad \text{and} \quad \pi'_{11} < \pi'_{12} < \cdots < \pi'_{1n'}.$$

Then it is clear that we have

$$F_Y(t) = \sum_{j=1}^{n} q_j f_t(\pi_{1j}), \; F_{Y'}(t) = \sum_{k=1}^{n'} g'_k f_t(\pi'_{1k}).$$

Then

$$\sum_j q_j g(\pi_{1j}) = \sum_s c_s F_Y(t_s) + ar_1 + b,$$

$$\sum_k q'_k g(\pi'_{1k}) = \sum_s c_s F_{Y'}(t_s) + ar_1 + b,$$

since

$$\sum q_j \pi_{1j} = \sum q_k \pi'_{1k} = r.$$

Therefore condition (φ) is equivalent to condition (F), since $c_s \geqq 0$.

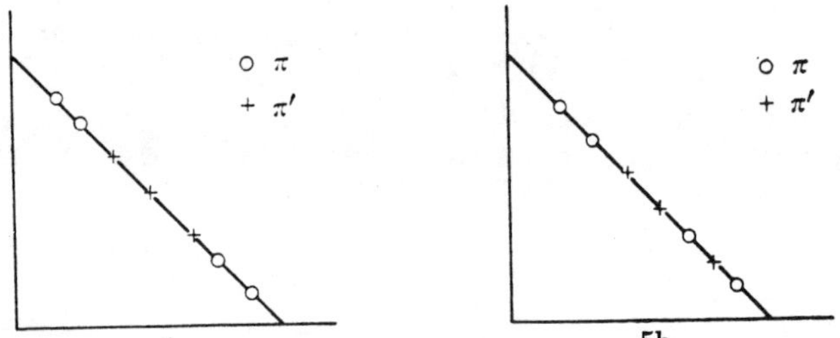

5a 5b

FIGURE 5

DICHOTOMIES: $m = 2$

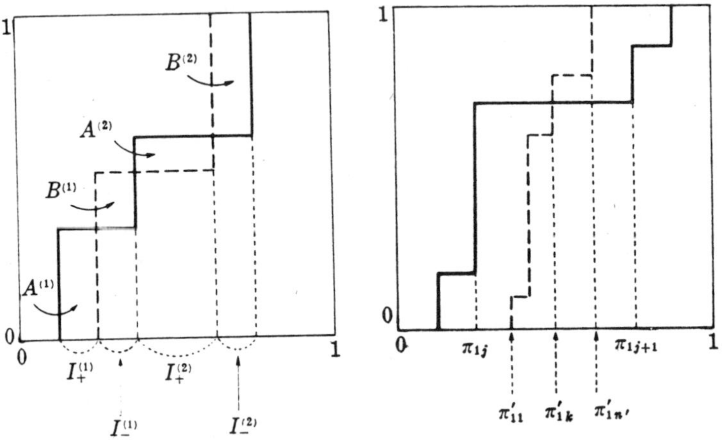

6a 6b

FIGURE 6

$\cdots < \pi'_{1n'}$. First, we shall prove (c) $\Rightarrow$ (Π). For a fixed j, we have by condition (c)

(14.10) $$\pi_{1j} \leqq \pi'_{11} < \cdots < \pi'_{1n'} \leqq \pi_{1j+1} .$$

Let q, q' be any vectors such that (14.1) holds. Then $G_Y(\pi_{1j}) < 1 = G_{Y'}(\pi'_{1n'})$. Therefore, there exists an index k such that

(14.11) $$G_{Y'}(\pi'_{1k-1}) \leqq G_Y(\pi_{1j}) \leqq G_{Y'}(\pi'_{1k}) ,$$

(where, when $k = 1$, we consider only the right-hand inequality). Then from the monotonicity of $G_Y(t)$ and $G_{Y'}(t)$ (see Figure 6b)

(14.12) $$\begin{aligned} G_Y(t) &\geqq G_{Y'}(t) , & 0 < t < \pi'_{1k} , \\ G_{Y'}(t) &\leqq G_Y(t) , & \pi'_{1k} \leqq t \leqq 1 . \end{aligned}$$

Therefore, all intervals $I_+^{(1)}, I_+^{(2)}, \cdots$ are located on the left-hand side of π'_{1k}

and all the intervals $I_-^{(1)}, I_-^{(2)}, \cdots$ are located on the right-hand side of π'_{1k}. Therefore by (14.9) and the definitions of $F_Y(t)$ and $F_{Y'}(t)$, clearly, condition (F) holds. Then by Theorem 14.2, it follows that (c) $\Rightarrow$ (II).

Next, in order to prove that (II) $\Rightarrow$ (c), suppose that (c) does not hold. Then there exists at least one pair of points among $\pi'_{11}, \cdots, \pi'_{1n'}$, — say π'_{1k} and π'_{1k+1}—such that the interval (π'_{1k}, π'_{1k+1}) contains at least one point of $\{\pi_{11}, \cdots, \pi_{1n}\}$ —say $\pi_{1j}, \cdots, \pi_{1j+s}$, $s \geqq 0$. We shall show that there exists a pair of vectors $q \equiv (q_1, \cdots, q_n)$, $q_j > 0$, $\sum q_j = 1$ and $q' \equiv (q'_1, \cdots, q'_{n'})$, $q'_k > 0$, $\sum q'_k = 1$ such that

$$\Pi q = \Pi' q' , \tag{14.13}$$

and for the two corresponding information systems Y and Y', the respective functions $F_Y(t)$ and $F_{Y'}(t)$ do not satisfy condition (F). Then by Theorem 14.2, we can conclude $(\Pi, q) \not\succ (\Pi', q')$, i.e., (II) does not hold.

We can choose $q \equiv (q_1, \cdots, q_n)$ and $q' \equiv (q'_1, \cdots, q'_{n'})$ so as to satisfy (14.9) and the following conditions (14.14.1)-(14.14.5):

$$0 < q_g \ll q_h , \qquad g = 1, \cdots, j-1, j+1, \cdots, j+s-1, j+s+1, \cdots, n, \quad h = j, j+s , \tag{14.14.1}$$

$$\sum_{g=1}^{n} q_g = 1 \tag{14.14.2}$$

$$0 < q'_g \ll q'_h , \qquad g = 1, \cdots, k-1, k+2, \cdots, n', \quad h = k, k+1 , \tag{14.14.3}$$

$$\sum_{h=1}^{n'} q'_h = 1 , \tag{14.14.4}$$

$$\sum_{g=1}^{j-1} q_g < \sum_{h=1}^{k} q'_h < \sum_{g=1}^{j+s} q_g , \tag{14.14.5}$$

where for two positive numbers a and b, $a \ll b$ denote that a is infinitesimally small compared to b. Now, in numbering the intervals $I_+^{(\alpha)}$ and $I_-^{(\beta)}$, let us define $I_+^{(1)}$ and $I_-^{(1)}$ by $I_+^{(1)} \equiv [\pi_{1j+s}, \pi'_{1k+1}]$, $I_-^{(1)} \equiv [\pi'_{1k}, \pi_{1j}]$. Then

$$A^{(1)} \equiv (\pi'_{1k+1} - \pi_{1j+s})(G_Y(t) - G_{Y'}(t)), \qquad \pi_{1j+s} \leqq t \leqq \pi'_{1k+1} , \tag{14.15}$$

$$B^{(1)} \equiv (\pi_{1j} - \pi'_{1k})(G_{Y'}(t) - G_Y(t)) , \qquad \pi'_{1k} \leqq t \leqq \pi_{1j} . \tag{14.16}$$

Then in addition to (14.9), by (14.14.1) and (14.14.3), we have

$$A^{(2)} + A^{(3)} + \cdots \ll A^{(1)} , \tag{14.17}$$

$$B^{(2)} + B^{(3)} + \cdots \ll B^{(1)} . \tag{14.18}$$

Then by (14.9)

$$A^{(1)} - B^{(1)} = (B^{(2)} + B^{(3)} + \cdots) - (A^{(2)} + A^{(3)} + \cdots) . \tag{14.19}$$

Therefore, by (14.17), (14.18), $A^{(1)} - B^{(1)}$ is almost zero. Accordingly by (14.17)

$$A^{(2)} + A^{(3)} + \cdots \ll B^{(1)} . \tag{14.20}$$

This implies that we cannot have $F_Y(t) \geqq F_{Y'}(t)$ over the whole sub-interval (π'_{1k}, π_{1j}). We have thus shown that if (c) does not hold, then (F) does not hold and by Theorem 14.2, (II) cannot hold. Hence (II) $\Rightarrow$ (c), completing the proof of the theorem.

15. SUMMARY

Given the set X of states of nature, described in unlimited detail and with a probability measure defined on it, we consider its partitions: Z (set of events z) and $Y, Y', Y'', \cdots$ (information systems, i.e., sets of mutually exclusive messages denoted by y in Y, y' in Y' etc.). The set Ω_Z consists of all payoff function ω for which Z is a payoff-adequate (i.e., not too coarse) partition of X. Let the set of feasible decisions d entering the argument of ω be D^ω; thus ω is a real valued function on $Z \times D^\omega$. The (gross) expected payoff of an information system Y is

$$U(Y;\omega) = \sum_{z,y} \Pr(x \in z \cap y) \cdot \omega(z, d_y) ,$$

where d_y is a decision responding optimally to message y; that is,

$$\sum_z \Pr(x \in z \cap y)[\omega(z, d_y) - \omega(z, d)] \geqq 0 , \qquad \text{all } d \in D^\omega .$$

A class of partially ordering relations is defined on the set of information systems $Y, Y', \cdots$, as follows: Y is said to be more informative than Y', as revealed by a given property of the distribution on $Z \times Y \times Y'$, if this property implies that

$$U(Y;\omega) \geqq U(Y';\omega) , \qquad \text{all } \omega \in \Omega_Z .$$

In particular, greater informativeness of Y relative to Y' may be revealed by comparing the (bivariate) distributions on $Z \times Y$ and on $Z \times Y'$; by comparing the matrix of likelihoods $\Lambda \equiv [\lambda_{zy}] \equiv [\Pr(x \in z \cap y)/\Pr(x \in z)]$, with the correspondingly defined matrix Λ'; or by comparing the matrix of posterior probabilities, $\Pi \equiv [\pi_{zy}] \equiv [\Pr(x \in z \cap y)/\Pr(x \in y)]$, with the correspondingly defined matrix Π. The latter comparison is the strictly stronger one (Theorem 5.3) except in the important case when the messages of the more informative system (each message being represented by a column of Π, or of Λ) are linearly independent: Theorems 9.5, 9.7. The numerical criteria for comparison of informativeness, given in Theorem 13.2 are all equivalent, and are strictly stronger than that of Theorem 9.1; but they are all equivalent in the case of linear independence between messages. This case applies in particular to information systems that are noiseless with respect to—i.e., are sub-partitions of—the set Z of events (Section 11); or are binomial—the case of two messages,—or binary—the case of two messages and two events (Section 10). Furthermore, for the "dichotomy" cases (i.e., the case of only two events), a certain property of posterior probabilities is proved to be necessary and sufficient for Y to be more informative than Y' (Section 14). The "equivocation" parameter of classical information theory, as well as its generalization to any other convex operator on posterior probabilities, is shown to be a necessary but not sufficient criterion of comparative informativeness; but a stronger criterion involving *all* convex operators on posterior probabilities is shown to be both sufficient and necessary (Section 12).

Statements on comparative informativeness can also be derived from the knowledge, not of the numerical properties of the probability distribution of events and messages, but of the process by which messages constituting one information system are generated from those of another system. Thus it is shown that "garbling," of Y into Y', a well-defined property of some distributions on $Z \times Y \times Y'$, can never make Y' more informative than Y. A special case of garbling is "collapsing" information, and a still more special case is dis-"joining" it: Theorem 7.3. Moreover, in the case of garbling of linearly independent messages, the Markov matrices used in some of the criteria of informativeness and relating the distribution on $Z \times Y$ to that on $Z \times Y'$ receive an insightful interpretation in terms of conditional probabilities of the messages of one system, given the message of another: Theorem 9.3.

To use our results for a definitive economic comparison of information systems one would have to know information costs. Unless these are additive, one would have to discard the concept of gross payoff functions (Section 4). One should, moreover, characterize the feasible set Δ_φ of decision rules (rather than the set D^m of feasible decision), and take account of the cost which is associated with a decision rule; this cost, too, is in general non-additive, thus calling for a further re-definition of (net) payoffs.

In addition to these open questions of an economic nature, the mathematician will notice that by confining ourselves to finite sets of events and messages, we have neglected measure-theoretical difficulties which were attacked by other authors (see footnote 14).

More general studies are therefore necessary. We hope the present study contributes to stimulating and preparing them.

University of California, Los Angeles, U.S.A.
and University of Tokyo, Japan

REFERENCES

[1] ABRAMSON, NORMAN, *Information Theory and Coding* (New York: McGraw-Hill, 1963).

[2] BLACKWELL, DAVID, "Comparison of Experiments," in J. Neyman, ed., *Proceedings of the Second Berkeley Symposium on Mathematical Statistics and Probability* (Berkeley: University of California Press, 1951), 93-102.

[3] ———, "Equivalent Comparisons of Experiments," *Annals of Mathematical Statistics*, XXIV (June, 1953), 265-73.

[4] ——— and M. A. GIRSHICK, *Theory of Games and Statistical Decisions* (New York: John Wiley and Sons, 1954).

[5] BOHNENBLUST, H. F., L. S. SHAPLEY and S. SHERMAN, "Reconnaissance in Game Theory," Research Memorandum RM-208 (The RAND Corporation, 1949).

[6] DEGROOT, M. H., "Uncertainty, Information and Sequential Experiments," *Annals of Mathematical Statistics*, XXXII (June, 1962), 602-5.

[7] FEINSTEIN, AMIEL, *Foundations of Information Theory* (New York: McGraw-Hill, 1958).

[8] HALMOS, PAUL R., *Measure Theory* (Princeton, N.J.: Van Nostrand, 1950).

[9] KARLIN, SAMUEL, *Mathematical Methods and Theory in Games, Programming, and Economics*, Vol. II (Reading, Mass.: Addison-Wesley, 1959).

[10] MARSCHAK, JACOB, "Remarks on the Economics of Information," in *Contributions to Scientific Research in Management* (printed privately).

[11] ———, "The Payoff-Relevant Description of States and Acts," *Econometrica*, XXXI (October, 1963), 719–29.

[12] ——— and R. RADNER, "Economic Theory of Teams," Chapter II, Working Paper, No. 82 (Center for Research in Management Science, University of California, Berkeley, 1959).

[13] MCGUIRE, C. B., "Comparisons of Information Systems," Cowles Foundation Discussion Paper No. 71 (1959).

[14] MIYASAWA, KOICHI, "Information Structures in Adaptive Programming," Working Paper No. 61 (Western Management Science Institute, University of California, Los Angeles, 1964).

[15] RAIFFA, HOWARD and R. SCHLAIFER, *Applied Statistical Decision Theory* (Cambridge, Mass.: Harvard University Press, 1961).

[16] SAVAGE, LEONARD J., *The Foundations of Statistics* (New York: John Wiley and Sons, 1954).

II

Application to Managerial Accounting

SECOND LECTURE

JOEL S. DEMSKI

Our goal in this second session of the seminar is to use the state-act-outcome paradigm and the notion of consistent choice (represented by the expected utility hypothesis) to examine various issues traditionally associated with managerial accounting. (Of course, at this level of abstraction the distinction between managerial and financial accounting becomes quite blurred.)

The presentation is structured around single- versus multiperson questions. In the former, we shall examine the basic question of cost "assessment" and the meaning of the term "cost." In the latter, we shall examine the question of "optimal" design of performance evaluation systems. Hopefully this will give some insight into how the basic assumptions are employed in this arena.

Single-Person Analysis

In the previous lecture we dealt with a single, isolated individual playing a game (if you like) against "Nature." We can apply this story directly to, say, a sole proprietorship and examine a number of questions. For example, suppose our individual collects cost data today because analysis of such data is useful in tomorrow's decision making. How should these data be *aggregated?* Reliance on a homogeneity criterion is popular in our literature. And it should be clear that we would directly apply the Blackwell Theorem at this point (see [Feltham, 1977]).

For example, apply this analysis to the full (absorption) versus direct (variable) costing controversy. How do we respond when our students want to know whether we are direct or full costers? Using the Blackwell Theorem, we can say that we are direct costers, and we can always convert to full (absorption). Conversely, we can be full costers, but will display the component of inventory that is a fixed cost so we can convert to direct costing. The point is that we view accounting data as information and proceed to select the most preferred accounting method (or information structure) using the Blackwell Theorem.

For another example, suppose we are called upon to construct an "approximate" cost curve. This cost curve is close enough to support analysis, but in the interest of the cost of cost accounting, we stop short of an ideal complete analysis. Precisely, we begin with some choice problem with expected utility representation: $\{p, S, A, U, \phi\}$. This particular statement of the problem is not unique; S may not be payoff relevant, U is subject to positive linear transformation, and so on. Indeed, we partition the possible transformations into those that are guaranteed to select a most preferred act (termed *modification*) and those that carry no such guarantee (termed *simplification*).

Modification

The idea behind modification is to transform one statement of the problem into an alternative statement of the problem. This transformation has the property that the optimal solution to the transformed problem is the optimal solution to the original problem. For example, if the decision makers are risk-neutral, they can legitimately focus on expected incremental returns just by going to first differences.

Simplification

Another form of transformation, which is the complement of modification, is simplification. In this transformation, the ability to guarantee selection of the optimal act is lost. For example, suppose decision makers are risk-averse, but we assume for analysis that they are risk-neutral. As the transformation does not guarantee selection of the optimal act, you might ask why we would ever simplify. One answer is that you would never move beyond a modification if analysis were a free good, but recognizing the cost of analysis you might adroitly select a simplified transformation of your problem.

For example, consider the game of chess. Chess is really a very simple game. Uncertainty is limited to actions of your opponent; yet we don't know what an optimal strategy is. Indeed, the first theorem in game theory assures us that either white wins, black wins, or a draw is forced. (And we don't know much beyond that [Simon, 1972].) So we resort to simplification because the number of combinations in chess is so large.

Now let's apply this idea to cost accounting questions. Initially we must introduce some notion of cost. Opportunity cost quickly comes to mind, but it doesn't lead to the questions we typically have to answer.[1] In fact, minimizing opportunity costs is a modification of maximizing utility. Instead, we generally focus on outcomes of the firm, such as cash flows and net income. So instead of focusing on opportunity cost, we focus on outcome cost and noncost (benefit?) components. We might use an ordered pair: $x = (x^B, x^C)$. Further, suppose the acts have a natural structure of (a, a_B, a_C), where a_C exclusively affects x^C, etc. Thus,

$$p(s, (a, a_B, a_C) = (p^B(s, a, a_B), p^C(s, a, a_C)).$$

For example, a might be aggregate output and a_C might be a particular detailed production plan.

Observe that if the individual is risk-neutral, we can modify the choice problem so that it calls for construction of a cost representation. In particular, let $\bar{p}^C(a) = \min Ep^C(s, a, a_C)$, where the minimization is taken over all a_C that are consistent with supporting a. The benefit side is open to similar modification, leading to $\bar{p}^B(a) = \max Ep^B(\ldots)$. We now describe the choice problem in terms of

$$\max_a \bar{p}^B(a) - \bar{p}^C(a).$$

This is but a superficial condensation of the full analysis (see Demski and Feltham [1976]); but I hope it is sufficient to motivate the following discussion.

We would generally agree that materials used in the production process are "costly" and therefore somehow captured by $\bar{p}^C(a)$. We would also be inclined to engage in the net realizable value, replacement cost, and exit value debate.

Consider a firm with two products, a and b, where $a \in \{0, 1\}$ and $b \in \{0, 1, 2\}$. The revenue from producing a and b is

$$p^B(s, a, b) = a(500 - 50a) + b(400 - 50b);$$

and the cost of any production schedule is

$$p^C(s, a, b, DL, DM) = 100 + 100\,DL + 200\,DM$$

$$\text{if} \begin{cases} DL\,(\text{direct labor}) \geq a + b; \\ DM\,(\text{direct materials}) \geq a + b - 1, \end{cases}$$

where the latter constraint reflects a beginning inventory of one unit. Of course, optimal $a_C = (DM, DL)$ behavior requires $DL = a + b$ and $DM = a + b - 1$. As shown in Exhibit 2.1, the obvious choice of our analysis is one unit of a and one unit of b.

Exhibit 2.1

a	b	DM^*	DL^*	$p^B(\cdot)$	$p^C(\cdot)$	x
0	0	−1	0	0	−200 + 100	100
0	1	0	1	350	100 + 100	150
0	2	1	2	600	400 + 100	100
1	0	0	1	450	100 + 100	250
1	1	1	2	800	400 + 100	300
1	2	2	3	1050	700 + 100	250

Suppose, however, that we vary the modification theme once more so that the analysis focuses only on the a product. (This is the classic special order problem that we are all so fond of.) The idea is to define $p(s, a) = p(s, a, b^*(a))$ where $b^*(a)$ is the best choice of $b \in \{0, 1, 2\}$ *given* a. Clearly $b^*(0) = 1$ and $b^*(1) = 1$. We therefore have

$$\begin{aligned} p(s, a) &= p^B(s, a, 1) - p^C(s, a, 1) \\ &= (350 - 100 - 100) + a(500 - 50) - 300a \\ &= 150 + a[(500 - 50) - 100 - 200]. \end{aligned}$$ [2]

Observe, however, that this is an illustration of the neoclassical economic story: factor markets are perfect, production is separable, the cost of a product is the cost of its factors, and the factor cost is its market price.[3] As a result, this is a particularly sterile setting in which to deal with cost accounting. But remember that this is the source of much of our thinking.

Suppose, then, that the factor market is imperfect, with selling and buying prices different. The material can be sold for 150 or bought for 300. The data are shown in Exhibit 2.2.

Exhibit 2.2

a	b	DM^*	DL^*	$p^B(\cdot)$	$p^C(\cdot)$	x
0	0	−1	0	0	−50	50
0	1	0	1	350	200	150
0	2	1	2	600	600	0
1	0	0	1	450	200	250
1	1	1	2	800	600	200
1	2	2	3	1050	1000	50

To modify the analysis and to focus directly on the special order, we now have $b^*(0) = 1$ and $b^*(1) = 0$. Hence,

$$p(s, 0) = 350 - (100 + 100);$$
$$p(s, 1) = 450 - (100 + 100);$$

or

$$p(s, a) = a[(500 - 50a) - 100] - (a - 1)(250) - 100$$
$$= 250 + a(500 - 50a) - 100a - 250a - 100.$$

Why is the cost of *DM* equal to 250 in this case? We call this net realizable value, utilization cost, or service potential in best internal use foregone.

Alternatively, suppose you have factor market imperfection and the revenue from b is $100b - 50b^2$, as shown in Exhibit 2.3.

Exhibit 2.3

a	b	$p^B(\ )$	$p^C(\ )$	x
0	0	0	−50	50
0	1	50	200	−150
0	2	0	600	−600
1	0	450	200	250
1	1	500	600	−100
1	2	450	1000	−550

Modification to focus on the special order leads to

$$p(s, a) = a[(500 - 50a) - 100] - 100 - (a - 1)150$$
$$= 150 + a(500 - 50a) - 100a - 150a - 100$$

which has an exit value interpretation.

In turn, the original revenue structure with *DM* exit price = 150 and replacement price = 200 will produce a modification that relies on replacement cost.

In sum, the (x^B, x^C) structure allows us to speak of the outlay cost of some act (given S). This act may be described in terms of inputs and outputs, which is itself a modification question. And, if so, we express the action cost in terms of the cost of the requisite factors. In turn, modifying the analysis to suppress the act components leads to the cost of factor questions. Fundamentally, this familiar question arises in the determination of $b^*(a)$ and subsequent construction of $p(s, a) = p(s, a, b^*(a))$.[4]

This theme allows us to analyze a number of familiar issues:

- Incremental or relevant cost analysis may or may not be part of a modification. (Consider the risk-averse case.)
- Allocating a "sunk" cost may (or may not) proxy quite well for the modified cost of using a facility.
- The direct-indirect cost distinction also arises naturally as part of a modified analysis. However, the key is to carry along a sufficient description to support the modification. Further, the specification is likely to be far from unique.
- It is possible to lay out social accounting proposals in this manner. Quite simply, we seek a modification of society's resource allocation problem so that each local entity "sees" the secondary effects of its behavior. This leads us into multiperson issues that we deal with in the third lecture.

By way of summary, then, I have tried to present an extremely brief overview using the economics of uncertainty to examine familiar cost accounting problems. I hope you are convinced that such a line of inquiry is possible (and even insightful). But the topic is not that popular; and the set-up cost for a thorough analysis is nontrivial.

Multiperson Analysis

A familiar and unsettled question is how to evaluate someone's performance. We think of this in terms of evaluation systems and address such questions as whether budgets are useful, whether standards should be "tight," whether costs should be allocated, and so forth. Note that the basic idea is to set up *at the time of choice* some provision for retrospective analysis of the choice and its (state-dependent) outcome.

Now consider the various choice settings in which evaluation might be an issue:

- *The (1, 1) case.* Here we have one person and one final choice. Performance evaluation would not be useful because it cannot be used for any choices.
- *The (1, $\geq$ 2) case.* Here we have one person but at least two final choices. Analysis of tomorrow's cost might be useful for improving the quality of the day after tomorrow's choice. (And, in general, we come back to the Blackwell Theorem.)
- *The (2, 1) case.* Here we have one final choice, but two individuals. One, called a *principal,* has delegated choice of $a \in$

A to another, called an *agent.* Performance evaluation is of interest here because it is a key step in motivating the agent.

In particular, we generally view the principal and agent in a noncooperative sense. The agent acts in *his* or *her* best interest and therefore will not necessarily do what the principal wants—even if he or she so promises. Rather, self-interest explains his or her behavior. The key for the principal is to work on the agent's self-interest. We do this, of course, by specification of some employment contract. For such a contract to be incentive-compatible, however, its domain is limited by what is jointly observed by the contracting parties. For example, we don't see salvation contracts; defense contracts depend on "cost," but not how "hard" the contractor worked; tenure depends on published results; today's reward doesn't depend on what will happen tomorrow; and so on. This is the key to performance evaluation. It is useful here to the extent that it provides a basis for improved contracting between the principal and the agent.

- *The (≥2, ≥2) case.* This is the general case of multiple agents and multiple periods.

In summary, it should be clear that in the one-person, two-period case your motivation for performance evaluation is to improve next period's choice. Your motivation in the two-person, one-period case is to improve your contracting arrangements with the agent and thereby improve this period's choice. In the general case with at least two agents and at least two periods, performance evaluation (1) motivates the agent, (2) informs the agent, and (3) informs the principal. This implies that we have both a motivation and a future choice problem operating simultaneously.

We now look more closely at the principal-agent model. The initial major work here is Wilson's "On the Theory of Syndicates" [1968]. His paper deals with risk sharing and the conditions under which members of an organization would be unanimous in their selection among risky projects. If unanimity obtains, we have solved the organization's incentive problems. If we examine the contracting arrangements that support optimal risk sharing, we are able to say something about our controllability theme. For example, shielding a manager from random variations in the returns of his division (or that of another manager) may in fact be inconsistent with efficient risk sharing [Demski, 1976].

More generally, we tend to worry about nonpecuniary as well

as pecuniary returns (as in Jensen and Meckling [1976]). The agent picks an act and is paid by the owner or principal. The owner receives the actual outcome less what he paid the agent. His preferences reflect only his residual return. But to capture the idea of a nonpecuniary return, the agent's preferences reflect what he is paid *and* the act he selected.[5]

This basic idea is exploited in the Demski and Feltham [1978] budgeting paper. The outcome structure is $x = p(s, a, q)$, where a is the agent's effort and q is the owner's capital. The agent's utility depends on outcome, x_w, and effort, $U_w(x_w, a)$; and he is generally risk- and work-averse. We also regard the owner as risk-neutral and treat $p(.,.,.)$ as exhibiting constant stochastic returns to scale.

Performance evaluation questions arise in specifying the contracting arrangement. $\eta : S \times A \times Q \rightarrow Y$ denotes the jointly observed information. Hence the domain of the contract is limited to $y : x_w = \mathscr{I}(\eta(s, a, q))$. Varying $\eta(\cdot)$ amounts to varying the performance evaluation system. In general, $\mathscr{I}$ shall depend on η.

The specific question now addressed is the use of budgets—where by budget we mean a partition of Y into favorable and unfavorable regions and the use of a distinct reward function over each region. As both parties must agree to such an arrangement, the question is structured in terms of equilibrium contracting arrangements in the labor market.

Somewhat more precisely, with some $(\mathscr{I}, \eta)$ pair the worker's behavior is represented by

$$\max_{a \in A} \int U_w(\mathscr{I}(\eta(\cdot)), a)\phi(s)ds.$$

And with a^* = the act the worker will select here, the owner's evaluation is

$$\int [p(s, a^*, q) - \mathscr{I}(\eta(\cdot))]\phi(s)ds,$$

where homogeneous beliefs are assumed. The question then asked is: for some specific η_0, what will be the allocation (contracts and effort) at equilibrium?

A parallel exercise deals with unobservable skill differentials in the labor market and the ability of budget mechanisms to induce the individuals to sort themselves. The idea is that workers know their skills but employers don't. What can employers do to get workers to reveal their skills? An analogy can be drawn with insurance contracts. Suppose an auto insurance company offers \$50-deductible and \$250-deductible insurance contracts. The more risk-prone will self-select the $50-deductible; thus the insurance company would use different actuarial rates for the different contracts. In summary, employers offer different contracts and get workers to self-select. Their selection reveals their skill level. The results are summarized in Exhibit 2.4.

Exhibit 2.4

Moral Hazard Case	Adverse Selection Case
$x = p(s, a, q = 1)$	$x = p(s, a_1, q_1, 1) + p(s, a_2, q_2, 2)$
P1: $\eta = (s, a, q, x)$. Wage contracts are efficient, with all the usual interpretations.	P7: $\eta = (s, a, q, h, x)$. Skill-dependent wage contracts are efficient, with all the usual interpretations.
P2: $\eta = (s, q)$. Rental and insurance contracts give first-best solution.	P8: $\eta = (s, q)$. Rental and insurance contracts give first-best solution.
P3: Budgets useful implies don't jointly observe s or a.	P9: Budgets useful implies don't jointly observe a and h or s.
P4: Budgets useful implies workers are risk-averse.	P10: Budgets useful implies workers are risk-averse.
P5: Constant stochastic returns to scale and Cobb-Douglas production functions imply budget-based contracts dominate linear contracts.	P11: Budget-based contracts dominate separating linear contracts.
P6: Budget-based contracts with conditional investigation dominate linear contracts.	P12: Budget-based contracts with conditional investigation dominate separating linear contracts.

Hopefully, some insight into the use of budgets is available from the exercise. In particular, consider questions of employee participation in budgeting, use of an "attainable" standard, applicability of mechanical quality control procedures, and the controllability notion.

The budget mechanism comes into play to compensate for lack of contracting information. And, in effect, you trade off some risk sharing to gain incentive effects. But further note that two types of results are presented. First, conditions are noted in which less than complete contracting information is present, but a first-best (or informationally unconstrained) solution is available. Indeed, this argument applies to any form of monitoring of the agent, as discussed in the Harris and Raviv [1978] paper.

Second, conditions are noted in which budget mechanisms are superior to linear contracts. While it is comforting to know that a linear contract can be improved upon, we would prefer to know what an optimal contract looks like here.

Mirrlees [1976] has proposed a somewhat different statement of the problem that allows us to say quite a bit about the optimal use question. The trick is to state the problem in terms of picking an *act-conditioned outcome distribution.* Let $\phi(x|a)$ denote the outcome density given act $a \in A$. Also let the owner be risk-neutral and the worker risk- and work-averse with a *separable utility* function $U_w(x_w, a) = U(x_w) - V(a)$. Adopting a partial equilibrium setting, we have the following problem when only x is jointly observed:

$$E(U_0|\eta) = \max_{\substack{a \in A \\ \underline{\mathscr{I}} \leq \mathscr{I} \leq \overline{\mathscr{I}}}} \int x\phi(x|a) - \int \mathscr{I}(x)\phi(x|a)dx$$

subject to:

$$\int U(\mathscr{I}(x))\phi(x|a)dx - V(a) \geq \theta$$
$$\int U(\mathscr{I}(x))\phi_a(x|a)dx - V'(a) = 0$$

The first constraint is a minimum utility condition on the agent and is meant to capture the idea of making sure the employment arrangement is attractive. The second constraint is the first-order condition for the agent or worker to select act a. Let λ be the multiplier associated with the first constraint, and μ the multiplier with the second constraint. Pointwise maximization then gives us

$$\frac{1}{U'} = \lambda + \mu \frac{\phi_a(x|a)}{\phi(x|a)}.$$

Regularity issues are nontrivial here. The best reference I know of is a recent Stanford GSB dissertation by Holmstrom, "On Decentralization, Incentives, and Control in Organizations" [1977].[6]

An example will probably be helpful at this point. Let

$$U_w(x_w, a) = 2\sqrt{x_w} - a^2 \quad \text{and} \quad \phi(x|a) = \frac{1}{a} e^{-x|a} (a > 0, x \geq 0).$$

A first-best solution is given by:

- Optimal effort, a^*, = .6300.
- Contractual payment, $\mathscr{I}$, = constant = .6300.
- Principal's utility, $E(U_0)$, = 0.
- Worker's utility, $E(U_w)$, = 1.1905.

Now suppose the principal observes only $x\,(\eta = x)$, the outcome. The agent can shirk without being caught. What is the optimal contract under these arrangements? We have

$$\begin{aligned}\sqrt{\mathscr{I}(x)} &= \lambda + \mu\phi_a(\cdot)/\phi(\cdot)\\ &= \lambda + \mu\frac{(x-a)}{a^2}.\end{aligned}$$

Solving the constraints provides $\mu = a^3$ and $\lambda = 1/2(\theta + a^2)$. With $\theta = 1.1905$ we have:

- Optimal effort, a^*, = .4520.
- Contractual payment, $\mathscr{I}(x)$, = $.2431 + .4458\,x + .2043\,x^2$.
- Principal's utility, $E(U_0)$, = $-.0761$.

Suppose you can introduce an additional performance measure y with joint distribution

$$\phi(y, x|a) = \left(\frac{1}{a}e^{-x/a}\right)\left(\frac{1}{a}e^{-y/a}\right).$$

We then readily determine:

- Optimal effort, a^*, = .5086.
- Contractual payment, $\mathscr{I}(x,y)$, = $.2171 + .2370\,(x + y) + .0647\,(x + y)^2$.
- Principal's utility, $E(U_0)$, = $-.0499$.

Indeed, with n such signals we would have

$$\sqrt{\mathscr{I}(x,y)} = \hat{\lambda} + \frac{\hat{\mu}}{a^2}\left[(x-a) + \sum_{i=1}^{n}(y_i - a)\right]$$

and the solution converges to the first-best solution as n becomes arbitrarily large.

Suppose, now, that the outcome is jointly observed. What property must some evaluation system have if it is to be useful in motivating the agent? It must be used in the corresponding optimal contract.

THEOREM 5 (HOLMSTROM). *A necessary condition for some evaluation system to be strictly desirable when x is jointly observed is that*

$$\frac{\phi_a(x|a)}{\phi(x|a)} \neq \frac{\phi_a(x,y|a)}{\phi(x,y|a)}.$$

This follows directly from the first-order condition noted earlier [Holmstrom, 1977, 1979]. Indeed, a Blackwell-type statement is also available here.

THEOREM 6. *Consider two costless evaluation systems, η and η', for which there exists a function $g : Y' \to Y$ such that $y = \eta(\cdot) = g(\eta'(\cdot))$. Then $E(U_o/\eta') \geq E(U_o/\eta)$.*

The proof follows directly from the maximization problem that we previously discussed. In effect, $\mathscr{I}$ is constrained under η relative to under η' and the maximal expected utility cannot be lower.[7]

Now apply these ideas to our old friend, responsibility accounting. To keep the discussion as simple as possible, suppose we have *two* agents and an *additive* outcome structure of:

$$p(s, a_1, a_2) = p^1(s, a_1) + p^2(s, a_2).$$

The owner remains risk-neutral and each manager is risk- and work-averse with separable utility functions. What do we typically say here?

To check this thinking with our model, we need to be somewhat precise about what we mean by responsibility accounting. One way to do this is to assume that $x = p^1(\cdot) + p^2(\cdot)$ is jointly observed by the owner and *each* manager. An evaluation mechanism that would support responsibility accounting would then be one that reported $p^1(\cdot)$ and $p^2(\cdot)$. We will term the former η and the latter η^R.[8] Now suppose x^1 and x^2 are *independent:* $\phi(x^1, x^2|a) = \phi(x^1|a^1)\phi(x^2|a^2)$. What is gained by movement from η to η^R? From our previous analysis, but with *two* managers, we know that $\phi_{a_i}(\cdot)/\phi(\cdot)$ is the key.

Under η^R, independence then provides

$$\frac{1}{U_i'(\cdot)} = \lambda_i + \mu_i \frac{\phi_{a_i}(x^i|a_i)}{\phi(x^i|a_i)}$$

And we have precise confirmation of our dogma; that is, there are gains to moving from η to η^R *and* optimal use of the information entails confining manager i's evaluation to outcome x^i.

More interesting is the case when x^1 and x^2 are partially correlated.

A variation on Theorem 5 (moving to the two-agent case) will guarantee strictly positive returns to moving from η to η^R. But the main point is the source of these returns.

An example may be insightful. Suppose $\phi(x^1, x^2|a)$ is multivariate normal with $E(x^i|a_i) = 8a_i$ and $\sigma_{x^1} = \sigma_{x^2} = 1$ and a correlation between x^1 and x^2 of .60. The utility of each worker is

$$\sqrt{x_w^i} - a_i^2.$$

Let $\theta_i = 0$ and assume $\mathscr{I}^i \geq 0$. With only x reported we find

$$a_i^* = .88$$

$$2\sqrt{\mathscr{I}^i(\cdot)} = \lambda_i + \frac{\mu_i}{3.2}(x - 8a_i),$$

when $\mathscr{I}^i > 0$ and $E(U_0|\eta) = 4.40$. (Also $\lambda_i = 1.01$ and $\mu_i = 1.06$.) In contrast, with η^R we find

$$a_i^* = .88$$

$$2\sqrt{\mathscr{I}^i(\cdot)} = \hat{\lambda}_i + \frac{\hat{\mu}_i}{0.64}(x^i - E(x^i|x^j, a)),$$

when $\mathscr{I} > 0$ and $E(U_0|\eta^R) = 5.62$. (Also, $\lambda_i = 1.53$ and $\mu_i = .14$.)

In short, we use x^1 *and* x^2 to evaluate each manager. x^2 tells you something about a_1, and you must employ η^R to obtain the information. Separation is, thus, the key. But optimal use is more subtle than we generally admit. The best example I can think of here is "comparison" of branch managers.

Another place to apply these ideas is in the area of standard cost variance analysis. Would variance analysis be useful here? Suppose x = price times quantity = $p(s) \times q(s, a)$. Factoring out the price effect would produce a less risky evaluation of the manager's behavior. On the other hand there would be no point to the exercise if $p(s)$ is a constant.

Extensions

For another aspect of this story, consider the idea that if the variance is "large" we investigate. Again we can set this up in the principal-agent model, but I have been unsuccessful at finding any results here.[9]

Two other excursions are probably worth additional efforts in this area, as well. One deals with incentives to honestly transmit private information, as when managers self-report time allocations, demand or cost expectations, and so forth. The other is the extension of the principal-agent story to what we might recognize as financial reporting, which is the subject of the third lecture.

Notes

1. See Demski and Feltham [1976, Chapter 4] for further analysis.
2. What is the cost of material in the special order? What is the cost of the special order?
3. $p^B(\cdot)$ is strictly concave to keep $p^C(\cdot)$ linear; you might interpret it as net of distribution "cost."
4. For example, consider the "cost" of a stockout.
5. An interpretation is to view the act as effort, an undesirable.
6. Subsequently reported in Holmstrom [1979]. Also see Shavell [1979].
7. More precisely, $\mathscr{I}(y')$ is constant for all y' such that $g(y') = y$ for some $y \in Y$ in the η model.
8. What does Theorem 6 say about η vs. η^R?
9. In subsequent work, Baiman and Demski [1980] report a result guaranteeing the optimality of a nonrandomized investigation strategy.

References

Baiman, S., and Demski, J. "Variance Analysis Procedures and Motivation Devices." *Management Science,* in press.

Demski, J. "Uncertainty and Evaluation Based on Controllable Performance." *Journal of Accounting Research,* Autumn 1976.

———, and Feltham, G. *Cost Determination: A Conceptual Approach.* Ames, Iowa: Iowa State University Press, 1976.

———. "Economic Incentives in Budgetary Control Systems." *The Accounting Review,* April 1978.

Feltham, G. A. "Cost Aggregation: An Information Economic Analysis." *Journal of Accounting Research,* Spring 1977.

Harris, M., and Raviv, A. "Some Results on Incentive Contracts with Applications to Education and Employment, Health Insurance and Law Enforcement." *American Economic Review,* March 1978.

Holmstrom, B. "On Decentralization, Incentives and Control in Organizations." Ph.D. diss., Stanford University Graduate School of Business, 1977.

———. "Moral Hazard and Observability." *Bell Journal of Economics,* Spring 1979.

Jensen, M. C., and Meckling, W. H. "Theory of the Firm: Managerial Behavior, Agency Costs and Ownership Structure." *Journal of Financial Economics,* Oct. 1976.

Mirrlees, J. "The Optimal Structure of Incentives and Authority within an Organization." *Bell Journal of Economics,* Spring 1976.

Shavell, S. "Risk Sharing and Incentives in the Principal and Agent Relationship." *Bell Journal of Economics,* Spring 1979.

Simon, H. A. "Theories of Bounded Rationality." In *Decision and Organization,* ed. by C. B. McGuire and R. Radner. New York: American Elsevier, 1972.

Wilson, R. "On the Theory of Syndicates." *Econometrica,* Jan. 1968.

A SIMPLE CASE OF INDETERMINATE FINANCIAL REPORTING

JOEL S. DEMSKI

Financial accounting theorists have long sought to specify the content of financial reports. Frustrations emerge when we observe scholars making inconsistent and/or unimplemented recommendations; and the majority conjecture is that these inconsistencies and rejections are driven by the complexity of the task at hand.

For example, consider a firm that holds a single asset, say cash in the form of twenty $1 bills (U.S. currency). The argument is that we would *all* surely agree that the firm's assets could be described by a total of $20 (U.S. currency as of the date in question). And the obvious implication is that stripping away complexity brings us to a point of fundamental agreement.[1]

Unfortunately, such encounter with the siren begs the question of economic returns to financial reporting. With nontrivial resources devoted to financial reporting, addressing the question of how to report presupposes some specification of how the resulting data are to be used as well as alternative use of the resources devoted to reporting. And, as we shall see, explicitly adding the economic return dimension to our simple setting considerably clouds the situation.

The purpose of this paper, then, is to pose a simple one-asset firm and address the question of economic returns to financial

Note: This research was sponsored by the Stanford Program in Professional Accounting, major contributors to which are: Arthur Andersen & Co.; Arthur Young & Co.; Coopers & Lybrand; Ernst & Ernst; Peat, Marwick, Mitchell & Co.; and Price Waterhouse & Company. Helpful comments of David Kreps, Jerry Feltham, Lynn Marples, and David Ng are gratefully acknowledged.

reporting for that firm. The analysis proceeds in three stages. Initially, we examine our mythical reporting firm in a one-period setting. Extension to the multiperiod case is then illustrated by repeating the analysis in a two-period setting. Finally, numerous extensions of the basic analysis are briefly sketched.

The Single-Period Setting

Consider a two-person, one-asset firm with one period of existence. One individual, an *owner,* has invested in the firm and the second individual, a *manager,* will operate the firm by making critical decisions and by providing labor services. The manager is compensated for his services and the owner occupies a residual position. (Note that under appropriate conditions the owner may be viewed as a group of individuals, as in Wilson [1968].)

An example is provided by a taxi company. The owner has provided a cab and the manager will operate the cab. At the end of the period all necessary maintenance will be performed and the cab will be sold. The maintenance is subcontracted and—for simplicity—no maintenance choices are entertained. The manager does, however, make two critical decisions: he selects a search procedure to hunt for fares and a level of "care" that will impact on maintenance costs. And the fundamental question posed is what financial reporting should be engaged in. (An additional question of moral hazard on the fares charged and collected is, for the moment, assumed away.)

To be more specific, we envision some overall outcome arising from the firm's operations, denoted $x \in X$. The manager is paid some amount x_M and the owner receives the residual amount $x_O = x - x_M$. For example, after the taxi firm is liquidated the cash balance is x; x_M is then paid to the manager, and x_O is received by the owner.

The firm's outcome, in turn, depends on the owner's investment, denoted $q \in Q$, and the manager's decision, denoted $a \in A$. Also, to introduce uncertainty into the production process, we envision some state $s \in S$ as ultimately obtaining and influencing the productive outcome. We then have the functional representation[2]

$$x = p(s, a, \bar{q}). \qquad (1)$$

$\bar{q} \in Q$ is fixed, by assumption in this section, and a will be selected by the manager before s obtains. (The question of specifying $\bar{q}$ will be addressed in the following section.)

Financial reporting in this simple setting consists of some retrospective analysis of the firm's productive outcome. Some report will be prepared and distributed to both individuals *after* a is chosen and s and x obtain. By properly specifying the state variable we may view such a reporting mechanism as a mapping into some signal space F:[3]

$$\mathscr{F} : S \times A \times Q \times X \rightarrow F \tag{2}$$

To introduce the cost of this reporting, denoted $C(\mathscr{F})$, we adopt an expositionally convenient additive formulation and replace (1) by:

$$x = p(s, a, \bar{q}) - C(\mathscr{F}). \tag{3}$$

Observe, now, that the setting is purposely constructed to limit the motivation for financial reporting. The owner has already invested $\bar{q} \in Q$ and, upon liquidation, no new investments will be entertained (and the report is not desired for its own sake). Thus, we have a strict *stewardship* motive at this point. The purpose of the reporting is to provide information about the manager's use of the asset, $\bar{q}$, entrusted to him. In particular, the only choice variables open in this setting are the manager's behavior, choice of $a \in A$, and choice of the contracting arrangement between the owner and manager. Presumably, choice of $a \in A$ will be determined by the manager's own self-interest; otherwise, we have no interest in stewardship reporting.

The contractual arrangement, in turn, is a key determinant of the particular manager's behavior. Here we assume (to maintain incentive compatibility) that contracting arrangements are limited by what is jointly observable by the manager and the owner. That is, the contract cannot be conditioned on variables not observable by both of the parties. For example, the contract cannot rest on a specific decision a (for example, a specific search procedure and driving style) unless the owner is able to verify the implementation of the particular decision (procedure and style). Similarly, the contract cannot rest upon net liquidation proceeds if the manager is to be paid before such proceeds are realized.

To make this contracting arrangement more precise, let η^O denote the information system possessed or accessed by the owner and η^M that possessed or accessed by the manager. The respective signals are observed after the manager's decision is selected but before x_M is determined. (Both systems are mappings from $S \times A \times Q$

$\times X$ into some signal space.) And with each signal privately observed, the contract is limited to functions over the common signal in the two systems. We let $\hat{\eta}$ denote the common elements in the two systems and $\hat{y}$ the corresponding common signal. In turn, with financial reporting system $\mathscr{F}(\cdot)$ we expand the information on which employment contracting is possible. That is, with financial reporting system $\mathscr{F}(\cdot)$ the manager's remuneration may be a function of both $\hat{y} = \hat{\eta}(s, a, q, x)$ and $f = \mathscr{F}(s, a, q, x)$. Denote this function or contracting arrangement by $x_M = \mathscr{I}(\hat{y}, f)$. It is this basis for contracting that provides the motivation for financial reporting *in this particular case.*

Several additional assumptions will provide sufficient structure to explore this reporting motivation. First, we assume that the outcome is always observed by both individuals (x is included in $\hat{y}$). This appears to be a reasonable assumption in that both could observe, say, the firm's bank balance. On the other hand, we might consider this a form of financial reporting. But it appears best to reserve such reporting for something more sophisticated than a cash flow total. And in any event, the assumption is made for expositional reasons. The ensuing analysis can be readily extended to the non-outcome-observed case.

Second, we assume individual preferences are represented by the expected utility hypothesis. This allows the reporting motivation to be directly linked to the perceived "well-offness" of the individuals. The owner is concerned only with his realized net return, x_O, and is risk-neutral. He therefore evaluates alternative contracting arrangements in terms of the expected value of his return, preferring more to less. On the other hand, the manager's preferences depend on his pecuniary return, x_M, as well as the act taken; we encode them in the additive (and differentiable) representation $U_M(x_M, a) = U(x_M) - V(a)$. Also, the manager is regarded as generally risk- and work-averse.[4]

The act $a \in A$ is admitted as an item of concern here in order to capture the idea of the manager preferring—*ceteris paribus*—leisure to work. Otherwise, as we shall see, motivation issues are far more simple. Moreover, this notion of "disutility" for work or effort is subject to a broad nonpecuniary return interpretation and can be made precise by introducing the notion of consumption at work, as in Stafford and Cohen [1974] and Jensen and Meckling [1976].[5]

Finally, we assume the manager and owner share homogeneous beliefs concerning the productive and reporting uncertainties. To simplify the notation, let $\eta = (\hat{\eta}, \mathscr{F})$ denote the entire reporting system when joint structure $\hat{\eta}$ and financial reporting system $\mathscr{F}$ are present. Also denote the combined signal by the pair $(x,y) = (\hat{y},f)$ where y denotes all jointly observed signals except the outcome, x. The individual's beliefs concerning the productive and reporting uncertainties are then assumed encoded in the (differentiable) conditional joint density of outcome x and report y given the choice of $a : \phi(x,y|a)$.[6]

Individual evaluations

Now consider the manager's behavior under some combined reporting system η and employment contract $x_M = \mathscr{I}(x,y)$. His choice behavior will reflect his tastes for the pecuniary and nonpecuniary returns involved in the contracting arrangement. Presuming suitable regularity, we describe his choice of $a \in A$ by:

$$E(U_M|\mathscr{I},\eta,a) = \int\int U(\mathscr{I}(x,y))\phi(x,y|a)dxdy - V(a) \tag{4}$$

$$a^*(\mathscr{I},\eta) = \operatorname*{argmax}_{a\in A} E(U_M|\mathscr{I},\eta,a) \tag{5}$$

where $a^*(\mathscr{I},\eta)$ is the set of maximizers of the expected utility measure in (4). With alternate optima, the manager is, of course, strictly indifferent among the members of $a^*(\mathscr{I},\eta)$.

In a similar manner, the owner's evaluation of his residual position in this arrangement is given by:

$$E(x_O|\mathscr{I},\eta,a^{**}) = \max_{a\in a^*(\mathscr{I},\eta)} \int\int (x - \mathscr{I}(x,y))\phi(x,y|a)dxdy - C(\mathscr{F}) \tag{6}$$

where we assume the manager will select any $a \in a^*(\mathscr{I},\eta)$ desired by the owner.

Note here that the assumed solution concept is a perfect Nash equilibrium. The owner specifies the possible returns available to the manager, by specifying $\mathscr{I}(\cdot)$ and $\mathscr{F}(\cdot)$, and the manager then selects his most preferred act given the selected and observed $\mathscr{I}(\cdot)$ and $\mathscr{F}(\cdot)$. But he does not engage in any threat strategies in an attempt to influence the selection of $\mathscr{I}(\cdot)$ and $\mathscr{F}(\cdot)$. (Also note that the manager is assumed not to have financial reporting options in this setting.)[7]

In turn, the owner's options in specifying $\mathscr{I}(\cdot)$ and $\mathscr{F}(\cdot)$ are not unlimited. He must offer an employment arrangement that is attractive to the manager. We recognize this by presuming a minimum utility constraint, $E(U_M|\mathscr{I},\eta,a^{**}) \geq \theta$. Given a particular reporting system $\eta = (\hat{\eta},\mathscr{F})$, then, the choice of remuneration scheme is described by:

$$E(x_O|\eta) = \max_{\mathscr{I}(\cdot)} E(x_O|\mathscr{I}, \eta, a^{**}) \qquad (7)$$
$$\text{s.t. } E(U_M|\mathscr{I}, \eta, a^{**}) \geq \theta$$

And finally, we term financial reporting system $\mathscr{F}(\cdot)$ weakly preferred to system $\hat{\mathscr{F}}(\cdot)$ if $E(x_O|(\hat{\eta}, \mathscr{F})) \geq E(x_O|(\hat{\eta}, \hat{\mathscr{F}}))$.

With these behavioral descriptions before us, we now examine the question of returns to financial reporting.

The first-best solution

Initially consider the case where all pertinent variables are jointly observable, $\hat{\eta} = \eta^f = (s, a, x)$. The Pareto optimal allocations with such extensive observability are readily determined. The risk-indifferent owner shoulders 100 percent of the productive risk; and the manager therefore receives a constant wage (say k^*) regardless of the productive outcome. In exchange, the manager provides a particular act (say a^*). Moreover, the act and wage are such that the expected marginal product of the manager's act is equal to the manager's marginal rate of substitution between income and acts or effort.[8]

We term this the *first-best solution* to the stewardship problem. Quite clearly, no financial reporting scheme could do better; and none would be used if this allocation could be achieved in its absence.

Necessary conditions for usefulness of financial reporting

With the first-best allocation before us, we now consider what conditions are necessary for costly financial reporting to be employed. Following Harris and Raviv [1978], we isolate conditions under which the first-best allocation is achievable without additional information. The absence of these circumstances then provides the desired necessary conditions.

First consider the case where both parties observe the agent's act as well as the outcome, $\hat{\eta}(\cdot) = (a, x)$. A contract paying the agent $\mathscr{I}(a) = k^*$ if a^* is taken and nothing (or worse) in its absence will clearly guarantee selection of a^* and attainment of the first-best solution. We term this a *wage contract* and have

LEMMA 1. *In the basic stewardship model with the act and outcome jointly observed, an appropriate wage contract will produce the first-best solution.*

Alternatively, suppose only the state and the outcome are jointly observed, $\hat{\eta}(\cdot) = (s, x)$. Use of an insurance contract guaranteeing an income of k^* if a^* is selected will surely give us the desired allocation. And $\mathscr{I}(s,x) = x - p(s,a^*,\bar{q}) + k^*$ does precisely this. Terming this arrangement an *insurance contract* we have[9]

LEMMA 2. *In the basic stewardship model with the state and outcome jointly observed, an appropriate insurance contract will produce the first-best solution.*

Now suppose the only jointly observed variable is the outcome, $\hat{\eta}(\cdot) = x$. If the manager is also risk-neutral and has sufficient resources to acquire the firm by paying the owner his expected return in the first-best allocation, we again produce the first-best solution. In other words, with no risk sharing to worry about, selling the firm to the agent completely internalizes the effort allocation decision. Terming this the *takeover contract* we have[10]

LEMMA 3. *In the basic stewardship model with the manager risk-neutral (and no binding bankruptcy constraint), an appropriate takeover contract will produce the first-best solution.*

Finally, note that with the manager work-neutral ($V(a)$ = constant) and presumably willing to implement the owner's preferred act, $\mathscr{I}(\cdot) = k^*$ will produce the first-best solution. Terming this a *salary contract* we have

LEMMA 4. *In the basic stewardship model with the manager work-neutral, an appropriate salary contract will produce the first-best solution.*

Combining these four lemmata in obvious fashion we obtain Harris and Raviv's [1978] monitoring conditions, here specialized to a financial reporting setting:[11]

PROPOSITION 1. *Necessary conditions for returns to financial reporting to exist in the basic stewardship model with the outcome jointly observed are (i) that the jointly observed variables include neither the act nor the state; (ii) that the manager be strictly risk-averse (assuming no binding bankruptcy constraint); and (iii) that the manager be strictly work-averse.*

The outcome-observed case

Now consider more closely the case in which both parties observe only the final outcome, $\hat{\eta}(\cdot) = x$. The manager is also assumed to be work- and risk-averse. We first give an example, inspired by Gjesdal [1976], to demonstrate that the conditions in Proposition 1 are not sufficient to support returns to financial reporting.

Example 1

Consider a case where $p(s, a, \bar{q}) = 4(1 + s)\sqrt{a}$ with s uniformly distributed over the interval $[-1/2, 1/2]$. We then have

$$\phi(x|a) = \begin{cases} 1/(4\sqrt{a}) & \text{if } x \in [2\sqrt{a}, 6\sqrt{a}]; \\ 0 & \text{otherwise.} \end{cases}$$

Also, $U_M(x_M, a) = ln(x_M - 1) - a^2$. A first-best solution is given by

$$a^* = 1, \mathscr{I}^*(\cdot) = k^* = 2, E(U_0|\eta^f) = 2, \text{ and}$$
$$E(U_M|\eta^f, \mathscr{I}, a^*) = -1.$$[12]

Suppose, however, that only the outcome is observed. If a^* is actually selected by the manager the subsequently observed outcome will be in the interval $[2,6]$. But for any $a < a^*$ the smallest possible outcome of $2\sqrt{a}$ is less than 2. Hence, for all $a < a^*$ there is a chance that the observed outcome will be inconsistent with $a = a^*$. Capitalizing on this fact, the following penalty contract ensures selection of a^* and attainment of the first-best solution:[13]

$$\mathscr{I}(x) = \begin{cases} 2 & \text{for all } x \geq 2; \\ 1 + 10^{-10} & \text{otherwise.} \end{cases}$$

Selecting $a = a^*$ completely avoids the penalty; there is no incentive to select $a > a^*$; and the penalty is sufficiently severe that there is no incentive to chance fate by selecting $a < a^*$.

Thus, with the appropriate technology (a lower bound moving with the act) and sufficient penalties, fear of the penalty ensures attainment of the first-best solution. And we have a case in which returns to financial reporting, in spite of satisfying the necessary conditions in Proposition 1, are precisely nil.[14]

Of course, jointly observing the outcome need not provide a basis for producing the first-best solution. This is demonstrated in our second example.

Example 2[15]

Consider a setting in which $U_M(x_M, a) = 2\sqrt{x_M} - a^2$ and $\phi(x|a) = (1/a)e^{-x/a}$ (with $a > 0$ and $x \geq 0$). The outcome is exponentially distributed with a mean (and standard deviation) given by the manager's act. One particular first-best solution is given by $a^* = .6300$, $k^* = .6300$, $E(U_O|\eta^f) = 0$, and $E(U_M|\eta^f, \mathscr{I}, a^*) = 1.1905$. But with only the outcome observed, this allocation cannot be achieved.

To locate the best allocation with $\hat{\eta}(\cdot) = x$, we follow the formulation in relations (4) through (7) and maximize the owner's expected return subject to a minimum utility constraint for the manager and subject to satisfaction of the manager's first-order condition for choice of $a \in A$:

$$\max E(x_O|\mathscr{I}, a) = a - \int \mathscr{I}(x)\phi(x|a)dx$$
$$\text{s.t. } E(U_M|\eta,\mathscr{I}, a) = 2\int \sqrt{\mathscr{I}(x)}\,\phi(x|a)dx - a^2 = \theta$$
$$\frac{\partial}{\partial a}E(U_M|\eta,\mathscr{I}, a) = 2\int \sqrt{\mathscr{I}(x)}\,\phi_a(x|a)dx - 2a = 0$$

where $\phi_a(x|a) = \partial\phi(x|a)/\partial a$. Let λ be the multiplier associated with the minimum utility constraint and μ that with the first-order condition constraint.

Pointwise maximization over the remuneration scheme provides

$$\sqrt{\mathscr{I}(x)} = \lambda + \mu\frac{\phi_a(x|a)}{\phi(x|a)} = \lambda + \frac{\mu(x-a)}{a^2}. \tag{8}$$

Holding the manager at the illustrated first-best position of $\theta = 1.1905$, we readily obtain[16]

$$\mathscr{I}^*(x) = .2431 + .4458x + .2043x^2$$

with $a^* = .4520$ and $E(x_O|\hat{\eta}) = -.0761 < E(x_O|\eta^f) = 0$. Note, in particular, that the optimal solution calls for the manager to absorb some of the production risk (even though the owner is risk-neutral) and that the effort supplied is less than in the first-best solution. We thus readily observe an unambiguous and strictly positive *potential* return to financial reporting in this case.

The next question is how the introduction of financial reporting will affect this particular allocation. In one extreme, the report might be either pure noise or a direct transformation of the jointly observed outcome and thus supply no additional information.[17] In the other extreme, the report might serve to identify the manager's act and thus provide a basis for producing the first-best allocation (via Lemma 1). The intermediate case is illustrated below.

Example 3

Consider the same setting as in Example 2, but with a financial reporting system characterized by

$$\phi(x, f|a) = \left(\frac{1}{a}e^{-x/a}\right)\left(\frac{1}{a}e^{-f/a}\right).$$

We interpret this as a reporting mechanism that produces a report less than perfectly indicative of the manager's behavior. But, for convenience, the noise in the reporting system is independent of the outcome.

Proceeding as in the previous example and holding the manager at the illustrated first-best solution of $\theta = 1.1905$, we obtain:

$$\mathscr{I}^*(x, f) = .2171 + .2370\,(x + f) + .0647\,(x + f)^2, \quad \text{with}$$

$$a^* = .5086 \quad \text{and} \quad E(x_O|\eta) = -.0499 > E(x_O|\hat{\eta}) = -.0761.$$

A final question concerns the nature of the financial reporting scheme that gives rise to positive reporting returns. With the outcome jointly observed, any report that provides a mechanical transformation of the outcome would surely be valueless.[18] Similarly, the missing information that precludes attainment of the first-best solution is the owner's lack of knowledge of the manager's choice behavior. And by implication, the feature of the reporting scheme that is critical is learning something additional about the manager's behavior.

Note that the owner strictly prefers the reporting scheme in Example 3 (as long as its cost is not excessive) because it provides a contracting arrangement that is indifferent to the manager while at the same time inducing the manager to behave in a manner more beneficial to the owner. (Conversely, we could demonstrate indifference by the owner but strict preference by the manager.) Indeed, repeatedly sampling the manager's behavior along these lines will arbitrarily approximate the first-best solution.[19]

This intuition can, in fact, be made more precise by examining the first-order condition on the optimal contracting arrangement in the above two examples. If the optimal arrangements are identical in the two cases, the additional signal is not being used, nothing has changed, and the reporting system is therefore valueless. But from relation (8) it is clear that we must have $\phi_a(x|a)/\phi(x|a) \neq \phi_a(x, f|a)/\phi(x, f|a)$ if the two arrangements are to differ, simply because $\sqrt{\mathscr{I}^*(x)}$ is the best linear function of the former and $\sqrt{\mathscr{I}^*(x, f)}$ of the latter. Otherwise nothing is altered through introduction of the report.

Indeed, this observation extends well beyond our examples. Holmstrom [1977] provides extensive discussion of the conditions that are necessary for a reporting system to be valuable in the outcome-observed case; and, with suitable regularity, it is relatively easy to see[20]

PROPOSITION 2. *A necessary condition for financial reporting system $\mathscr{F}(\cdot)$ to have positive value in the basic stewardship model with $\hat{\eta}(\cdot) = x$ is that $\phi_a(x|a)/\phi(x|a) \neq \phi_a(x,f|a)/\phi(x,f|a)$.*

Thus, an accrual procedure in our setting must, in one way or another, reflect something about the manager's behavior that is not discernible from the observed outcome. For example, separating capital gains from the net outcome may be desirable *if* excluding them provides a more informative measure.

The Two-Period Setting

Now consider a two-period version of the basic setting discussed above. Admitting to a second period adds two dimensions to the problem. First, at the time of initial period payment to the manager, the outcome is not, by definition, completely observed. Second, an abandonment decision may also be feasible at that time. (An additional dimension of replacing the manager may also be feasible but is not entertained at this point.)

The motivation problem in the face of incomplete outcome observation is merely a variation on the theme discussed above. With a vector interpretation of acts and outcomes we could directly repeat the necessary-conditions argument for existence of returns to stewardship reporting. And when returns do exist, the central feature of a valuable reporting scheme is additional information about the manager's choice behavior.

Analysis of the abandonment decision, in turn, leads to a straightforward discussion of value of information (and Blackwell's Theorem).[21] Here returns to financial reporting exist to the extent such reporting can improve the quality of the (subsequent) abandonment or second-period productive decisions. And, of course, economies of scale may exist in which a single reporting scheme has value in both the stewardship and abandonment-production senses.

Example 4

To begin illustrating these observations, we return to the structure of Example 1 but extend it to a two-period setting. The problem's time structure is represented by time indexing ($t = 1,2$) the state, act, and outcome variables, as in Figure 1: $s = (s^1, s^2)$, $a = (a_1, a_2)$, $x = (x^1, x^2)$, $x_M = (x_M^1, x_M^2)$, and $x_O = (x_O^1, x_O^2)$. The two states are independent and identically distributed with a uniform distribution

Time:	$t = 0$	$t = 1$	$t = 2$
Choice:	$a_1 \in A_1$	$a_2 \in A_2$ $q \in Q$	
Outcomes:		$x^1 = p^1(s^1, a_1, \bar{q})$	$x^2 = p^2(s^2, a_1, a_2, q)$
Individual Returns:		$x_M^1 = \mathscr{I}^1(x^1, y^1)$ $x_O^1 = x^1 - x_M^1$	$x_M^2 = \mathscr{I}^2(x^2, y^2)$ $x_O^2 = x^2 - x_M^2$

Fig. 1. Two-period setting.

over $[-1/2, 1/2]$. The first period outcome is given by $x^1 = 4(1 + s^1)\sqrt{a_1}$ and the second by $x^2 = \alpha(1 + s^2)\sqrt{a_1} + 4(1 + s^2)\sqrt{a_2}$, where $\alpha \neq 0$ provides for a future period effect associated with the first period's act. The owner's preferences are represented by $U_O(x_O) = x_O^1 + .9x_O^2$ and the manager's by $U_M(x, a) = ln(x_M^1 - 1) - a_1^2 + .9(ln(x_M^2 - 1) - a_2^2)$. Also, the outcome and act are jointly observed each period: $\hat{\eta}(\cdot) = (\hat{\eta}^1, \hat{\eta}^2) = ((x^1, a_1), (x^2, a_2))$.

A first-best solution is readily determined by:[22]

$$\max E(U_O|\eta, \mathscr{I}) = E(x_O^1 + .9x_O^2) = 4\sqrt{a_1} - E\mathscr{I}^1(x^1, a_1) + .9[\alpha\sqrt{a_1} + 4\sqrt{a_2} - E\mathscr{I}^2(x^2, a_2)]$$

$$\text{s.t.} \quad E(U|\eta, \mathscr{I}, a) = E(ln(\mathscr{I}^1(\cdot) - 1)) - a_1^2 + .9(E(ln(\mathscr{I}^2(\cdot) - 1)) - a_2^2) = \theta$$

For a numerical illustration, with $\theta = -1.9$ and $\alpha = .25$, we have $a_1^* = 1.0267$, $a_2^* = .9900$, $\mathscr{I}^1(\cdot) = \mathscr{I}^2(\cdot) = k^* = 2.0153$, and $E(U_O|\hat{\eta}) = 4.0340$.

Observe that we might consider an accrual to account for the expected future effect of the first period act (i.e., $\alpha\sqrt{a_1} = .25\sqrt{1.0267} = .2533$). But there is no reason to do this. The accrual in this example would be based on information available at the end of the first period and therefore contributes no additional insight into the second period's state occurrence. Hence it cannot improve the quality of the a_2 selection. And it is also useless for motivation purposes because a first-best solution is attainable in its absence. Indeed, even with the joint information restricted to $\hat{\eta}(\cdot) = x$, we would not be interested in any financial reporting. The penalty structure illustrated in Example 1 could be used to produce the first-best solution.[23]

Thus, even with unobserved future effects we do not necessarily generate a positive demand for financial reporting. In terms of guiding future decisions, however, the story changes if we admit that the financial report is not some summarization or processing of the current (end of first period) information. In this case the prospect of useful additional information is raised.

Example 5

To illustrate, consider the owner's abandonment decision in the above example. At the end of the first period, he has the options of continuing (with an expected outcome of $x^2 = \alpha\sqrt{a_1} + 4\sqrt{a_2}$) or liquidating (with an expected outcome of $\alpha\sqrt{a_1} + P$, where P is the liquidation price). An exit value reporting system, $\mathcal{F}(\cdot) = P$, would have value at this point if the owner's abandonment decision varied with the signal. Of course, this implies that some type of market imperfection is present (otherwise the price would be known) and that the optimal decision will vary with the price.

Suppose, for a numerical illustration, that the price is either 0 or 6, with equal probability. In the above case ($\theta = -1.9$, $\alpha = .25$), the owner will continue into the second period in the absence of additional information (with an expected price of 3). But if the exit value will be reported at the end of the first period, the owner will liquidate if $P = 6$ obtains and continue if $P = 0$ obtains. Holding $\theta = -1.9$ (with $\alpha = .25$) the first-best solution under this information structure consists of $a_1^* = 1.1028$, a_2^* (with $P = 6$) $= 0$, a_2^* (with $P = 0$) $= 1.0633$, $k^* = 1.9120$, and $E(U_O|\eta) = 5.3601$. Note that such a prospect alters the production plan in both periods; and the owner would pay up to $(5.3601 - 4.0340) = 1.3261$ for such a reporting system. On the other hand, if the price varied between, say, 0 and 4, the reporting system would be useless.

Example 6

The reporting system's value can also be produced through correlation with the second period's production as opposed to liquidation outcomes. Consider, in the above example, a replacement type measure that says nothing whatever about current liquidation prospects, but by reflecting various actors' information reveals something about s^2. To be specific, suppose it partitions S into $f^1 = [-1/2, 0)$ and $f^2 = [0, 1/2]$. With the uniform distribution assumption, $E(s^2|f^1) = -.25$ and $E(s^2|f^2) = .25$. In the $\theta = -1.9$, $\alpha = .25$ case, with f^1 received the owner will take his chances in the liquidation "market" (with an expected price of 3), but will continue with f^2. The first-best solution now consists of $a_1^* = 1.0735$, a_2^* (with f^1) = 0, a_2^* (with f^2) = 1.2011, $k^* = 1.9496$, and $E(U_O|\eta) = 4.4892$.

Again note the altered production plans. Also, if one is forced to choose between the two systems, the exit measure is more valuable than the replacement cost measure. But altering the numerical assumptions will reverse the ranking. Indeed, the only way to provide a general ranking at this point is to appeal to Blackwell's Theorem and have one reporting system sufficient for the other.

Thus, admitting to a two-period setting allows for reporting returns that derive from improving the quality of decisions made subsequent to the signal's receipt (predecision information) and from improving the quality of the manager's decisions made prior to the signal's receipt (postdecision information). Relating back to Proposition 2, shifting $\phi_a(\cdot)/\phi(\cdot)$ is critical in the second instance and shifting $\phi(\cdot)$ is critical in the first. The nature of the returns, then, becomes clear in our simple setting. But the most desirable reporting system remains a situation-specific issue.

Possible Extensions

Numerous extensions are conceivable at this point. First, the single owner assumption is an extreme case in the financial reporting environment. Indeed, it would be desirable to consider a three-tier setting consisting of "inactive" owners, owners "active" in the firm's management (e.g., board of directors), and the manager. But the single owner assumption allows us to talk unambiguously about the "firm's" preferences, with an expected utility representation. Admitting to a multiple-ownership setting removes this feature of the analysis, via Arrow's Impossibility Theorem [1963]. It is important to note, however, that even with a well-defined preference structure for the firm the reporting question remains ambiguous.

Second, the single manager assumption could be relaxed. Multiple managers and task allocation among them could then be addressed. This would also permit analysis of manager turnover, in terms of replacement by the owner, promotion/demotion, and self-selection by the managers. Of course, all of this drives us away from the partial equilibrium setting assumed here. In turn, by allowing for multiple firms and information markets we could begin to consider regulatory issues.

Finally, the question of auditing the financial reports should also be addressed. This would entail some possibility of "cheating" or "bluffing" in the report production and verification by others (e.g., moral hazard on the fares in the taxi story). Precisely what conditions would produce something akin to our present institutional arrangements, however, remains an open question.

Summary

Focusing on a simple one-asset, one-manager, one-owner firm provides an unrealistic but somewhat analyzable setting in which to explore financial reporting issues. By focusing on the question of economic returns to reporting, however, the reporting question is seen to be largely indeterminate, even in the highly simplified context examined. The inherent nature of the reporting process that gives rise to returns, as well as the nature of the environment in which such returns are available, has been discussed. But, as with other factors of production, we ultimately analyze demand (or value or returns to) in terms of the tastes, opportunities, and relative prices at hand. General solutions remain in the realm of fiction.

Notes

1. To be sure, uniqueness questions also arise here. Is an additive measure in U.S. currency the only measure of the firm's assets? But the important point is that the $20 datum is obtained by application of a reporting method that all consider within the class of appropriate measurements.
2. An additional determinant, the manager's skill, could also be introduced. But the basic analysis and argument offered here are more straightforward without this elaboration. We will also assume throughout, for simplicity, that optimal acts are in the interior of A.
3. It seems unwise to be more precise at this point in specifying what we mean by financial reporting. Such reports are historical and presumably describe various aspects of the productive act and/or outcome. Precisely what language is used, whether the reports are audited, and so on, should, ultimately, be a product of our analyses. For this reason, I prefer the somewhat vague description in (2). However, we will ultimately have something to say about the properties $\mathscr{F}(\cdot)$ must possess if it is to be useful (or valuable).
4. Somewhat more precisely, unless otherwise noted we assume $U' > 0$, $U'' \leq 0$, $V' < 0$, and $V'' \geq 0$.
5. In a similar vein, the owner is assumed to be risk-neutral for expositional reasons. When nonpecuniary return considerations create a motivation problem, otherwise efficient risk sharing may be traded off to lessen the motivation problem. The trade-off is most easily

observed when a contracting arrangement between a risk-neutral owner and a risk-averse manager calls for the manager to bear part of the productive risk.

6. $\bar{q} \in Q$ and η also condition the joint density, but we view $\bar{q}$ as fixed in this section and η will be clear from the context. Also note that, presuming suitable regularity, we may view the joint density as being derived from the state density, $\phi(s)$. For example, with y a null signal we would have

$$\psi(x \leq \hat{x}|a) = \int_{s \in S(\hat{x},a)} \phi(s)ds$$

where

$$S(\hat{x}, a) = \{s \in S | p(s, a, \bar{q}) \leq \hat{x}\} \quad \text{and}$$

$$\phi(\hat{x}|a) = \frac{d}{d\hat{x}} \psi(x \leq \hat{x}|a).$$

7. There is some ambiguity here concerning who selects the financial reporting system. It is difficult to envision cooperative specification because noncooperative behavior is assumed in act selection. And because it is an integral component of the employment mechanism, I have modeled the choice as resting with the owner. But it is easy to envision the manager having such choice, as in government contracting. Of course, with moral hazard on the act we should also expect moral hazard on the reporting system. This then gives rise to auditing, which further complicates the analysis. We could also have moral hazard on the owner's part. In any event, it should be clear how the model can be extended to accommodate these considerations.

8. To see this, we maximize the owner's well-being subject to constant well-being for the manager.

$$\max_{\mathscr{I}(\cdot),a} \int\int (x - \mathscr{I}(x, a, s))\phi(x|a, s)\phi(s)dxds$$

$$\text{s.t.} \int\int U(\mathscr{I}(x, a, s))\phi(x|a, s)\phi(s)dxds - V(a) = \theta$$

Presuming suitable regularity, first-order conditions provide:

(i) $U'(\mathscr{I}^*(\cdot)) = \text{constant} = U'(k^*)$

and

(ii) $$\left.\frac{E\,\partial p(s, a, \bar{q})}{\partial a}\right|_{a^*} = \frac{V'(a^*)}{U'(k^*)}$$

where strict concavity of $U(\cdot)$ provides the wage interpretation of constant marginal utility of income for the manager. (Risk sharing would be an indifferent proposition with $U'' = 0$.)

9. The manager faces the following problem:

$$\max_{a \in A} \int\int U(\mathscr{I}(s, x))\phi(x, s|a, \eta)dxds - V(a)$$
$$= \max_{a \in A} \int U(p(s, a, \bar{q}) - p(s, a^*, \bar{q}) + k^*)\phi(s)ds - V(a).$$

And the first-order condition is satisfied at $a = a^*$ with

$$\left.\frac{E\,\partial p(\cdot)}{\partial a}\right|_{a^*} = \frac{V'(a^*)}{U'(k^*)}.$$

10. This is clear from Lemma 2. No insurance ($\mathscr{I}(s)$ = constant) is one possible solution with both parties risk-neutral; and risk sharing is not an allocative issue when both parties are risk-indifferent. Further note that the bankruptcy condition can, under certain conditions, be circumvented by a penalty contract in which the manager receives $k^1 > k^*$ if $x \geq \hat{x}$, and $k^2 < k^*$ otherwise. $\hat{x}$, k^1, and k^2 are set such that $a^* = \text{argmax } E(U_M|\mathscr{I}, \eta)$ and $Ex_M = k^*$. See Feltham [1978].

11. The basic point, of course, is that with any of the conditions present we can achieve the first-best solution. Hence, they must be absent for returns to financial reporting or, more generally, any monitoring of the agent's behavior. They must also, therefore, be absent for gains to use of budget-based contracting arrangements [Demski and Feltham, 1978].

12. Use of $U_M(x_M, a) = ln(x_M - 1) - a^2$ in this and subsequent examples presumes $\mathscr{I}(\cdot) > 1$. Also note here that $V'/U' = 2a(x_M - 1) = (E\,\partial p(s, a, \bar{q}))/\partial a = 2/\sqrt{a}$ with $a^* = 1$ and $k^* = 2$.

13. The manager clearly has no incentive to select $a = 0$ or $a > a^*$. For $0 < a \leq a^*$, we have

$$\begin{aligned} E(U_M|\eta, \mathscr{I}, a) &= (ln\ 10^{-10})\,\phi(x < 2|a) + (ln\ 1)\,\phi(x \geq 2|a) - a^2 \\ &= (ln\ 10^{-10})(2 - 2\sqrt{a})/4\sqrt{a} - a^2. \end{aligned}$$

And maximization over $0 < a \leq a^*$ results in selection of $a = a^* = 1$, since (for $a \in (0, 1)$)

$$(\partial E(U_M|\eta, \mathscr{I}, a))/\partial a = -(ln\ 10^{-10})/4a^{3/2} - 2a > 0$$

and

$$(\partial^2 E(U_M|\eta, \mathscr{I}, a))/\partial a^2 = 3(ln\ 10^{-10})/8a^{5/2} - 2 < 0.$$

14. A similar argument, based on continuity considerations, is given by Mirrlees [1975]. He adopts a lognormal outcome distribution and shows that, with suitable regularity, use of a penalty contract with a severe penalty and very low outcome standard allows us to arbitrarily approximate the first-best solution.

15. This particular example, along with a rigorous discussion of the existence of a solution to this general class of moral hazard problem, is analyzed in Holstrom [1977].

16. Satisfaction of the two constraints provides $\mu = a^3$ and $\lambda = (1/2)(\theta + a^2)$. And, the owner's first-order condition on the act provides

$$1 - 2\lambda a - 4a^3 = 0.$$

17. This is readily checked by repeating the argument in Example 3.

18. Indeed, any report for which the outcome is sufficient in a statistical sense would be valueless.

19. With n such signals, identically and independently distributed, we would have

$$\phi(x, f|a) = \phi(x, f_1, \ldots, f_n|a) = \left(\frac{1}{a}e^{-x/a}\right)\left(\frac{1}{a}e^{-f_1/a}\right)\cdots\left(\frac{1}{a}e^{-f_n/a}\right).$$

Solution of the owner's problem, as in Example 2, then provides

$$\sqrt{\mathscr{I}(x,f)} = \lambda + \frac{\mu}{a^2}\left((x-a) + \sum_{i=1}^{n}(f_i - a)\right)$$

where λ is the multiplier on the manager's well-being constraint and μ is the multiplier on the manager's act selection constraint. We also obtain

$$\mu = a^3/(n+1) \text{ and } \lambda = (1/2)(\theta + a^2).$$

Notice that the owner now receives a payment whose square root is linear in the sum of the deviations from the expected outcome. And allowing the "sample size" n to grow without bound produces the first-best allocation (See Parzen [1960, p. 429] for a formal proof.)

20. A rigorous proof is provided by Holmstrom [1977]. (Also see Gjesdal [1976].) The basic logic is, however, quite straightforward. Positive value requires $\mathscr{I}^*(x) \neq \mathscr{I}^*(x,f)$. Otherwise the allocation is unaffected. Repeating the argument in Example 3 on pointwise determination of $\mathscr{I}^*(\cdot)$ with $U_M(x_1, a) = U(x_M) - V(a)$, we obtain $(U')^{-1} = g(\mathscr{I}(\cdot)) = \lambda + \mu\phi_a(z|a)/\phi(z|a)$ where $z = x$ or (x,f) and λ and μ are multipliers on the $E(U_M|\eta, \mathscr{I}, a) = \theta$ and $(\partial E(U_M|\eta, \mathscr{I}, a))/\partial a = 0$ constraints. And for $\mathscr{I}^*(x)$ to differ from $\mathscr{I}^*(x,f)$, $\phi_a(x|a)/\phi(x|a)$ must differ from $\phi_a(x,f|a)/\phi(x,f|a)$.

21. Marschak and Miyasawa [1968] and McGuire [1972].

22. First-order conditions provide

$$\mathscr{I}^1(\cdot) = \mathscr{I}^2(\cdot) = k$$
$$(2 + .45\alpha)/\sqrt{a_1} = 2a_1(k-1)$$
$$2/\sqrt{a_2} = 2a_2(k-1)$$

which are subject to the usual efficiency interpretation. Also note that a richer setting would provide for interperiod borrowing.

23. These comments apply even if the manager may be replaced after the first period.

References

Arrow, K. J. *Social Choice and Individual Values.* New York: John Wiley, 1963.

Demski, J. S., and Feltham, G. A. "Economic Incentives in Budgetary Control Systems." *Accounting Review,* April 1978.

Feltham, G. A. "Optimal Incentive Contracts: Penalties, Costly Information and Multiple Workers." Unpublished working paper, University of British Columbia, 1977.

Gjesdal, Froystein. "Accounting in Agencies." Unpublished paper, Stanford University Graduate School of Business, 1976.

Harris, M., and Raviv, A. "Some Results on Incentive Contracts." *American Economic Review,* March 1978.

Holmstrom, B. "On Decentralization, Incentives and Control in Organizations." Ph.D. diss., Stanford University Graduate School of Business, 1977.

Jensen, M. C., and Meckling, W. H. "Theory of the Firm: Managerial Behavior, Agency Costs and Ownership Structure." *Journal of Financial Economics,* Oct. 1976.

Marschak, J., and Miyasawa, K. "Economic Comparability of Information Systems." *International Economic Review,* June 1968.

McGuire, C. B. "Comparisons of Information Structures." In *Decision and Organization,* ed. by McGuire and Radner. New York: North Holland, 1972.

Mirrlees, J. A. "Notes on Welfare Economics, Information and Uncertainty." In *Essays on Economic Behavior under Uncertainty,* ed. by Balch, McFadden, and Wu. New York: North Holland, 1974.

———. "The Optimal Structure of Incentives and Authority within an Organization." *Bell Journal of Economics,* Spring 1976.

Parzen, E. *Modern Probability Theory and Its Applications.* New York: John Wiley, 1960.

Stafford, F. P., and Cohen, M. S. "A Model of Work Effort and Productive Consumption." *Journal of Economic Theory,* March 1974.

Wilson, R. "On the Theory of Syndicates." *Econometrica,* Jan. 1968.

DISCUSSION SUMMARY

The paper addresses the question of economic returns to financial reporting for a one-asset firm. The analysis is carried out in a one-period setting and is then extended to two periods.

The firm, which has one asset, is owned by a single individual who is risk-neutral. A manager operates the firm by making the decisions and providing labor services. The manager is assumed to be risk-averse. The owner and manager share homogenous beliefs concerning the productive and reporting uncertainties.

The contractual arrangement between the owner and the manager determines the manager's behavior. In this setting, financial reporting provides information about the manager's use of the asset, i.e., the stewardship function.

The manager will attempt to maximize his expected utility on the basis of his preferences for the pecuniary and nonpecuniary returns involved in the contracting arrangement. In turn, the owner will attempt to maximize his expected utility on the basis of his residual position in the arrangement. The manager is assumed not to have financial reporting options.

The paper then develops the conditions necessary for financial reporting to have value. These conditions are summarized in Proposition 1:

PROPOSITION 1. *Necessary conditions for financial reporting to exist in the basic stewardship model with the outcome jointly observed are (i) that the jointly observed variables include neither the act nor the state; (ii) that the manager be strictly risk-averse (assuming no binding bankruptcy constraint); and (iii) that the manager be strictly work-averse.*

Although these conditions are necessary for economic returns to financial reporting, they are not sufficient. A first-best solution may be achieved in the case of a jointly observed outcome under moving support conditions and a penalty contract. However, in the case of a jointly observed outcome alone (no penalty contract), the first-best solution cannot be obtained and financial reporting does have a positive potential return. If the financial report is either pure noise or if it is a direct transformation of the jointly observed outcome, it will provide no additional information and hence have no value. If, however, it does help to identify the manager's act, then the report would support movement toward the first-best solution and therefore have a positive return.

Introduction of a second period adds two dimensions to the problem. First, when the manager is paid at the end of period 1, the outcome is not completely observed, i.e., only period 1's outcome is observed. Second, a decision to abandon the operation may be made at the end of period 1. In the incomplete outcome observation case, returns to reporting exist when the financial report provides additional information about the manager's choice behavior. This is similar to the single period setting. In the case of the abandonment decision, returns to financial reporting exist when such reporting improves the quality of the abandonment or the second-period production decisions. There may also be economies of scale in which a single reporting scheme has value in both the stewardship and abandonment-production senses.

Three examples are presented. In the first, financial reporting has no value although there are unobserved future effects. This is true if the report is just a summarization of the first period's information. The second example demonstrates that an exit value system will produce economic returns, and the third argues for a replacement cost type of system. In order to choose between these two systems one has to rank them. However, the ranking changes depending upon the numerical values used, so no general rule can be used. Selection between the two systems is a situation-specific issue.

THE AMERICAN ECONOMIC REVIEW
VOL. 68 NO. 1 MARCH 1978

Success Indicators in the Soviet Union: The Problem of Incentives and Efficient Allocations

By MARTIN LOEB AND WESLEY A. MAGAT*

> ... [T]he correct combination of the interests of the controlling and the controlled levels of production is one of the most important tasks of an optimally controlled economy. It is quite possible (and even highly probable!) that the liquidation of the striving of the lower levels to hide their productive possibilities, the orientation of the interests of the masses to the search for new, better variants of production and many other consequences of such a combination, at the present time conceals bigger reserves for the growth of the socialist economy, than the use of mathematical programming with the preservation of the former relations between the controlling and the controlled levels of the economy.
>
> *Viktor V. Novozhilov* [p. 32][1]

As Novozhilov recognized in 1969, elimination of the incentives for Soviet managers to act contrary to the interests of society would yield significant gains in the value of output produced by Soviet enterprises. Realizing the importance of incentives for motivating behavior which is consistent with plans, Soviet planners have long struggled with the problem of designing good success indicators.[2] Success indicators should induce enterprises to act efficiently in carrying out state plans. They should also motivate enterprises to send accurate forecasts to the Central Planning Bureau (*CPB*) so that socially desirable plans may be constructed and capital efficiently allocated.

*Assistant professor, department of economics and business, North Carolina State University, and assistant professor, Graduate School of Business Administration, Duke University, respectively.

[1]This quote was taken from Michael Ellman (1973b, p. 40).

[2]See Alec Nove.

Forecasts are particularly important in a centralized economy because the *CPB* cannot be expected to possess detailed knowledge of the enterprises' production functions. Nove presents a convincing argument which explains why enterprises are constantly presented with a range of alternative decisions, that is, why the *CPB* is incapable of centrally planning all aspects of the production process. He also provides some examples of how poor success indicators provide incentives for enterprises to produce inefficiently, or to otherwise act contrary to the best interests of the *CPB*, and thus the Soviet state.

As Joseph Berliner has explained (pp. 401, 402), Soviet planners cannot reasonably expect managers to act as *Homo Sovieticus*, the party man who carries out all directives and makes all decisions in the best interests of his country. *Homo Economicus*, the manager who acts in his own best interests, provides a more reliable model for studying the behavior of the Soviet manager, for his operating rules are derived primarily from the incentive structure and may differ considerably from the formal decision rules. As an example, the ratchet problem which has plagued Soviet planning can only be explained by reference to an incentive structure which penalizes managers by assigning them higher plans in subsequent years if they overfulfill their current year's plans by too great a margin. As David Granick concludes,

> Soviet leaders have viewed intermediate and lower-level managers as "economic men"—much as top decision makers in capitalist firms are viewed in orthodox neoclassical economic theory. They have perceived their own problem as being that of creating a combined incentive and de-

cision-rule system which would lead such managers, in their own personal and narrow self-interest, to act in the fashion desired by the central policy makers. [p. 37]

Our work takes this same view in analyzing the "bonus-maximizing" behavior of Soviet managers. We do not distinguish between the behavior of the enterprise and that of its managers, since bonuses are the prime source of income over which managers have control and bonuses are tied closely to the enterprise bonus fund. In addition, the earnings of the managerial and professional staff are also dependent upon the size of the bonus fund, so bonus maximization helps to foster a pleasant working atmosphere and to retain reliable staff members.[3]

Western economists have recently begun to analyze the incentive properties of success indicators employed in the Soviet Union. The growing literature on resource allocation mechanisms[4] has also spurred renewed interest in the design and analysis of new success indicators with desirable incentive properties. Ellman (1971, 1973a, b) provides an algebraic characterization of the bonus formulas incorporated in the 1965 Soviet economic reform. Martin Weitzman offers a formulation of the success indicators utilized in the 1971 reform and a careful analysis of their incentive properties, both in the certainty and uncertainty cases. On the design side, Liang-Shing Fan has proposed a success indicator to motivate desirable behavior on the part of Soviet enterprise managers which also possesses desirable incentive properties.

This paper accomplishes three main purposes. First, we show that the reform of 1971, in so far as it relates to the static incentive properties of enterprise success indicators, is merely cosmetic and has the same properties as those given by the 1965 reform. The Weitzman indicators are shown to be only a slight generalization of the Ellman indicators. Furthermore, we observe that Fan's proposal is not new, since the Fan indicators are a subset of the Ellman indicators (and, hence, also a subset of the Weitzman indicators).

Our second purpose is to show that the Fan, Ellman, and Weitzman success indicators actually possess *undesirable* incentive properties. While Fan, Ellman, and Weitzman all recognize the desirability of motivating accurate forecasts, their models do not explain how the *CPB* uses these forecasts. Their analyses implicitly assume that enterprises ignore the effects of forecasts on *CPB* allocations to the enterprises. Our model recognizes that the *CPB* uses forecasts to make allocations. We also allow enterprises to take this knowledge into account when sending forecasts to the *CPB*. Under such circumstances, we show that using the success indicators studied by Fan, Ellman, and Weitzman, enterprises can individually gain by transmitting inaccurate forecasts, to the detriment of society as a whole.

The third purpose of this paper is to present a new success indicator which motivates accurate forecasts and efficient behavior in the context of our more general model.

In Section I we show that the set of Fan success indicators is a subset of the Ellman indicators, which in turn comprise a subset of the Weitzman indicators. Section II contains a description of the problem which arises when the *CPB* uses forecasts to allocate capital to the enterprises. We define the incentive problem in terms of a game in which enterprises are motivated by success indicators to play strategies consisting of forecasts and operating decisions. Section III provides an example to demonstrate that the Fan, Ellman, and Weitzman indicators actually encourage the transmittal of biased forecasts. Section IV contains a presentation of a new success indicator designed to overcome the problems associated with the Weitzman, Ellman, and Fan indicators.

I. The Weitzman, Ellman, and Fan Success Indicators

Weitzman has supplied a major contribution to the study of Soviet incentive

[3]See Granick, pp. 37–41.

[4]For a review of this literature, see Leonid Hurwicz.

systems by formally modeling the success indicators imbedded in the recent 1971 Soviet economic reform.[5] He is careful to explain that his "aim is to focus directly on the *analytical essence* of the new reward structure" (p. 252, emphasis added). Our work follows in the spirit of his paper, since we believe that any complex reward system cannot be expected to motivate socially desirable behavior unless, when reduced to its barest essentials, it possesses the necessary incentive properties.

We recognize that there are several enterprise incentive funds (each based on more than one variable, such as sales or profit rate), that managers receive additional bonuses related to such activities as development and assimilation of new technology, and that enterprises face a considerable amount of administrative uncertainty. Further, a success indicator which possesses desirable incentive properties within the context of a certainty model that incorporates only a single bonus fund may not actually induce the socially desired behavior in this more complex environment. However, we cannot expect to understand the effects of complicated reward systems until we first understand the properties of the simpler incentive systems on which they are based.

Weitzman describes a three-stage process. In the preliminary phase, planners assign each enterprise a tentative target π° and a tentative bonus $\bar{B}$, where the target may reflect profit rate, value of output, or labor productivity. The enterprises are also assigned bonus and penalty coefficients, α, β, and γ, where $0 < \alpha < \beta < \gamma$. In the planning phase, each enterprise must choose a plan target π^F, which could differ from the tentative target π°. If the enterprise actually produced the targeted amount π^F, then the enterprise would receive the planned bonus $\hat{B}$, where

$$(1) \qquad \hat{B} = \bar{B} + \beta(\pi^F - \pi^\circ)$$

In the implementation phase the enterprises produce some amount π^A and are rewarded on the basis of the success indicator S, where

(2)

$$S(\pi^F, \pi^A) = \begin{cases} \hat{B} + \alpha(\pi^A - \pi^F), \text{ if } \pi^A \geq \pi^F \\ \hat{B} - \gamma(\pi^F - \pi^A), \text{ if } \pi^A < \pi^F \end{cases}$$

Weitzman does distinguish between the *static* problem described above and the *dynamic* problem which arises when planners use current performance to revise the coefficients of future success indicators (such as the coefficients α, β, and γ). In the static problem enterprises are assumed to maximize the success indicator S, whereas in the dynamic problem they aim to maximize a time-discounted sum of current and future values of S. The 1971 reform was most significant in that it reduced the size of the ratchet effect which is characteristic of the dynamic problem, for it froze the fixed targets (π° and $\bar{B}$) and the coefficients (α, β, and γ) for the entire ninth five-year plan (1971–75). Thus managers were no longer faced with a penalty for excessive overfulfillment of plans, at least in the first three or four years of the five-year planning period. We follow Weitzman in considering only the static problem.

Using equation (1), we can rewrite (2) as

$$(3) \quad S(\pi^F, \pi^A) = \begin{cases} \bar{B} + \beta(\pi^F - \pi^\circ) \\ \qquad + \alpha(\pi^A - \pi^F), \text{ if } \pi^A \geq \pi^F \\ \bar{B} + \beta(\pi^F - \pi^\circ) \\ \qquad - \gamma(\pi^F - \pi^A), \text{ if } \pi^A < \pi^F \end{cases}$$

Now define $\mathcal{S}^W$ as the set of all Weitzman success indicators. That is $\mathcal{S}^W$ is the set of all $S(\pi^F, \pi^A)$, as in (3), with $\bar{B} \geq 0$, $\pi^\circ \geq 0$, and $0 < \alpha < \beta < \gamma$.

When the forecast π^F affects S, but not the actual amount selected π^A, the Weitzman indicators possess desirable incentive properties. As shown by Weitzman, in the case of perfect certainty about production and market possibilities, enterprises are motivated to send truthful forecasts. Given these forecasts, they also have incentives to increase actual performance π^A as much as possible.

[5] See Weitzman for a more detailed description of the success indicator.

Next consider the subset $\mathcal{S}^E$ of $\mathcal{S}^W$ defined by setting $\bar{B} = \pi° = 0$ (i.e., eliminating the preliminary phase of the three-phase planning process). A member of $\mathcal{S}^E$ is, therefore, written as

$$(4) \quad S(\pi^F, \pi^A) = \begin{cases} \beta\pi^F + \beta(1 - \epsilon_1)(\pi^A - \pi^F), \text{ if } \pi^A \geq \pi^F \\ \beta\pi^F - \beta(1 + \epsilon_2)(\pi^F - \pi^A), \text{ if } \pi^A < \pi^F \end{cases}$$

where ϵ_1 and ϵ_2 are defined by $\epsilon_1 = 1 - \alpha/\beta$ and $\epsilon_2 = \gamma/\beta - 1$, with $0 < \epsilon_1 < 1$ and $\epsilon_2 > 0$. Equation (4) can be rewritten as

$$(5) \quad S(\pi^F, \pi^A) = \beta\pi^F - k\beta(\pi^F - \pi^A)$$

where $k = (1 - \epsilon_1)$ if $\pi^A \geq \pi^F$ and $k = (1 + \epsilon_2)$ if $\pi^A < \pi^F$. Note that equation (5) is the Ellman indicator (represented by equation (3) in his 1973 paper).[6] Ellman presents (5) as a formalization of the success indicators employed by the Soviet planners in the 1965 reform. We have shown that $\mathcal{S}^E$ is a subset $\mathcal{S}^W$, so that the 1971 reform indicators represent only a slight generalization of the 1965 reform indicators.

Even this, however, overstates the contribution of the 1971 reform. Success indicators are merely used as a *basis* on which to reward enterprises. Hence, a monotonic transformation of an indicator belongs to the same equivalence class, that is, has the same incentive properties. The Weitzman indicators merely add $\bar{B}$ and $\beta\pi°$ to the Ellman indicators (a monotonic transformation) and replace the *CPB*'s control variables, ϵ_1, ϵ_2, and β, with α, β, and γ. Thus the 1965 and 1971 success indicators are essentially the same; the 1971 reform does not represent a significant step in solving the static incentive problem.[7]

Consider the subset $\mathcal{S}^F$ of $\mathcal{S}^E$ defined by setting $\epsilon_1 = \epsilon_2 = \epsilon$, where $0 < \epsilon < 1$. Substituting into (4), we can represent a member of $\mathcal{S}^F$ as

$$(6) \quad S(\pi^F, \pi^A) = \begin{cases} \beta\pi^F + \beta(1 - \epsilon)(\pi^A - \pi^F), \text{ if } \pi^A \geq \pi^F \\ \beta\pi^F - \beta(1 + \epsilon)(\pi^F - \pi^A), \text{ if } \pi^A < \pi^F \end{cases}$$

Equation (6) can be written as

$$(7) \quad S(\pi^F, \pi^A) = \beta[\pi^F + (\pi^A - \pi^F) - \epsilon\,|\,\pi^A - \pi^F\,|\,]$$

or

$$(8) \quad S(\pi^F, \pi^A) = \beta[\pi^F + (1 + \epsilon \cdot sgn(\pi^F - \pi^A)) \cdot (\pi^A - \pi^F)]$$

When π^A and π^F are interpreted to mean actual and forecasted *profit*, then equation (8) represents the success indicator given by Fan.[8] Thus, his proposed indicator is merely a special case of ones already in use.

For future reference the Fan indicator is further simplified by rewriting (7) as:[9]

$$(9) \quad S(\pi^F, \pi^A) = \beta[\pi^A - \epsilon\,|\,\pi^F - \pi^A\,|\,]$$

We note that this indicator has been studied elsewhere in the context of management performance evaluation in a firm.[10]

II. Incentives and Allocations

A major problem with the theory of Soviet success indicators is its failure to consider the uses of enterprise forecasts. Weitzman, for example, argues that planning is needed for coordination and that forecasts are indispensible for tightly coordinated plans; however, he does not explain how these forecasts are to be used in coordinating the activities of several enterprises. In the (unusual) special case when the information (forecasts) received by the *CPB* is used for decisions which do *not*

[6]Note that in claiming (5) to be the Ellman indicator, we are assuming that the *CPB* uses the *enterprise* forecast π^F as *its* target plan for rewarding the enterprise.

[7]As we mentioned earlier, the 1971 reform is significant in that it did partially resolve the *dynamic* incentive problem.

[8]Fan does not require that $\epsilon < 1$; however, his incentive structure only motivates profit maximization when ϵ is less than one. We also note that while Fan was aware of Ellman's work, he did not explicitly relate his success indicator to those employed in the Soviet Union. His paper is quite confusing on this point.

[9]After this paper was essentially completed, a paper by John Bonin appeared that also reduces Fan's indicator to this equation and analyzes another variant of the Weitzman indicator.

[10]See Yuji Ijiri et al. and Loeb (1974, 1975).

affect the enterprises' measured performance (π^A), then the Weitzman success indicators do possess some desirable properties, as claimed. They motivate enterprises to report truthful forecasts and to operate as efficiently as possible once these forecasts have been made.

We show in Section III that in the more general case where forecasts are used to make decisions affecting measured performance (for example, the allocation of capital to the enterprises), the Weitzman, Ellman, and Fan indicators motivate enterprises to send biased forecasts.

Before illustrating this weakness of the Weitzman, Ellman, and Fan indicators, we first must explain the incentive problem which arises when the *CPB* makes allocations to the enterprises based on their forecasts.[11] Consider a *CPB* with n enterprises under its control. Let us take the index of performance π^A for each enterprise to be enterprise profit. Assume that enterprises take prices as fixed, that is, each enterprise believes that its forecasts and actual profits will not affect the *CPB*'s determination of prices.[12] We also assume that the *CPB* uses enterprise forecasts to make all allocations of capital to the enterprises.

The profits of the ith enterprise depend upon K_i the amount of capital it is allocated and on L_i a vector of local enterprise decisions.[13] The ith enterprise's profits are denoted by $\bar{\pi}_i^A(K_i, L_i)$, and are gross of any charge for capital. We assume that allocations of capital are made prior to local decisions. To insure that enterprise managers act efficiently in their local operations (i.e., they maximize $\bar{\pi}_i^A(K_i, L_i)$ with respect to L_i) we restrict our attention to success indicators which are increasing in an enterprise's own realized profits. Note that the Weitzman indicators satisfy this requirement.

We may now focus on the functions $\pi_i^A(K_i)$, defined by:

$$(10) \quad \pi_i^A(K_i) = \max_{L_i} \bar{\pi}_i^A(K_i, L_i), \qquad i = 1, 2, \ldots, n$$

These functions are assumed to exist for each $K_i \geq 0$ and belong to the set of functions Π, defined as:

$$(11) \quad \Pi = \{\pi : R^+ \rightarrow R \mid \pi(\ ) \text{ is continuous and nondecreasing}\}$$

The *CPB* is assumed to have a fixed quantity $\bar{K}$ of capital to allocate to the n enterprises.[14] It collects contingency forecasts from each enterprise showing the projected profits of that enterprise for various allocations of capital from the *CPB*. The contingency forecasts for the ith enterprise are represented by a function $\pi_i^F(K_i)$. The forecasts $\pi_i^F(\ )$ are also assumed to belong to the set Π.

The *CPB* allocates capital to maximize the sum of the enterprises' forecasted profits. That is the *CPB* selects $\hat{K}_1, \hat{K}_2, \ldots, \hat{K}_n$ such that

$$(12) \quad \hat{K}_1, \hat{K}_2, \ldots, \hat{K}_n \text{ maximize} \sum_{i=1}^{n} \pi_i^F(K_i)$$

subject to $\sum_{i=1}^n K_i \leq \bar{K}$ and $K_i \geq 0$, $i = 1, 2, \ldots, n$. Notice that each $\hat{K}_i$ is a function of *all* of the enterprises' forecasts. We therefore use the notation $\hat{K}_i = \hat{K}_i(\pi^F)$, where $\pi^F \equiv (\pi_1^F, \ldots, \pi_n^F)$, and where the arguments of each π_j^F have been suppressed. While the

[11] In what follows, we make the simplifying assumption that the *CPB* imposes no charge on the enterprises for their capital allocation. Joseph Berliner, p. 433, indicates that the enterprises are required to pay to the State Treasury a charge of 15 percent of the value of their fixed and working capital. It can easily be shown that the incentive problem still exists when capital charges are made.

[12] We are also implicitly assuming that the *CPB* selects "correct" prices which account for externality effects that may occur. Under these circumstances, enterprises seeking to maximize profits act in the best interests of society.

[13] While we interpret K_i as the ith enterprise's allocation of capital, it more generally may be interpreted as a vector of resources, "public inputs," or decisions with externalities. See Loeb (1975) and Theodore Groves and Loeb.

[14] Edward Ames has pointed out to us in personal correspondence that the planning board can increase, but in practice not decrease the amount of capital which an enterprise has. Our argument could be modified to account for this constraint by treating $\bar{K}$ as the *increment* in capital available for distribution to the enterprises.

indicated maximum may not be unique, the decision rules $\hat{K}_1(\pi^F)$, $\hat{K}_2(\pi^F)$, ..., $\hat{K}_n(\pi^F)$ represent a particular maximizer.

The value of the ith enterprise's success indicator depends on its realized profits π_i^A, a real number. However, realized profits are a function of the enterprise's rationed capital, itself a function of the enterprises' contingency forecasts, π^F. For this reason we write enterprise i's success indicator as $S_i(\pi_i^A; \pi^F)$.

As mentioned above, if $S_i(\ )$ is increasing in π_i^A, then the ith enterprise has an incentive to act efficiently in choosing its local decisions. We would also like to choose $S_i(\ )$ so that it motivates accurate forecasts. As a minimal test, we require that if a manager is rewarded on the basis of his success indicators and if he has perfect knowledge of his profit function π_i^A, then he should be motivated to send $\pi_i^A(\ )$ as his forecast.[15] Now the definition of an optimal success indicator can be given.

DEFINITION: The success indicator $\hat{S}_i(\pi_i^A; \pi^F)$ is said to be *optimal* if, and only if:

(a) it is *operationally desirable:* for all π^F belonging to the n-fold Cartesian product of Π and for all real numbers π^1 and π^2, $\pi^1 > \pi^2$ implies $\hat{S}_i(\pi^1; \pi^F) > \hat{S}_i(\pi^2; \pi^F)$;

(b) it is *message desirable:* for all π^F belonging to the n-fold Cartesian product of Π and for all π_i^A belonging to Π, $\hat{S}_i(\pi_i^A[\hat{K}_i(\pi^F/\pi_i^A)]; \pi^F/\pi_i^A) \geq \hat{S}_i(\pi_i^A[\hat{K}_i(\pi^F)]; \pi^F)$, where $\pi^F/\pi_i^A \equiv (\pi_1^F, \ldots, \pi_{i-1}^F, \pi_i^A, \pi_{i+1}^F, \ldots, \pi_n^F)$.

Condition (a) requires that an optimal success indicator be increasing in the enterprise's realized profits. Condition (b) requires that "telling the truth" be a dominant strategy equilibrium for the enterprises. That is, each enterprise can not independently gain by reporting inaccurate forecasts no matter what forecasts the other enterprises send. Thus when it employs a message desirable incentive system the *CPB* has justification for accepting the enterprise forecasts as truthful, avoiding the gaming involved in attempting to correct for forecast bias. Notice that with an optimal indicator each enterprise's evaluation is independent of the local decisions of the other enterprises.

[15]Actually, it need only be required to send forecasts with the same marginal efficiency of capital schedule as its actual profit function, since such forecasts will lead to socially optimal allocations.

III. Nonoptimality of the Weitzman, Ellman, and Fan Indicators

In this section we show that the success indicators given by Weitzman, Ellman, and Fan do not meet the optimality criteria established in Section II. While their indicators do motivate enterprises to maximize profits (i.e., they are operationally desirable), they encourage enterprises to send biased forecasts (i.e., they are not message desirable). To demonstrate this last weakness, we present a simple counterexample showing that when an enterprise is rewarded on the basis of a Weitzman-Ellman-Fan indicator, the manager has an incentive to send biased forecasts, even if all other managers report truthfully. Thus, sending accurate forecasts is not a dominant strategy equilibrium; it is not even a Nash equilibrium.[16]

Consider a *CPB* which has two units of capital to allocate between two enterprises. Suppose each enterprise's actual profit function is

$$\text{(13)} \qquad \pi_i^A(K_i) = \sqrt{K_i} \qquad i = 1, 2$$

Let enterprise 1 be rewarded on the basis of the following success indicator:

$$\text{(14)} \quad S_1(\pi_1^A; \pi_1^F, \pi_2^F) = \pi_1^A(\hat{K}_1) - \epsilon \,|\, \pi_1^F(\hat{K}_1) - \pi_1^A(\hat{K}_1) \,|$$

where $0 < \epsilon < 1$ and $\hat{K}_1 = \hat{K}_1(\pi_1^F, \pi_2^F)$ represents the *CPB*'s allocation to enterprise 1. Recall that, by definition,

[16]A Nash equilibrium only requires enterprises to report truthfully when all other enterprises act likewise. Hurwicz uses the term "incentive compatibility" to refer to this property of resource allocation mechanisms which lead to behavioral patterns in which "truthful" reporting constitutes a Nash equilibrium.

(15) $\hat{K}_1, \hat{K}_2$ maximize $\pi_1^F(K_1) + \pi_2^F(K_2)$ subject to $K_1 + K_2 \leq 2, K_1 \geq 0$, and $K_2 \geq 0$

Comparing equation (14) to equation (9), we see that enterprise 1 is being rewarded on the basis of a Fan indicator. As $\mathcal{S}^F \subset \mathcal{S}^E \subset \mathcal{S}^W$, it is also being rewarded on the basis of an Ellman and a Weitzman indicator.

Suppose both enterprises send accurate forecasts, that is, send $\pi_i^F(K_i) = \pi_i^A(K_i)$, $i = 1, 2$. One easily verifies that the *CPB* would then set $\hat{K}_1 = \hat{K}_2 = 1$. The profits of enterprise one would equal 1, as would the value of its success indicator (14).

Now suppose enterprise 2 continues to send accurate forecasts, $\pi_2^F(K_2) = \sqrt{K_2}$, but enterprise 1 sends the biased forecast:

$$(16) \quad \pi_1^F(K_1) = K_1 - (1\tfrac{3}{4} - \sqrt{1\tfrac{3}{4}})$$

Using the decision rules given by (15), the *CPB* would then set $\hat{K}_1 = 1\frac{3}{4}$ and $\hat{K}_2 = \frac{1}{4}$. The profits of enterprise 1 increase from 1 to $\sqrt{1\frac{3}{4}}$, as does the value of the success indicator (14). Thus, enterprise manager 1 individually gains by sending biased forecasts, even if enterprise manager 2 reports truthfully, indicating that the Fan, Ellman, and Weitzman indicators are not optimal.[17]

IV. A Class of Optimal Success Indicators

In this section we present a class of success indicators which meet the criteria for optimality given in Section III. Versions of this scheme were independently discovered by William Vickrey, Groves (1969), and Edward Clarke, and have been put forth as an incentive compatible means of allocating both private and public goods.[18]

Consider the following class of success indicators:

(17)
$$\hat{S}_i(\pi_i^A, \pi^F) = \pi_i^A(\hat{K}_i) + \sum_{j \neq i} \pi_j^F(\hat{K}_j) - A_i$$

where $\hat{K}_1, \hat{K}_2, \ldots, \hat{K}_n$ are defined by (12) and $A_i = A_i(\pi_1^F, \ldots, \pi_{i-1}^F, \pi_{i+1}^F, \ldots, \pi_n^F)$ is any real value calculated *independently* of enterprise *i*'s forecast.

Success indicator (17) consists of the *i*th enterprise's realized profits (at its allocated level of capital) plus the *forecasted* profits of all other enterprises at their allocated levels of capital, less an amount calculated independently of enterprise *i*'s forecast. Clearly, this success indicator is operationally desirable. In the Appendix, we prove that it is also message desirable; hence, it is optimal.[19] The message desirability of (17) may be explained by examining the enterprise's problem of selecting a forecast. Enterprise *i* selects a forecast π_i^F to maximize indicator (17), which is equivalent to maximizing

$$(18) \qquad \pi_i^A(\hat{K}_i) + \sum_{j \neq 1} \pi_j^F(\hat{K}_j)$$

since A_i is independent of π_i^F. The forecast π_i^F affects the indicator only through the capital allocations $\hat{K}_1, \hat{K}_2, \ldots, \hat{K}_n$. When enterprise *i* reports its true profit function $\pi_i^F = \pi_i^A$, then from (12) the *CPB* will choose capital allocations that maximize enterprise *i*'s success indicator. Thus by reporting truthful forecasts, the *i*th enterprise ensures that the *CPB* will act to maximize the *i*th enterprise's own success indicator.

As the term A_i does not depend on enterprise *i*'s forecast, it does not affect individual (noncooperative) behavior. However, for a meaningful interpretation of the success indicator which some planners might believe insures an equitable distribution of rewards across enterprises, we suggest the following definition of A_i:

$$(19) \quad A_i \equiv \max_{(K_1,\ldots,K_{i-1},K_{i+1},\ldots,K_n)} \left\{\sum_{j \neq i} \pi_j^F(K_j)\right\}$$

[17] It is interesting to note that with this particular example, the *CPB* cannot detect that enterprise 1 reported a biased forecast, since

$$\pi^F(1\tfrac{3}{4}) = \pi^A(1\tfrac{3}{4}) = \sqrt{1\tfrac{3}{4}}$$

[18] For a survey of this literature, see Loeb (1976).

[19] This result is well known in the literature surveyed in Loeb (1976). An earlier proof appears in Groves and Loeb.

subject to $\sum_{j \neq i} K_j \leq K$ and $K_j \geq 0, j \neq i$

With A_i defined as in (19), the ith enterprise's success indicator measures the contribution that it makes to total profit. When enterprises respond with accurate forecasts, $\hat{S}_i$ will equal the sum of all enterprises' profits less the maximum profits all others could obtain if enterprise i were to be eliminated.[20] That is, $\hat{S}_i$ represents the opportunity cost of abandoning the ith enterprise.

As the indicators of the form (17) are optimal, sending accurate forecasts is a dominant strategy equilibrium. These success indicators therefore solve all incentive problems of a noncooperative game theoretic nature. In addition, Groves (1976) shows that under suitable regularity conditions sending truthful forecasts forms a unique dominant strategy equilibrium, and Jerry Green and Jean-Jacques Laffont show that every indicator with the dominance property can be written in the form given in (17).

Appendix

We must show that the success indicator given by equation (17) is message desirable, but first we introduce some additional notation. Let $\mathcal{K} \equiv \{(K_1, \ldots, K_n) \mid K_j \geq 0,\ j = 1, 2, \ldots, n \text{ and } \sum_{j=1}^{n} K_j \leq \bar{K}\}$, $\pi_{-i}^F \equiv (\pi_1^F, \ldots, \pi_{i-1}^F, \pi_{i+1}^F, \ldots, \pi_n^F)$, $\hat{K}_i^1 \equiv \hat{K}_i(\pi^F / \pi_i^A)$ and $\hat{K}_i^2 \equiv \hat{K}_i(\pi^F)$. Then

$$\hat{S}_i(\pi_i^A(\hat{K}_i^1); \pi^F/\pi_i^A) - \hat{S}_i(\pi_i^A(\hat{K}_i^2); \pi^F)$$

$$= \left[\pi_i^A(\hat{K}_i^1) + \sum_{j \neq i} \pi_j^F(\hat{K}_j^1) - A_i(\pi_{-i}^F)\right]$$

$$- \left[\pi_i^A(\hat{K}_i^2) + \sum_{j \neq i} \pi_j^F(\hat{K}_j^2) - A_i(\pi_{-i}^F)\right]$$

$$= \left[\pi_i^A(\hat{K}_i^1) + \sum_{j \neq i} \pi_j^F(\hat{K}_j^1)\right]$$

$$- \left[\pi_i^A(\hat{K}_i^2) + \sum_{j \neq i} \pi_j^F(\hat{K}_j^2)\right]$$

$$= \max_{(K_1, \ldots, K_n) \in \mathcal{K}} \left\{\pi_i^A(K_i) + \sum_{j \neq i} \pi_j^F(K_j)\right\}$$

$$- \left\{\pi_i^A(\hat{K}_i^2) + \sum_{j \neq i} \pi_j^F(\hat{K}_j^2)\right\} \geq 0$$

where the last inequality follows by the definition of a maximum and the fact that $(\hat{K}_1^2, \ldots, \hat{K}_n^2) \in \mathcal{K}$. This completes the proof.

[20] By the phrase "if enterprise i were to be eliminated," we mean that enterprise i receives a zero capital allocation and earns a zero profit.

References

Joseph Berliner, *The Innovation Decision in Soviet Industry*, Cambridge, Mass. 1976.

J. Bonin, "On the Design of Managerial Incentive Structures in a Decentralized Planning Environment," *Amer. Econ. Rev.*, Sept. 1976, *66*, 682–87.

E. Clarke, "Multipart Pricing of Public Goods," *Publ. Choice*, Fall 1971, *11*, 17–33.

Michael Ellman, *Soviet Planning Today: Proposals for an Optimally Functioning Economic System,* London 1971.

———, (1973a) "Bonus Formulae and Soviet Managerial Performance: A Further Comment," *Southern Econ. J.*, Apr. 1973, *39*, 652–53.

———, (1973b) *Planning Problems in U.S.S.R.*, London 1973.

L.-S. Fan, "On the Reward System," *Amer. Econ. Rev.*, Mar. 1975, *65*, 226–29.

D. Granick, "Soviet Introduction of New Technology: A Depiction of the Process," unpublished paper, Stanford Res. Inst., Jan. 1975.

J. Green and J. Laffont, "Characterization of Satisfactory Mechanisms for the Revelation of Preferences for Public Goods," *Econometrica,* Mar. 1977, *45*, 427–38.

T. Groves, "The Allocation of Resources Under Uncertainty: The Informational Incentive Roles of Prices and Demand in a Team," Center Res. in Manage. Sci., tech. rep. no. 1, Univ. California-Berkeley, Aug. 1969.

______, "Information, Incentives, and Internalization of Production Externalities," in Steven Lin, ed., *Theory and Measurement of Economic Externalities*, New York 1976.

______ **and M. Loeb,** "Incentives and Public Inputs," *J. Publ. Econ.*, Aug. 1975, *4*, 211–26.

L. Hurwicz, "The Design of Mechanisms for Resource Allocation," *Amer. Econ. Rev. Proc.*, May 1973, *63*, 1–30.

Y. Ijiri, J. Kinard, and F. Putney, "An Integrated Evaluation System for Budget Forecasting and Operating Performance with a Classified Budgeting Bibliography," *J. Accounting Res.*, Apr. 1968, *6*, 1–28.

M. Loeb, "Comments on Budget Forecasting and Operating Performance," *J. Accounting Res.*, Autumn 1974, *12*, 363–66.

______, "Coordination and Informational Incentive Problems in the Multidivisional Firm," unpublished doctoral dissertation, Northwestern Univ. 1975.

______, "Alternative Versions of the Demand-Revealing Process," *Publ. Choice*, Spring 1977, Suppl., *29*, 15–26.

V. Novozhilov, "Khozraschetnaya Sistema Planirovaniya," in *Optimal'noe Planirovanie I Sovershenstvovanie Upravlenie Narodnym Khozyaistvom,* Moscow 1969.

A. Nove, "The Problem of 'Success Indicators' in Soviet Industry," *Economica,* Feb. 1958, *25*, 1–13.

W. Vickrey, "Counterspeculation, Auctions, and Competitive Sealed Tenders," *J. Finance*, May 1961, *16*, 8–37.

M. Weitzman, "The New Soviet Incentive Model," *Bell J. Econ.*, Spring 1976, *7*, 251–57.

DISCUSSION SUMMARY

In the classical Soviet incentive structure, there is a tendency for managers to understate their productive possibilities. The bonus, which is the prime source of income over which managers have control, is linked to the degree of fulfillment of the production plan set forth by the Central Planning Bureau (CPB). Managers send forecasts of their production capabilities to the CPB. The CPB analyzes these forecasts and determines the level of production based upon these forecasts and upon the overall plan. In order to maximize their bonuses, managers send inaccurate forecasts to the CPB, thus resulting in a socially suboptimal plan.

The paper by Loeb and Magat attempts to design a system of incentives which encourages managers to act in a manner that is socially desirable. The authors show that the success indicators developed by Weitzman are a generalization of the Ellman indicators, which in turn include the Fan indicators as a subset. When the targeted amount of production affects the success indicators, but not the actual production, the Weitzman indicators possess socially desirable incentive properties. Managers will be motivated to send truthful forecasts in the case of perfect certainty about production and market possibilities. However, when forecasts are used to make decisions affecting measured performance, the Weitzman, Ellman, and Fan indicators motivate managers to send biased forecasts.

For a success indicator to be optimal, it should be (i) operationally desirable, i.e., it should increase with the enterprise's realized profits; and (ii) message desirable, i.e., managers should not be able to benefit by reporting inaccurate forecasts regardless of what forecasts the other enterprises send. This will ensure that the CPB receives truthful forecasts and not biased ones.

Section IV of the paper develops a class of success indicators which meet the criteria set forth in the preceding paragraph. It consists of the ith enterprise's realized profits (at its allocated level of capital) plus the forecasted profits of all other enterprises at their allocated levels of capital, less an amount calculated independently of enterprise i's forecast. This success indicator is both operationally desirable and message desirable.

THE ACCOUNTING REVIEW
Vol. LIII, No. 2
April 1978

Economic Incentives in Budgetary Control Systems

Joel S. Demski and Gerald A. Feltham

ABSTRACT: This article explores conventional questions of why and how budgets should be employed for motivation purposes in an economic setting. The authors focus on the types of employment contracts that are associated with equilibrium allocations in the labor market. Market incompleteness is a necessary condition for use of budgets in the employment contract. Beyond this, issues of controllability, management by exception, and tightness of standards are observed to depend on the contracting environment faced by the individual agents.

THE use of standard costs and budgeted profits or costs in performance evaluation has long been advocated in management accounting. Comparison of actual results with some "norm," it is argued, provides a basis for motivating performance and for identifying situations requiring corrective action.

The purpose of this paper is to explore conditions that may induce the use of budgetary control systems in an economic setting. Basically, these conditions take the form of a market incompleteness [Radner, 1974]. Recognition of this incompleteness provides entry to explicit consideration of such questions as the type of standards that should be used, whether the evaluation should be confined to factors controllable by the subordinate, and the extent to which participation in setting the standards is desirable.

We begin with a general discussion of delegation in an incomplete market setting. Our basic model is then presented and analyzed. Exploration of pure moral hazard and adverse selection questions identifies conditions that may induce the use of budgetary control systems.

PRELIMINARY OBSERVATIONS

The basic question we explore is why we observe budgets and standards being used as motivation devices. They are often expensive to install and maintain, and the dysfunctional behaviors they may induce are well known.[1] Nevertheless, their use is both widespread and generally advocated by textbook literature.

We examine the use of these devices from both the employer's and employee's perspective. We translate our basic question into one of identifying factors that will induce an equilibrium in the demand and supply of labor such that contracting

We gratefully acknowledge the considerable help of John Dickhaut, an anonymous reviewer, and, especially, Lynn Marples and the financial help of the Canada Council and the Stanford Program in Professional Accounting (major contributors to which are: Arthur Andersen & Co.; Arthur Young & Company; Ernst & Ernst; Peat, Marwick, Mitchell & Co.; and Price Waterhouse & Co.).

[1] For example see Argyris [1952], Ridgeway [1956], Stedry [1960], Schiff and Lewin [1970], Hopwood [1972], Itami [1975], and Swieringa and Moncur [1975].

Joel S. Demski is Professor of Accounting, Stanford University; Gerald A. Feltham is Professor of Accounting, University of British Columbia.

for (some) labor services is based on a standard of performance.

The basic feature of such contracting is that the compensation paid for labor services depends, in part, on the relationship between actual and standard performance. This payment may, of course, be somewhat indirect if we consider a multi-period setting with promotion contingent on current performance relative to standard. Compensation is a broad concept embracing direct cash payments, stock options, club memberships, pride, self-satisfaction, and so on.

In general, a standard may be expressed in terms of either the "quality" of the input provided or the outcome that results from its use. Contracts based on input quality are very common in the acquisition of physical goods such as wheat, beef steak, fabric and fertilizer, for which there are well developed quality "standards" expressed in terms of observable attributes of those goods. We term such contracting arrangements commodity contracts.

Commodity contracts may also be used in conjunction with labor services, the quality of which depends on both the worker's skill and the effort he expends. Skill may be assessed through examination (references and tests) while supervisory personnel may be used to assess effort. Thus, we observe contracts in which accountants are paid a fixed salary for specific tasks, and machine operators are paid a constant wage per hour of labor provided.

The costliness of precisely observing skill and effort levels, however, leads to other forms of contracts. For example, machine operators are sometimes compensated on a piece-rate basis; service station operators rent their facilities from oil companies, and salesmen have mixed contracts in which they receive a salary plus a bonus based on their total sales. Of particular interest here are budget-based contracts in which worker compensation depends, at least in part, on the relationship between actual and budgeted performance where performance is expressed in terms of some observable attribute(s) of the outcome of worker actions.

More specifically, we define an employment contract as budget-based when

1. the worker's compensation is, in part, a function of some observable attribute(s) of the outcome resulting from his actions;
2. the contract specifies a budgeted (standard) outcome (attribute) level that partitions the set of possible outcomes into favorable and unfavorable subsets; and
3. the worker's compensation function consists of two functions, one defined over the favorable subset and the other over the unfavorable subset.[2]

An example is a contract in which a manager is paid a basic wage if some measure of profit (the outcome attribute) is below a specified budget and a higher wage (basic wage plus bonus) if profit is at or above the specified budget.

Contracting Incentives

Clearly, a necessary condition for budget-based contracts is that employers must be motivated to acquire labor services and workers must be motivated to sell their services. We briefly discuss these

[2] Obviously, we are not limited to a binary partition of the set of outcomes. Indeed, a budget-based contract is a contingent claims contract. and it can be contingent on more than just the outcome. It can depend, for example, on observed attributes of the worker's action or uncontrollable factors (state elements) that influence the outcome. The budgeted outcome may depend on these factors or they may only be observed if the outcome is unfavorable (or favorable). Flexible budgets and investigation of unfavorable variances are obvious examples.

motivations in terms of the "benefits" and "costs" associated with employment contracts, without, as yet, considering the specific type of contract into which the parties will enter.

Consider the extreme case of a sole proprietorship. The owner's benefit from acquiring labor services may take the form of increased income and, hence, increased consumption or increased work-related consumption. An increase in net income is likely if expansion permits the owner to use more effectively his capital and his own efforts. This may result from specialization, both in production in the narrow sense (Adam Smith's pin factory) and in decision-making. For example, information processing advantages may be available, as when a product-line manager acquires considerable local information. Also, specialization is likely to be particularly beneficial when workers possess complementary skills that can be matched to the tasks at hand.

The returns from expanding the firm's work force need not take the form of increased income to be desirable to the owner. He may choose to use such returns to obtain work-related consumption such as leisure, companionship, office decor, and so on (see Stafford and Cohen, 1974, and Jensen and Meckling, 1976). In our formal analysis later in the paper, we assume that the owner contracts for labor services so that he can obtain a return from his capital without expending any effort. (He achieves maximum leisure.)

The worker's benefit from selling his labor services may take the form of increased income or work-related consumption. His costs may include foregone self-employment opportunities and leisure. Additionally, some aspects of the job may be undesirable *per se*. Economies of scale from specialization, matching of complementary skills, and efficient use of capital are likely to result in larger returns from the sale of labor services than from self-employment. The worker's return probably depends on his skill and the effort he expends. He cannot change his skill (at least in the short run), but effort is under his immediate control and he must trade off the return from additional effort and his personal cost from expending it.

Contracting in a Perfect and Complete Market Setting

The nature of the contracts induced by the owners' and workers' preferences is readily sketched in a setting of complete and perfect markets. Here, each conceivable commodity, including each conceivable type of labor service (skill and effort combination), is traded in an organized perfect market. Thus, in surveying the delegation opportunities, the sole proprietor has access to a specific known price for each possible employment task. The same holds for a worker. Assuming an expected utility representation of preferences for the "benefits" and "costs," each maximizes his subjective expected utility with respect to work-derived consumption goods and leisure. We arrive at the thoroughly classical result that, at equilibrium, marginal rates of substitution are equated and the allocation is Pareto optimal. Moreover, employment contracting is predicated on commodity contracts. No budget-based contracting is observed. Rather, we have an extreme case in which the worker is compensated only if the contracted labor services actually are supplied. Put another way, the worker supplies a specific commodity and is compensated accordingly. Implicitly, we assume that the type of labor service provided is costlessly verified and payment of contracts is costlessly enforced; otherwise such contracting may not be efficient.

Contracting in an Incomplete Market Setting

The situation changes drastically once we admit that some aspect of the above skill-task-effort dependent commodity contract is not observable by both parties. With such an information void, the parties cannot contract on the basis of these variables. For example, if only the worker knows his skill type or effort expended, contracting based on skill or effort is not available because of lack of enforceability. This, in turn, creates information production incentives. But if the cost is prohibitive, less than complete observation will be employed, and we arrive at the incomplete markets case. Certain types of trades, in other words, may be unavailable. It is here that we encounter incentives to use budget-based contracts.

Moral Hazard Issues[3] First consider the case in which it is too costly for the owner to observe worker effort, but where both can costlessly observe the worker's skill, the state (uncontrollable factors that influence the outcome) and the outcome. Non-observability of worker effort precludes a contract that directly pays a specific wage for a specific task involving a specified minimum effort level. However, the same contract can be indirectly constructed if, for a given state and skill, the task outcome is uniquely determined by the effort level. In particular, the wage would be paid if the observed outcome is at least as desirable to the owner as the outcome that would have resulted from the specified minimum effort level given the worker's skill and the state that occurred. In short, an *ex post*, standard (flexible budget) is used to obtain the allocation that would have been achieved with perfect and complete markets.

Though an admittedly extreme and simple case, this illustrates the basic idea of a budget-based contract: we employ the outcome to learn something about the worker's behavior. Indeed, the information available in this case is sufficient to learn precisely what effort was expended. In general, however, the requisite information is not costlessly available; various aspects of worker performance can be observed for a price and the fundamental question reduces to one of what information to obtain. Indeed, if the owner can observe the state or worker effort by providing some of the labor service himself, he may choose to forego some leisure and obtain this information by delegating less than the entire amount of labor services to hired workers.

Now, consider the opposite extreme in which the owner has no knowledge whatever of what state obtains or what effort the worker expends. (The cost of such knowledge is prohibitive.) Under these conditions, the two may "agree" upon a particular effort-price combination, but the worker has no incentive to honor such an agreement. The worker prefers less effort to more and random state occurrence will likely mask at least some shirking by the worker [Alchian and Demsetz, 1972 and Becker and Stigler, 1974]. Thus, pure wage contracts are unlikely in this case. One alternative, which avoids the shirking problem entirely, is a rental contract in which the owner rents his capital to the worker for a fixed fee. Under this contract the owner, obviously, is indifferent as to the worker's effort level and the

[3] In many contracted arrangements some actions that influence the outcome are not specified because observation of these actions is too costly. The moral hazard phenomenon arises in these contexts when the agent in question is personally motivated to take actions other than those that would have been specified in the contract if such specification had been possible. For example, the insured in a fire insurance contract is likely to expend less effort or money on safety precautions since the costs of those precautions fall directly on him, whereas the cost of a fire falls primarily on the insurer.

worker is induced to expend effort because he receives all returns in excess of the rental fee.

Despite the avoidance of shirking, a rental contract may be less desirable than a wage contract (with complete information) because a rental contract imposes risk on the worker whereas a wage contract does not. Of course, this risk does not present a problem if the worker is risk neutral or can offset it with insurance (or a diversified portfolio of investments). But risk neutrality is a limiting case and complete insurance will not be provided unless the state is observable.[4] Consequently, non-observability of the state and the worker's effort level (coupled with worker risk aversion) forces the owners and workers to agree to contracts which provide a balance between risk sharing and incentive effects.

One obvious means of balancing risk sharing and incentive effects is a mixed contract in which the worker pays a smaller rent than in the pure rental case and in turn gives the owner some portion of the output. In the extreme, the rent is zero, and we have, in effect, a piece-rate or pure profit-sharing contract.[5] In any event, with the worker risk averse and the owner risk neutral, use of mixed contracts in this case imposes some risk on the worker in order to provide an incentive for the worker to expend some agreed level of effort. We demonstrate later that a budget-based contract may induce more effort with less worker risk, and in such a manner that both parties are better off relative to the mixed contract. In one such contract, the worker is offered a fixed wage if the outcome is above some standard, but the mixed contract terms apply if the outcome is below standard. Thus, relative to the mixed contract, the budget-based contract provides the worker with partial insurance against state occurrence risk.

Also note that in this setting the owner is motivated to select information systems that balance the gains from improved contracting against the information costs. (See Arrow [1974], Stiglitz [1974] and [1975]. Williamson *et al.* [1975], and Jensen and Meckling [1976].) One system, familiar in accounting, is to use sequential analysis in which costly investigation is performed only if inexpensively monitored outcome statistics indicate that such activity is warranted. This is the familiar "when to investigate a variance" problem [Kaplan, 1975]. Another strategy is more clearly identified with organization design variables. Managers, or owners, may engage in some productive acts simply because crucial worker monitoring information is provided as a by-product of such activity [Alchian and Demsetz, 1972].

Finally, owners as well as workers may engage in shirking behavior. A contract calling for sequential investigation may, for example, not be honored by the owner. The incentive effects of a potential investigation are achieved prior to the investigation and if the owner believes the desired effort level has been induced he will choose to avoid the costs of investigation.[6]

Adverse Selection Issues[7] Another issue

[4] The absence of state observability raises the familiar moral hazard problem discussed in the insurance literature. See Spence and Zeckhauser [1971] and Kihlstrom and Pauly [1971].

[5] If the rent is negative we have a "wage plus profit share" type contract. See Stiglitz [1974] for an extensive analysis of mixed contracts.

[6] The incentive to investigate may arise if we explicitly introduce multiperiod considerations (or some form of external enforcement agency).

[7] Adverse selection is a phenomenon in which members of a population self-select in response to a contractual offer, resulting in a set of respondees critically different from the population at large. Perhaps only "lemons" are offered for sale in the used car market; the unhealthy may subscribe to health insurance that is actuarially fair for the population at large; an unskilled manager may knowingly represent himself as skilled; and so on.

in labor services contracting arises when the worker's skill type is not observable. Efficiency in a perfect and complete market setting requires contracts that are contingent on the worker's skill. If these skills are not observable, the owner is likely to hire lower skilled applicants who falsely claim the requisite skill level [Akerlof, 1970]. The applicants' strategy will be masked by the fact that poor performance can be blamed on the state, provided it, too, is unobservable.

Both the owner and higher skilled workers, therefore, may have an incentive to obtain or provide costly information that will distinguish among skill types. (See Spence's 1973 signaling work.) Alternatively, appropriately designed contracts may achieve the desired matching of skills and tasks by inducing the workers to self-select contracts that achieve that matching. For example, a budget-based contract that would be too risky for lower skilled workers to self-select may accomplish the desired screening (but at a cost of increased risk for the higher skilled workers). Varying deductibility provisions in insurance contracts provides a similar example.[8] In turn, sequential investigation strategies may be desirable. Ultimately, of course, we again balance the cost of information against gains from improved contracting arrangements.

The More General Case

A more general case arises when we simultaneously admit to moral hazard and adverse selection phenomena in a multi-period setting. This is particularly interesting for two reasons. First, admitting to both phenomena simultaneously raises the question of distinguishing between them. And in the context of a budget-based contract, this distinction may be provided by the information contained in different variances. In a simplistic setting, for example, labor efficiency variances may address the effort question and material variances the skill question. The important point, however, is the motivation for developing subanalyses within the overall budgetary framework. Indeed, if decision-making costs were also introduced into the setting, we would likely encounter the traditional planning and control dichotomy, or management by exception framework. This, in turn, would lead to more detailed variances.

Second, the multiperiod framework vastly enriches the strategies that the parties have available. Short-run production schedules, for example, may be designed in part to provide information as to the employee's skill (as well as state occurrence). And both parties may agree to an initial short-run contract designed to provide the desired information. Similarly, direct information questions become more varied. Current decisions may have future period effects and, by definition, these effects are not costlessly observable in the short run. Contracts based strictly on observable events may not be satisfactory and the parties may be motivated to contract on the basis of estimates of future effects. Manipulation of these estimates presents obvious problems, and provides an inducement to have them produced by independent third parties.

In summary, formal performance evaluation systems, including budget-based contracts, are widely advocated in our literature. Movement away from a classical setting—in which only commodity contracts are observed—is a necessary condition for use of budget-based contracts to be desirable. More specific analyses are developed in the remaining sections of this paper. For convenience,

[8] See Rothschild and Stiglitz [1976] for an extensive discussion of adverse selection contracting and self selection in an insurance setting.

we assume the owner fully delegates the labor input activities to a worker. This disregards questions of optimal delegation and joint production of information, but is rich enough to explore the basic issues we seek to address.

THE BASIC MODEL

To explore the issues sketched in the preceding section, we consider a simple economy consisting of J capital owners and I workers. A worker contracts to use an owner's capital (or some portion thereof) in return for some share of the output. In the most general setting addressed, his output, denoted x, will depend on his effort, denoted a, the amount of capital he is provided, denoted q, his skill type, denoted h, and random state factors beyond the control of either the owner or the worker, denoted s. We denote the outcome function by $x=p(s, a, q, h)$.

The contract between the owner and the worker will be conditioned only on those factors that are observed by both. Those observed factors are denoted y and we express them as a function of the state, worker effort, capital, and worker skill: $y=\eta(s, a, q, h)$. The worker's output share is denoted $x_w=\mathscr{I}(y)$ and the owner's share, denoted x_0, is the residual less any information costs, which we denote $x_\eta=C(s, a, q, h, \eta)$; that is $x_0=x-x_w-x_\eta$.

Each individual's choice behavior is represented by the expected utility hypothesis. We assume the owner is only concerned with his residual outcome and denote his utility function $U_0(x_0)$.[9] The worker, on the other hand, is concerned with both his share of the outcome and his effort. Less effort is preferred to more effort. Consequently, we denote his utility function $U_w(x_w, a)$.[10]

The owners and the workers are assumed to have identical beliefs, encoded in the probability function $\phi(s)$.[11] The worker knows his own skill level, but the owner may be uncertain as to the skill of the worker who accepts his contract offer. The owner's beliefs are encoded in the probability function $\phi_0(h|\mathscr{C})$, where $\mathscr{C}=(q, \mathscr{I}, \eta)$ denotes the agreed contract.

The worker's expected utility is a function of the contract he signs, his skill and the effort he provides. In particular, for a worker of skill type h (and presuming suitable regularity) we have

$$E(U_{wh}|a, \mathscr{C}) = \int_S U_w(\mathscr{I}(\eta(s, a, q, h)), a)\phi(s)ds \quad (1a)$$

where S is the set of possible states. We let $a_h^*(\mathscr{C})$ denote his optimal effort given contract $\mathscr{C}$ and skill type h:[12]

$$E(U_{wh}|a_h^*(\mathscr{C}), \mathscr{C}) = \max_{a\in A} E(U_{wh}|a, \mathscr{C}) \quad (1b)$$

where A is the worker's set of feasible effort levels. The maximum of (1b) over the alternative contracts available provides the worker with his most preferred contract.

The owner's expected utility is a function of the contract he signs and his prediction of the worker effort it will induce. Assuming he predicts that a worker of skill type h will select effort $a_h^*(\mathscr{C})$, we have.[13]

[9] This could be the residual from more than one contract if he divides his capital among more than one worker. Also, other factors affecting his preferences may be viewed as implicit provided they are not influenced by the choices at hand. For example, the owner's effort level (possibly zero) is assumed constant across all contracting alternatives considered in this paper.

[10] The output share could come from more than one contract if he works for more than one owner.

[11] This implies that the worker is hired only for his skill and effort, and not for any specialized knowledge he may have about the state.

[12] Existence of a maximum is assumed.

[13] Again, if the owner contracts with more than one worker the outcome of interest will be the total from all his contracts. Vector interpretation of the effort and contract notation will accomplish this. Also, the notation

$$E(U_0|a^*(\mathscr{C}),\mathscr{C})=\int_H\int_S U_0(p(s,a_h^*(\mathscr{C}),q,h) - \mathscr{I}(\eta(s,a_h^*(\mathscr{C}),q,h)) - C(s,a_h^*(\mathscr{C}),q,h,\eta)) \cdot \phi(s)ds\,\phi_0(h|\mathscr{C})dh \quad (2)$$

where H is the set of possible skill types. And, parallel to the worker, maximizing (2) over the set of alternative contracts provides the owner with his most preferred contract.

The element of interest in our analysis is the particular contract that is agreed upon between the owner and worker. That agreement will depend on the nature of the outcome and information cost functions as well as the worker's and owner's preferences and opportunities. We consider primarily the implications of different information cost functions.

In much of our analysis we assume that s, a, q, h, and x are scalars, with x measured in monetary units.[14] Furthermore, the outcome function is a stochastic constant returns to scale function of the form[15]

$$x = p(s,a,q,h) = g(s)\psi_h F(a,q) = g(s)\psi_h f(a/q)q, \quad (3)$$

where $g(s)$ is the stochastic component, with $E(g(\cdot))=1$ and $\mathrm{Var}(g(\cdot))>0$ and finite. ψ_h is a positive scalar representing the skill level; $F(a,q)$ is homogeneous of degree one as well as an increasing concave (and differentiable) function with respect to any single component;[16] and $f(a)$ is the expected output from effort a by a worker with skill level $\psi=1$ and *one* unit of capital (*i.e.*, $f(a)=F(a,1)$). Each worker can supply any non-negative amount of effort ($A=\{a\geq 0\}$), and each owner has one unit of capital.

We also assume that the worker's differentiable utility function is increasing with respect to money ($\partial U_w(\cdot)/\partial x_w>0$) and that he may be either risk neutral ($\partial^2 U_w(\cdot)/\partial x_w^2=0$) or risk averse ($\partial^2 U_w(\cdot)/\partial x_w^2<0$). On the other hand, his utility function is decreasing and strictly concave with respect to effort ($\partial U_w(\cdot)/\partial a<0$ and $\partial^2 U_w(\cdot)/\partial a^2<0$). The owner, on the other hand, is assumed to be risk neutral ($U_0(x_0)=x_0$) so that we may focus on incentive issues; risk is imposed on the worker only if it is necessary to efficiently induce effort or reveal his skill.[17]

Moral Hazard Contracting

We now employ this basic model to examine contracting in a moral hazard setting. To limit the discussion to moral hazard effects, we assume in this section that all workers possess identical unit skill endowments, and since the skill does not vary, we suppress it in our notation. We also assume there are an equal number of owners and workers ($J=I$). This interpretation of the model in (1), (2), and (3) is termed the basic moral hazard model.

Table 1 provides the basic data of an example economy that will be used to obtain some specific results and to generate numerical examples.

The production function is a Cobb-Douglas function times a state that varies uniformly between 0 and 2. The worker's utility for money is a power function, as is his disutility for effort.

---

can be extended to reflect owner uncertainty as to the effort each type of worker will select upon agreement of a given contract.

[14] We can also interpret x as a single consumption good that is desired by both the owner and the worker.

[15] Excluding skill, this is the same form assumed by Stiglitz [1974] in his analysis of incentives and risk sharing.

[16] That is, $F(\lambda a,\lambda q)=\lambda F(a,q)$ for $\lambda>0$, $F_i(a,q)>0$ and $F_{ii}(a,q)<0$ for $i=a,q$. For example, we use a Cobb-Douglas function in our illustrations: $F(a,q)=\xi a^k \cdot q^{1-k}$ where $\xi>0$ and $0<k<1$.

[17] If both the owner and worker are risk averse, then a Parato optimal contract will require that they both share in the risk. For example, see Wilson [1968] and Gjesdal [1976].

TABLE 1

BASIC EXAMPLE ELEMENTS

Production Function:

$$F(a,q) = \xi a^k q^{1-k} \quad 0 < k < 1, 0 \leq q, \xi, a$$

$$g(s) = s \quad S = [0,2]$$

$$\phi(s) = \tfrac{1}{2}$$

$$\therefore \quad p(s,a,q) = s\xi a^k q^{1-k}$$

Worker's Utility Function:

$$U_w(x_w, a) = (\bar{x} + x_w)^\gamma - \theta a^r$$

$0 < \gamma < 1$ ($\gamma = 1$ is the risk neutral case.)

$0 < \bar{x}$ (the worker's current wealth)

$0 < \Theta, 1 < r$

Costless Action or State Information

We begin with the case where the worker's action is costlessly observable. This corresponds to the neoclassical theory of the firm in which information costs are ignored and it is implicitly assumed that everyone can costlessly observe the relevant aspects of the commodities (including labor skill and effort) being demanded and supplied. In this case, the owner and worker will contract on the level of effort to be supplied. Furthermore, if there are a large number of identical owners and workers interacting in a perfect labor market, we may view the resulting contract as an equilibrium wage (W^*) per unit of labor effort: $C(s, a, q, \eta) = 0$, $\eta(s, a, q) = a$, and $\mathscr{I}(a) = aW^*$.

The equilibrium solution has, presuming existence and an interior effort solution, three well-known properties:

Proposition 1:[18]

In the basic moral hazard model, if the risk neutral owner can costlessly observe the worker's action and all workers have identical skills (with $I = J$), then the competitive equilibrium based on wage contracts will have the following properties:

(i) the wage rate is equal to the worker's expected marginal product: $W^* = f'(a^*(W^*))$;

(ii) the worker will select his effort so that the wage rate equals the marginal rate of substitution between income and effort:

$$W^* = -(\partial U_w(\cdot)/\partial a) \div (\partial U_w(\cdot)/\partial x_w);$$

and

(iii) the resulting allocation is Pareto optimal.

This allocation mechanism depends critically upon knowledge of the worker's effort. However, costless observation of of the state and capital is sufficient to produce the same allocation. In this case, the owner and worker can enter into a combined rental and insurance contract that will result in precisely the same allocation as in Proposition 1. More specifically, consider $\eta(s, a, q) = (s, q)$ and $\mathscr{I}(s, q) = x - Rq - I(s)$ where $I(s)$ is an insurance policy such that $E(I(s)) = 0$.[19] The worker will request

$$I(s) = (g(s) - 1)F(a, q).^{20}$$

[18] (i) follows directly from the owner's first order conditions and (ii) follows directly from the worker's first order conditions, (iii) is obtained by focusing on one representative pair of individuals and maximizing the well-being of one while holding constant the well-being for the other:

$$\max_{x_w(\cdot), a} \left[\int_S U_w(x_w(s), a)\phi(s)ds \right] \text{subject to } f(a) - \int_S x_w(s)\phi(s)ds = \bar{U}_0.$$

First order conditions provide

$$f'(a^*) = -[\partial U_w(\cdot)/\partial a] \div [\partial U_w(\cdot)/\partial x_w].$$

[19] In this contract the worker receives the outcome x, but it is not an argument of $\mathscr{I}(\cdot)$ since the owner need not know the outcome—the worker operates the firm.

[20] This insurance policy guarantees the worker his expected profit. Note that the owner does not need to know or even infer the worker's effort; he need only be able to observe the state.

Denoting the equilibrium rent R^*, we then observe that the equilibrium solution is the same as in the effort observed case and therefore has the same properties. That is, again presuming existence and an interior effort solution, we have

Proposition 2:[21]

In the basic moral hazard model, if the risk neutral owner has sufficient wealth to provide insurance and both he and the worker can costlessly observe the state, then the competitive equilibrium based on rental and insurance contracts will have the following properties:

(i) the worker's average return per unit of effort is equal to his expected marginal product:

$$(f(a^*(R^*)) - R^*)/a^*(R^*) = f'(a^*(R^*));$$

(ii) the worker will select his effort so that his expected marginal product equals the marginal rate of substitution between income and effort:

$$f'(a^*(R^*)) = -(\partial U_w(\cdot)/\partial a) \div (\partial U_w(\cdot)/\partial x_w);$$

and

(iii) the resulting allocation is Pareto optimal from a complete information perspective.

Table 2 presents a numerical example of the effort observed and state observed cases using the model formulated in Table 1.

In conclusion we note that there is no incentive to develop budget-based contracts if either the worker's effort or the state are costlessly observable. That is, under either case a Pareto optimal allocation of productive effort and return is achieved without the use of budget-based contracts. Consequently, we have

Proposition 3:[22,23]

TABLE 2

ILLUSTRATION OF EFFORT OBSERVED AND STATE OBSERVED CASES

Parameter Values:

$k = .4, \xi = 200$

$\bar{x} = 400, \gamma = .5$

$\theta = 2, r = 2$

Effort Observed Case

$W^* = 106.7610$

$E(U_w|a^*(W^*), W^*) = 20.8227$

$a^*(W^*) = .6182$

$E(U_0|a^*(W^*), W^*) = 98.9995$

$f(a^*(W^*)) = 164.9991$

State Observed Case

$R^* = 98.9995$

$E(U_w|a^*(R^*), q^*(R^*), R^*) = 20.8227$

$a^*(R^*) = .6182$

$E(U_0|q^*(R^*), R^*) = 98.9995$

$f(a^*(R^*)) = 164.9991$

[21] The owner, obviously, will supply one unit of capital if R is positive. The first order condition for the worker's maximization problem given a rental contract specifying q units of capital, is

$$\frac{\partial U_w(\cdot)}{\partial x_w}\frac{\partial F(\cdot)}{\partial a} + \frac{\partial U_w(\cdot)}{\partial a} = 0.$$

Similarly, the first order condition on the contract variable (capital) is

$$\frac{\partial U_w}{\partial x_w}\left(\frac{\partial F(\cdot)}{\partial q} - R\right) = 0.$$

And if we set $q = 1$ we obtain conditions (i) and (ii). These are equivalent to the conditions in Proposition 1 when we view $(f(a) - R)/a$ as the effective wage per unit of effort. (iii) follows as in Proposition 1.

[22] The basic argument here is that costless observation of effort or state leads—with wage or rental and insurance contracts—to allocative efficiency. Hence, we must remove this condition to rationalize use of other types of

A necessary condition for a budget-based contract to be Pareto superior to all alternative contracts in the basic moral hazard model is that it be costly to observe both the worker's effort and the state.

Effort and State Not Observed

We now consider the other extreme case in which observing either the effort or state is so costly that neither is observed. The outcome and capital, on the other hand, are costlessly observable. Consequently, the contract information is $\eta(s, a, q) = (q, p(s, a, q))$ and we are faced with determining the form of the outcome sharing function $\mathscr{I}(q, x)$.

Ideally, we would consider the set of all possible sharing functions and identify those that are, given the information assumption, Pareto optimal. However, identifying the set of efficient sharing functions is beyond our scope; and instead we take a more modest approach. (See Mirrlees [1976].) In particular, we compare linear sharing functions with two types of budget-based contracts and seek conditions under which the latter are Pareto superior to the former.[24]

Linear Sharing Functions Stiglitz [1974] provides fairly extensive analysis of incentives and linear sharing functions of the form $\mathscr{I}(q, x) = \alpha x - Rq$. This function represents a variety of contract forms, including a pure salary contract ($\alpha = 0$ and $R < 0$), a pure rental contract ($\alpha = 1$ and $R > 0$), a pure piece rate contract ($0 < \alpha < 1$ and $R = 0$) and a mixed contract ($0 < \alpha < 1$ and $R \neq 0$).

The pure salary contract can be quickly discarded from our consideration in that it provides no incentives. If such a contract were signed in our model, the worker would take his salary and select an effort level of zero. (To be sure, this is a rather extreme result, but it would occur to some extent even if we modify the worker's preference function to reflect social norms that induce him to provide some effort for his salary.)

The other contracts all provide some incentive effect in that the worker's outcome share is dependent on the outcome, which in turn depends on his effort. This incentive effect is strongest in the pure rental contract. However, this contract imposes all of the risk on the worker since the state is not observed and thus the worker cannot obtain insurance as he did in the state observed case.[25] On the other hand, this presents no difficulty if the worker is risk neutral. To see this, return to Proposition 2 and note that if the worker is risk neutral, no insurance is an optimal arrangement, and the state need not be observed to obtain an efficient allocation. Hence, we have

Proposition 4:[26]

A necessary condition for a budget-based contract to be Pareto superior to all alternative contracts in the basic moral hazard model is that the worker be risk averse.

---

contracts. This applies to rationalization of budget-based contracts, as discussed here, or costly action monitoring systems, as discussed in Harris and Raviv [1976].

[23] More precisely, it must be costly to observe the effort and either the state or the capital assigned. However, we treat the capital as costlessly observable throughout our analysis.

[24] Contract $\mathscr{C}$ is Pareto superior to $\mathscr{C}'$ if $E(U_w | a^*(\mathscr{C}), \mathscr{C}) \geq E(U_w | a^*(\mathscr{C}'), \mathscr{C}')$, $E(U_0 | a^*(\mathscr{C}), \mathscr{C}) \geq E(U_0 | a^*(\mathscr{C}'), \mathscr{C}')$ and strict inequality holds for either the worker or the owner.

[25] Insurance based on the outcome instead of the state would not be acceptable because of the moral hazard problem. Once insurance was obtained, the worker would be motivated to select a low effort level and then claim the resulting low outcome was due to a "bad" state.

[26] Again, as in Proposition 3, the argument is one of allocative efficiency. If the worker is also risk neutral a Pareto optimal allocation of productive effort and returns is available with a pure rental contract. Hence, we must drop the risk neutrality assumption to obtain Pareto superior contracts of any kind, including those based on superior information about the worker's behavior (as in Harris and Raviv [1976]).

As a basis for comparison in the case where the worker is risk averse, we focus on a linear contract (i) that is Pareto optimal with respect to all other linear contracts and (ii) that induces a demand for and a supply of capital equal to unity. This contract, denoted $\mathscr{C}^{\ell}=(q^*=1, \alpha^*, R^*)$, represents an equilibrium contract that might be agreed upon if contracts were restricted to linear sharing functions.

Table 3 presents an equilibrium linear sharing function contract for the example formulated in Tables 1 and 2. Note that the worker's expected income per unit of effort is less than his marginal product. Also, his expected utility is lower than in the effort observed case, whereas the owner's expected profit is higher. The contract assigns over 80 percent of the outcome to the worker and thus imposes considerable risk on him. This is necessary in order to induce effort from him; even so, his effort is less than in the effort observed case.

TABLE 3

ILLUSTRATION OF LINEAR SHARING FUNCTION CONTRACT

$\alpha^* =$	.827		
$R^* =$	73.965	$E(U_w \mid a^*(\mathscr{C}^{\ell}), \mathscr{C}^{\ell}) =$	20.6819
$a^*(\mathscr{C}^{\ell}) =$	.53965	$E(U_0 \mid a^*(\mathscr{C}^{\ell}), \mathscr{C}^{\ell}) =$	101.0000
		$f(a^*(\mathscr{C}^{\ell})) =$	156.2697
Expected Worker Income per Unit of Effort $= [\alpha^* f(a^*(\mathscr{C}^{\ell})) - R^*]/a^*(\mathscr{C}^{\ell}) =$			102.4184
Expected Marginal Product $= f'(a^*(\mathscr{C}^{\ell}))$		$=$	115.8304

Budget-Based Contracts Consider use of budget-based contracts in this setting. Recall that the essential feature of such a contract is the use of an outcome standard to condition the manner in which payments are made. There are, of course, countless such contracts for any specific information system, varying in terms of the partitioning of the outcome into favorable and unfavorable categories and the form of the incentive function.[27] In the following discussion, the only non-outcome information is the capital, and it is assumed to be unity. Therefore, the budgeted outcome is a fixed amount, $\hat{x}$, and the outcome is favorable if it equals or exceeds this amount. We consider two forms of the incentive function, and explore whether such contracts can be Pareto superior to the linear contract $\mathscr{C}^{\ell}$.

In the first budget-based contract, the worker is paid a fixed wage if the outcome is above standard ($\mathscr{I}_1(x)=B_1$ for $x \geq \hat{x}$) and the amount he would have received under the linear contract $\mathscr{C}^{\ell}$ if below standard ($\mathscr{I}_2(x)=\alpha^* x - R^*$ for $x < \hat{x}$). This is termed a dichotomous contract and is denoted $\mathscr{C}^d=(q^*=1, \alpha^*, R^*, \hat{x}, B_1)$.[28] Note that it in effect reduces the risk incurred by the worker for favorable outcomes ($x \geq \hat{x}$).

Since the worker is risk averse we might expect that there exists an $\hat{x}$ and B_1 such that the dichotomous contract $\mathscr{C}^d$ is Pareto superior to the linear contract $\mathscr{C}^{\ell}$. Observe, however, that unless we set B_1 sufficiently high, the dichotomous contract will induce a lower effort

[27] Recall that the outcome budget may be a function of other information. An extreme case occurs when the capital, state, and outcome are costlessly observed. Then the allocation in Proposition 1 can be achieved with the following budget based contract:

$$\mathscr{I}(q^*, s, x) = \begin{cases} a^* W^* & \text{if } x \geq \hat{x}(q^*, s) = sF(a^*, q^*) \\ 0 & \text{if } x < \hat{x}(q^*, s). \end{cases}$$

Furthermore, worker performance can be assessed as favorable or unfavorable on the basis of information other than the outcome. See Harris and Raviv [1976] for an exploration of such contracts.

[28] This is somewhat similar to the dichotomous contracts considered by Harris and Raviv [1976]. However, they divide the performance into favorable and unfavorable on the basis of imperfect action information (other than the outcome).

level than the linear contract. In turn, $\hat{x}$ cannot be too low; and because of this, in our example we were unsuccessful in finding a Pareto superior contract for values of $\hat{x}$ that were achievable with the action induced by the linear contract. However, Pareto superior contracts were found when, exploiting the boundedness of s, we set $\hat{x}$ at the maximum possible outcome from the linear contract effort $(2f(a^*(\mathscr{C}^\ell))$ and then set B_1 sufficiently high to induce a higher level of effort from the worker. This is illustrated in Table 4.

TABLE 4

ILLUSTRATION OF A PARETO SUPERIOR DICHOTOMOUS SHARING FUNCTION

$\alpha^* =$	.827		
$R^* =$	73.965		
$\hat{x} =$	312.539	$E(U_w \mid a^*(\mathscr{C}^d), \mathscr{C}^d) =$	20.6846
$B_1 =$	200	$E(U_0 \mid a^*(\mathscr{C}^d), \mathscr{C}^d) =$	101.2442
$a^*(\mathscr{C}^d) =$	.56349	$f(a^*(\mathscr{C}^d)) =$	158.9954

Of course, if B_1 is set too high the additional effort will be more expensive to the owner than it is worth.

The above type of Pareto superior contract is available in any context represented by the model formulated in Table 1 (in which the state is bounded). More formally we have

Proposition 5:[29]

For the model formulated in Table 1 and assuming interior effort solutions, there always exists a dichotomous contract that is Pareto superior to a linear contract in which $0<\alpha<1$.

The second budget-based contract we illustrate is one in which the worker is paid a high income if the outcome is favorable ($\mathscr{I}_1(x)=B_1$ for $x \geq \hat{x}$) and a lower income if the outcome is unfavorable ($\mathscr{I}_2(x)=B_2$ for $x<\hat{x}$). We term such a contract bang-bang and denote it $\mathscr{C}^b=(q=1, \hat{x}, B_1, B_2)$. This contract is simple in its structure and has much the same appeal as the dichotomous contract.

We did manage to find a number of such contracts that are Pareto superior to the linear contract in Table 3. One such contract is presented in Table 5.

TABLE 5

ILLUSTRATION OF A PARETO SUPERIOR BANG-BANG SHARING FUNCTION

$\hat{x} =$	250		
$B_1 =$	193		
$B_2 =$	20	$E(U_w \mid a^*(\mathscr{C}^b), \mathscr{C}^b) =$	20.6842
		$E(U_0 \mid a^*(\mathscr{C}^b), \mathscr{C}^b) =$	101.8385
$a^*(\mathscr{C}^b) =$	.55282	$f(a^*(\mathscr{C}^b)) =$	157.7846

It is characterized by a rather high standard, and we were unsuccessful in finding Pareto superior contracts with "low" standards. If the standard is "low" the effort is "low" unless there is a large penalty (B_1-B_2) for not achieving the standard.[30] "High" standards have a strong incentive effect, but high incomes must be paid to offset the risk imposed on the worker.

[29] See appendix for proof.

[30] On the other hand, Mirrlees [1974] demonstrates that, with suitable regularity, employing a low $\hat{x}$ and an extreme penalty for not meeting the budget approximates the full information allocation. The only cost is an extreme penalty that falls on a small percentage of the workers (also see Harris and Raviv [1976]). (He also analyzes [1976] the case in which the full information equilibrium cannot be achieved.) In a similar vein, Gjesdal [1976] shows (assuming suitable regularity) that if the lower bound on the feasible outcome increases monotonically with effort then the full information contract can be approximated with a bang-bang contract. (In Table 1, for example, this would be available if $S=[\frac{1}{2}, \frac{3}{2}]$ instead of $S=[0, 2]$ and if the worker has a "large" initial wealth $\bar{x}$ that can be penalized, $B_2=-\bar{x}$.)

Effort or State Observed at a Cost

We conclude this section with a brief examination of the intermediate case where the effort or state can be observed at some "reasonable" cost. The capital and outcome are again costlessly observable; and we assume that any decision to observe the effort (or, equivalently, the state) can be conditioned on the observed capital and outcome. That is, effort (or state) observation is in the form of an *ex post* investigation of the causes of the outcome.

Many investigation policies are possible, but we restrict our discussion to those in which an investigation is made only if the outcome is below some standard $\hat{x}$. That is,

$$\eta(s, a, q) = \begin{cases} (q, p(s, a, q)) & \text{if } p(s, a, q) \geq \hat{x} \\ (q, a, p(s, a, q)) & \text{if } p(s, a, q) < \hat{x}. \end{cases}$$

There are, of course, many incentive functions that could be considered in conjunction with this information system. We restrict our discussion, however, to bang-bang sharing functions in which a high income (B_1) is paid if the outcome is favorable or the observed effort is not below some standard effort ($\hat{a}$), and a low income (B_2) is paid if the observed effort is below the standard. That is, we have a budget-based conditional investigation contract in which $\mathscr{I}_1(x) = B_1$ for $x \geq \hat{x}$ and

$$\mathscr{I}_2(x, a) = \begin{cases} B_1 & \text{if } a \geq \hat{a} \\ B_2 & \text{if } a < \hat{a} \end{cases} \quad \text{for } x < \hat{x}.$$

We denote this contract $\mathscr{C}^i = (q = 1, \hat{x}, \hat{a}, B_1, B_2)$.

For discussion purposes, we assume the worker will agree to any contract that provides an expected utility of at least $\overline{U}_w$. The owner selects the personally preferred contract given that constraint. And to illustrate our discussion we use our continuing example and let $\overline{U}_w = 20.6819$, the worker's utility from the linear contract in Table 3.

Note that if some standard action $\hat{a}$ is to be induced, the smallest possible worker income that will induce it and provide the worker with an expected utility of $\overline{U}_w$ is B_1^0, where

$$\overline{U}_w = U_w(B_1^0, \hat{a}).$$

(Implementing $\hat{a}$ guarantees, with conditional investigation, payment of B_1^0 to the worker.) Of course, $\hat{x}$ and B_2 must also be selected so that the worker prefers $\hat{a}$ to any lower effort. Obviously, the owner would like to select them so that he minimizes the expected cost of investigation. This is accomplished by first setting B_2 as small as possible and then letting $\hat{x}$ be as small as is consistent with inducing $\hat{a}$. The crucial question here is: How small can B_2 be?

Observe that if the worker selects $\hat{a}$, there is no chance he will receive B_2; therefore, it is irrelevant to him. Its lower bound must be determined either by the worker's wealth ($-B_2$ cannot exceed the amount collectible from the worker) or by institutional constraints (*e.g.*, negative wages may be illegal or minimum wage laws may be relevant).

To illustrate, we consider our example in Table 3 and let $\hat{a} = a^*(\mathscr{C}^\ell)$. Two minimum income levels are considered: (i) zero and (ii) minus the worker's wealth. The results are presented in Table 6. Observe that if the minimum income is zero, the probability of investigation is about .27 percent, and the owner would prefer this investigation contract to the linear contract if the investigation cost C is less than \$11.53. On the other hand, if the owner can collect all the worker's wealth if investigation reveals below standard effort, then the probability of investigation is only about .02 and the investigation contract is preferred if the

TABLE 6

ILLUSTRATION OF INVESTIGATION CONTRACTS

		(i)	(ii)
$\hat{a}=a^*(\mathscr{C}^\ell)$		.53965	.53965
$B_1^0=[\bar{U}+\theta\hat{a}^r]^{1/\gamma}-\bar{x}$			
$=[20.6819+2(\hat{a})^2]^2-400=$		52.17	52.17
B_2^0	-400.00	0	
$\hat{x}$		84	5
$\phi(x\leq\hat{x}\mid\hat{a})$		.2688	.0160
$E(U_w\mid a^*(\mathscr{C}^i),\mathscr{C}^i)$		20.6819	20.6819
$E(U_0\mid a^*(\mathscr{C}^i),\mathscr{C}^i)$		104.0997	104.0997
		$-.2688$C	$-.0160$C

investigation cost is less than \$193.73.

Several additional comments are in order.[31] First note that in both contracts the standard is significantly below the expected performance. Its role is to trigger an investigation, thereby conditioning the worker's payment. There is no intrinsic reason for the standard to be close to or far from the expected performance.

Second, whether this type of contracting will be preferred is very dependent on the information cost. Comparing it with those in the effort and state unobserved case, we are adding to the information on which the contracting is based. Indeed, with a very high standard, we approach the effort observable case. Thus, we would expect this contracting to be superior to, say, the linear contract in the effort unobserved case—provided the information is not too expensive. This is precisely the case if the worker is risk averse.[32] At a minimum, he would pay some positive amount to guarantee selection of some particular $\hat{a}$ and thereby shift outcome risk entirely to the owner. More formally, we have

Proposition 6:[33]

In the basic moral hazard model, if the owner is risk neutral and the worker is risk averse, then there exists a budget-based conditional investigation contract $\mathscr{C}^i$ that is Pareto superior to the linear contract $\mathscr{C}^\ell$ (with $a^*>0$ and $a^*(\mathscr{C})>0$) provided that the positive investigation cost is sufficiently small.

Third, as pointed out in the first section, the budget-based conditional investigation contract is not a Nash equilibrium without some external enforcement mechanism. The owner, but not the worker, has a unilateral incentive not to honor the agreement. Of course, with legal sanctions or a formal multiperiod structure this would not necessarily be the case.

31 In the contracts we have considered $\hat{a}=a^*(\mathscr{C}^\ell)$. However, the owner can increase his expected utility to $105.0586-C\phi(x\leq\hat{x}\mid\hat{a})$ if he increases $\hat{a}$ to .6206. That is, under an investigation contract it will be optimal to induce a higher effort level than under the linear contract.

32 See Harris and Raviv [1976] for an extensive discussion of conditions under which there are potential gains to observing the worker's effort. As in our analysis, such gains are not available if either the state is observed or the worker is risk neutral (assuming optimal contracting under those conditions). They demonstrate that there are potential gains to observing the effort if the worker is risk averse and the existing contract induces an effort in the interior of the set of possible effort levels. They do not directly consider conditional observation, but instead focus on unconditional observation (our full information case) and on contracts based on imperfect information about the effort.

Townsend [1976], on the other hand, considers observations that are conditional on outcomes known only by a single individual. This individual calls for an investigation if the outcome is in a specified region, and incentives are constructed such that it is in his best interest to honor such an agreement.

33 Proof: Set B_1^0 such that

$$U_w(B_1^0, a^*(\mathscr{C}^\ell)) = E(U_w\mid a^*(\mathscr{C}^\ell), \mathscr{C}^\ell),$$

$B_2=-R^*$, and $\hat{a}=a^*(\mathscr{C}^\ell)$. Then set

$$\hat{x} = \sup_{s\in S}\{p(s, \hat{a}, q)\}.$$

By construction $E(U_w\mid a^*(\mathscr{C}^i), \mathscr{C}^i)\geq E(U_w\mid a^*(\mathscr{C}^\ell), \mathscr{C}^\ell)$ and by Jensen's inequality $B_1^0<\alpha^* f(a^*(\mathscr{C}^\ell))-R^*$. Hence, the worker is, at worst, indifferent and the owner strictly prefers contract $\mathscr{C}^i$ provided that the cost is not too large.

Adverse Selection Contracting

Consider a setting in which the worker's effort is costlessly observed but, in general, neither his skill nor the state are. If skill varies among the worker population, a full information equilibrium may entail capital and labor combinations that reflect the individual worker's skills (with more skillful workers paid higher wages). Without skill differentiation, however, the lower skilled may have the incentive and the opportunity to misrepresent themselves.

To explore this issue we return to our basic model in (1), (2) and (3) and now assume there are I_1 unskilled ($h=1$) workers and I_2 skilled ($h=2$) workers with $I_1=I_2=J$ and $\psi_1<\psi_2$. The owner can split his capital between the two types of workers so that the output from his capital is

$$p(s, a, q)=p(s, a_1, q_1, 1)+p(s, a_2, q_2, 2)$$

where $a=(a_1, a_2)$, a_h is the effort of the type h worker, $q=(q_1, q_2)$, and q_h is the capital assigned to the type h worker. This interpretation of the model is termed the basic adverse selection model. The example economy in Table 1 is again used to illustrate our analysis, but with $p(s, a_h, q_h, h)=s\psi_h\xi a_h^k q_h^{1-k}$.

Costless Skill or State Information

If the owner can costlessly observe the worker's skill and effort, we may view the parties as contracting at a market wage (W_h) per unit of effort for each skill type: $C(\cdot)=0$, $\eta(s, a_h, q_h, h)=(a_h, q_h, h)$, and $\mathscr{I}(a_h, h)=a_h W_h$. Equilibrium requires equality between the labor demanded and supplied for each skill type. And our assumptions guarantee that each owner will employ one worker of each skill type. Denoting the equilibrium wage vector $W^*=(W_1^*, W_2^*)$, we illustrate an equilibrium in Table 7 and, presuming existence and interior effort solutions, summarize the essential properties with

Proposition 7:[34]

In the basic adverse selection model, if the risk neutral owner can costlessly observe each worker's skill and effort (with $I_1=I_2=J$), then the competitive equilibrium based on skill dependent wages will have the following properties:

(i) each wage rate is equal to the expected marginal product of the respective worker:

$$W_h^* = \psi_h \partial F(a_h^*(W^*), q_h^*(W^*))/\partial a_h;$$

(ii) each worker selects his effort so that his wage rate equals the marginal rate of substitution between income and effort:

$$W_h^* = -[\partial U_w(\cdot)/\partial a_h] \div [\partial U_w(\cdot)/\partial x_w];$$

(iii) the owner splits his capital between the skilled and unskilled workers so that the marginal rate of substitution is equal to the marginal rate of transformation (unity):

$$[\psi_1 \partial F(\cdot)/\partial q_1] \div [\psi_2 \partial F(\cdot)/\partial q_2]=1; \text{ and}$$

(iv) the resulting allocation is Pareto optimal.

As in the moral hazard case, costless observation of the capital and state will allow the same allocation. Again, the worker rents the capital from the owner and the owner also provides state insurance. That is,

$$C(\cdot)=0, \eta(s, a_h, q_h, h)=(s, q_h), \mathscr{I}(s, q_h)$$

[34] (i), (ii), and (iii) follow directly from the first order conditions for the workers and owner. (iv) follows, as in Proposition 1, from focusing on a representative trio of individuals and maximizing the well-being of one subject to constant well-being constraints for the other two.

TABLE 7

ILLUSTRATION OF ACTION AND SKILL OR STATE OBSERVED CASES

Parameter Values:		
$k = .4,$	$\xi = 200$	
$\bar{x} = 400,$	$\gamma = .5$	
$\theta = 2,$	$r = 2$	
$\psi_1 = .5,$	$\psi_2 = 1$	
Skill Observed Case:		
$W_1^* = 18.6333$	$W_2^* = 105.3727$	$E(U_{W1} \mid a_1^*(W^*), W^*) = 20.0271$
$a_1^*(W^*) = .1161$	$a_2^*(W^*) = .6113$	$E(U_{W2} \mid a_2^*(W^*), W^*) = 20.8029$
$q_1^*(W^*) = .0325$	$q_2^*(W^*) = .9675$	
$F(a_1^*(W^*), q_1^*(W^*)) = 5.41$		$E(U_0 \mid a^*(W^*), q^*(W^*), W^*) = 99.8664$
$F(a_2^*(W^*), q_2^*(W^*)) = 161.04$		
State Observed Case:		
$R^* = 99.8562$		$E(U_{w1} \mid a_1^*(R^*), q_1^*(R^*), R^*) = 20.0271$
$q_1^*(R^*) = .0325$	$q_2^*(R^*) = .9675$	$E(U_{w2} \mid a_2^*(R^*), q_2^*(R^*), R^*) = 20.8029$
$a_1^*(R^*) = .1161$	$a_2^*(R^*) = .6113$	$E(U_0 \mid q^*(R^*), R^*) = 99.8664$

$= x_h - Rq_h - I_h(s)$ and $E[I_h(s)] = 0$.[35]

Thus, presuming existence of an equilibrium with interior effort solutions at rental rate R^* (which equates the demand and supply for capital), we have

Proposition 8:[36]

In the basic adverse selection model, if the risk neutral owner has sufficient wealth to provide insurance and both he and the workers can costlessly observe the state and capital, then the competitive equilibrium based on rental and insurance contracts will have the following properties:

(i) each worker's average return per normalized unit of effort equals his expected marginal product:

$$(\psi_h f(n) - R^*)/n = \psi_h f'(n),$$

where

$$n = a_h^*(R^*)/q_h^*(R^*);$$

(ii) each worker selects his effort and capital so that his expected marginal product equals the marginal rate of substitution between income and effort: $\psi_h f'(a_h^*(R^*)) = -[\partial U_w(\cdot)/\partial a_h] \div [\partial U_w(\cdot)/\partial x_w]$;

(iii) $[\psi_1 \partial F(\cdot)/\partial q_1] \div [\psi_2 \partial F(\cdot)/\partial q_2] = 1$

(iv) the resulting allocation is Pareto optimal from a complete information perspective.

Table 7 presents a numerical example.

Finally, we note that Pareto optimality

[35] Again the worker receives x_h because he operates his part of the firm; and it does not appear as an argument of $\mathscr{I}(\cdot)$ since it is not observed by the owner.

[36] (i), (ii), and (iii) follow from first order conditions and (iv) follows as in Proposition 7.

can be achieved without budget-based contracting in the two cases discussed above, and we therefore conclude

Proposition 9:

A necessary condition for a budget-based contract to be Pareto superior to all alternative contracts in the basic adverse selection model is that it be costly to observe both the workers' skills and state.

Skill and State Not Observed

Consider the case in which neither the worker's skill nor the state can be observed, except at prohibitive cost. Only the worker's effort, capital and outcome are (costlessly) observed: $\eta(s, a_h, q_h, h) = (a_h, q_h, p(s, a_h, q_h, h))$ and $C(\cdot)=0$.

Determination of the sharing functions $\mathscr{I}(a_h, q_h, x_h)$ is important here because efficiency gains are generally available if the two worker classes can be distinguished, and some sharing functions may induce the workers to reveal their skill by their contract choices.

Initially, we consider the naive case in which a straightforward wage contract is offered, with $\mathscr{I}(\cdot)=a_iW$. With an inability to distinguish worker skill, the owner will split his capital between two workers. This contract clearly does not, in general, produce the allocation depicted in Propositions 7 and 8. See the illustration in Table 8 where we observe an incentive for the unskilled workers not to reveal their skill endowment.

The full information equilibrium can be achieved without skill or state information if the workers are risk neutral. This reduces to a special case of Proposition 8 in which the owner rents the capital to the workers but offers no insurance. Insurance is an indifferent proposition here, and not offering it obviates the need to observe the worker's state. Hence, (ignoring bankruptcy) we conclude

TABLE 8

ILLUSTRATION OF NONDIFFERENTIATION EQUILIBRIUM

$q_1^*(W^*) = q_2^*(W^*) = .500$

$E(U_0|a^*(W^*), q^*(W^*), W^*) = 83.0590$

$a_1^*(W^*) = a_2^*(W^*) = .4091$

$E(U_{wh}|a_h^*(W^*), W^*) = 20.3459$

$h = 1, 2$

$W_1^* = W_2^* = W^* = 67.6761$

Expected Marginal Product:

unskilled	45.1174
skilled	90.2348

Proposition 10:

A necessary condition for a budget-based contract to be Pareto superior to all alternative contracts in the basic adverse selection model is that the workers be risk averse.

Consideration of budget-based contracts in this setting, then, is motivated by a desire to identify the worker's skills to assure production efficiency. Offering a pair of contracts such that the unskilled self-select one and the skilled self-select another is one way of distinguishing the workers. (Examination and ex post investigation are alternative mechanisms.) Budget-based contracts may be efficient in promoting this self-selection.

To explore this theme, we adopt the strategy employed in the moral hazard case and compare budget-based with linear contracts. Initially, we note that it is possible to distinguish the workers by offering a pair of linear contracts. One such pair for our example economy is presented in Table 9 (see Table 7 for parameter values).[37]

[37] We make no attempt here to determine a Pareto optimal or equilibrium pair of linear contracts. We merely illustrate that differentiation can be achieved. Also note that offering the two wage contracts in Table 7 will not achieve differentiation; all would select the higher wage alternative.

TABLE 9

ILLUSTRATION OF SKILL DIFFERENTIATING CONTRACTS

	Contracts Preferred by		
	Unskilled (h=1)		*Skilled (h=2)*
Linear Contracts	$(\mathscr{C}_1^\ell)$		$(\mathscr{C}_2^\ell)$
q_h	.0325		.9675
a_h	.1161		.6113
$\mathscr{I}_h(a_h, q_h, x_h)$[38]	2.1633		$x_h - 80$
$E(U_{w1} \mid a_1^*(\mathscr{C}_h^\ell), \mathscr{C}_h^\ell)$	20.0271		19.2316
$E(U_{w2} \mid a_2^*(\mathscr{C}_h^\ell), \mathscr{C}_h^\ell)$	20.0271		21.0805
$E(U_0 \mid a^*(\mathscr{C}^\ell), \mathscr{C}^\ell)$		83.2450	
Dichotomous Contracts	$(\mathscr{C}_1^d = \mathscr{C}_1^\ell)$		$(\mathscr{C}_2^d)$
q_h	.0325		.9675
a_h	.1161		.6113
$\hat{x}_h$	—		161.0358
$\mathscr{I}_{h1}(a_h, q_h, x_h)$	2.1633		161.5536
$\mathscr{I}_{h2}(a_h, q_h, x_h)$	2.1633		$x_h - 80$
$E(U_{w1} \mid a_1^*(\mathscr{C}_h^d), \mathscr{C}_h^d)$	20.0271		19.2316
$E(U_{w2} \mid a_2^*(\mathscr{C}_h^d), \mathscr{C}_h^d)$	20.0271		21.0907
$E(U_0 \mid a^*(\mathscr{C}^d), \mathscr{C}^d)$		83.2450	

The difficulty with separation via linear contracts, however, is their implicit cost. They are inherently risky and, with the risk neutral owner, we trade off risk sharing for separation effects. Under the assumptions of our example economy, budget-based contracts can generally accomplish the same separation but with less risk allocated to the worker. Quite simply, with $\psi_2 > \psi_1$, a bounded state, and $\alpha > 0$, partial insurance always can be offered to the skilled worker without affecting the separation and without encountering a moral hazard problem (because a_h is observed). More specifically, we have

Proposition 11:[39]

For the example economy formulated in Table 1 with two equal sized skill groups ($\psi_1 < \psi_2$) and with each worker's action, capital, and outcome costlessly observed, there always exists a dichotomous contract $\mathscr{C}_2^d$ such that the pair of contracts $(\mathscr{C}_1^\ell, \mathscr{C}_2^d)$ is Pareto superior to the pair of skill differentiating contracts $(\mathscr{C}_1^\ell, \mathscr{C}_2^\ell)$ in which α_2, $a_2, q_2 > 0$.

[38] Payment is, of course, conditional on the observed effort level being at least the contracted level.

[39] We prove the proposition by illustrating a Pareto superior dichotomous contract. With $\psi_2 > \psi_1$, there exists a non-empty interval in the outcome space that, for any $0 < a, q$, will contain the skilled worker's outcome with nonzero probability but will contain the unskilled worker's outcome with probability zero; *i.e.*, the interval $(2\psi_1 F(a, q), 2\psi_2 F(a, q)]$. Let $\hat{x}_2 = 2\psi_1 F(a_2, q_2)$, $\mathscr{I}_{21}(a_2, q_2) = B_{21} = \alpha_2(\psi_2 + \psi_1)F(a_2, q_2) - R_2$, and $\mathscr{I}_{22}(a_2, q_2) = \alpha_2 x_2 - R_2$, where a_2, q_2, α_2, and R_2 are as specified in $\mathscr{C}_2^\ell$. The unskilled worker still prefers $\mathscr{C}_1^\ell$ and therefore is indifferent; the risk neutral owner's expected profit is unaffected and he, therefore, is indifferent; and Jensen's inequality guarantees that the skilled worker strictly prefers the dichotomous contract.

Table 9 provides an example of a Pareto superior dichotomous contract.

Skill or State Observed at a Cost

Finally, we briefly consider the case where the worker's skill or state can be observed at some "reasonable" cost. Each worker's effort, capital, and outcome are costlessly observable and observation activities can be conditioned on these variables.

As in the moral hazard case, the desirability of a conditional investigation contract will depend on the investigation costs and the type of sharing function employed. In general, however, investigation provides a strict increase in the amount of information on which the contracting is based and, thus, in general, we expect positive value to be associated with such a contract. Indeed, with the skilled worker forced into a risk position to gain separation from the unskilled worker, he will pay to shift that risk to the owner. Conditional investigation will accomplish this without dulling self-selection incentives. More formally, we have

Proposition 12:[40]

In the basic adverse selection model, if a risk neutral owner uses a pair of skill differentiating contracts (based on costless observation of the worker's effort, capital, and outcome) that impose risk on one of the two risk averse worker groups, then there is a pair of budget-based conditional investigation contracts that is Pareto superior to those existing contracts provided the positive investigation cost is sufficiently small.

As noted in the moral hazard case, however, conditional investigation contracts are not, in the absence of exogenous enforcement, Nash equilibria. Hence, we must expand our setting to fully rationalize such contracting procedures.

Concluding Remarks

Use of budget-based contracts, such as standard cost systems, can be analyzed in terms of conscious choice by both parties to the contract. We have demonstrated that market incompleteness (in terms of costly effort or skill observability) and risk aversion are necessary conditions for such contracting to be Pareto superior to other contracting alternatives. We have identified some conditions under which budget-based contracts are Pareto superior to linear contracts. Of course, our observations must be viewed as tentative in that they are based on a model of a simple economy. But it is clear that budget-based contracts can be rationalized in a market setting.

In concluding, we briefly relate our analysis to some of the debates in the accounting literature as to how budget-based contracts should be designed. (See Ronen and Livingstone [1975] for a recent review of this literature.) One continuing debate is whether the standard should be reasonably attainable. In our analysis attainability is not a direct issue. Furthermore, in the numerical cases examined, the standard is below expected performance when nonperformance triggers an investigation and above expected performance when no additional information is to be obtained. In each case, the budget-based contracts

[40] Let X^n be the set of possible outcomes for which one of the worker types incurs risk under the existing contracts. Investigating if $x \in X^n$, paying zero if the observed skill is not as represented but the conditional expected payment otherwise, provides a strictly superior budget-based conditional investigation contract. The owner is indifferent, the worker in question is strictly improved (by Jensen's inequality), and the remaining worker is unaffected. A similar contract can be constructed for the other worker, but there will be no improvement for him if X^n is null.

arise because of information voids, and when viewed in terms of the contracting arrangements that will be efficient, there is no reason to expect the standard to be reasonably attainable. Indeed, we are looking at market based allocations here and the contracting arrangements are jointly determined by the owners' and workers' tastes, beliefs, and opportunities.

To reinforce this point, recall the dichotomous contract with a high standard in Proposition 5. In this case the worker voluntarily increases his effort so as to have some chance of attaining the high standard because the compensation for doing so is sufficiently attractive. In many discussions of standards, the compensation aspects are largely ignored. Alternative standards will be associated with different compensation functions, and the preferences for one standard over another must reflect the changes in those functions. A *ceteris paribus* comparison is incomplete. On the other hand, discussions of standards often stress motivational aspects which we have ignored. In particular, we have ignored the possibility that the outcome relative to standard provides some form of non-pecuniary income to the worker.

A second issue in the design of budget-based systems is the degree of participation by the workers in establishing the standards. In our analysis, all aspects of a contract, including the standard, are unanimously agreed upon by both parties. But, of course, given our market setting, it is an equilibrium analysis interpreted in terms of the market forces that ultimately produce that agreement. More formal examination of participation in an economic model would require explicit recognition of contracting costs, information asymmetries, and internal labor markets.[41]

A third issue is the frequency or conditions under which management should investigate the causes of poor performance. In much of the accounting literature, that issue is explored in the context of simple analytical models that view the system as being either "in control" or "out of control." (See Kaplan [1975] for a review of this literature.) We provide a somewhat different view. In our analysis, system performance is not mechanistic, but is influenced by the worker; and the threat of investigation (and its consequences) is used to ensure that the worker provides the effort required by his wage contract. This "management by exception" may appear to be somewhat negative, but, in fact, the worker may benefit by obtaining a share of the larger returns such a system will provide if investigation costs are sufficiently small. (Note, however, that no non-pecuniary aspects of the owner-worker relationship were admitted in the analysis.)

A final issue is whether performance measures should encompass only that which is controllable by the worker. An affirmative answer is accepted dogma in much of the accounting literature (though risk sharing issues do arise). In the limiting case of costless information, that is what we observe in our analysis: the worker is responsible only for the effort he exerts with known skill. But recognition of information costs may result in contracts that leave the worker subject to the risks of factors beyond his control. In those cases, the worker would be worse off if he insisted on the controllability principle since the available returns with which to pay him would be smaller if the owner was forced to incur the in-

[41] See Doeringer and Piore [1971] for extensive development of the concept of internal labor markets. This concept gives formal recognition to the fact that while market forces are important at entry level positions, they are less important for many of the existing employees in a firm.

formation costs. On the other hand, the budget-based conditional investigation contract does effectively implement the controllability principle in the face of "reasonable" information costs.

In sum, budget-based contracts can be rationalized as labor allocation/employment devices when desirable information upon which to base the allocations is costly. This, in turn, adds insight into the nature and role of the standards and budgets that might be used.

Appendix

Proof of Proposition 5

We set $\hat{x}=2f(a^*(\mathscr{C}))$, where $\mathscr{C}=(1, \alpha, R)$ is the linear contract in question, and consider $B_1 \geq \alpha\hat{x}-R$.

Then

$$E(U_w|a^*(\mathscr{C}^d), \mathscr{C}^d) \geq E(U_w|a^*(\mathscr{C}), \mathscr{C}^d) = E(U_w|a^*(\mathscr{C}), \mathscr{C}).$$

And with $a^*(\mathscr{C}^d) \geq a^*(\mathscr{C})$, the optimal effort may be determined by differentiating the following:

$$\begin{aligned} E(U_w|a, \mathscr{C}^d) = {} & [(\gamma + 1)\alpha 2\xi a^k]^{-1}\{[\alpha\hat{x} + \bar{x} - R]^{\gamma+1} - [\bar{x} - R]^{\gamma+1}\} \\ & + [\bar{x} + B_1]^{\gamma}(1 - \hat{x}/2\xi a^k) - \theta a^r \end{aligned}$$

and setting it equal to zero. Let $a(B_1)$ denote the optimal effort:

$$a(B_1) = a^*(\mathscr{C}^d) = \left[\frac{k}{2\xi r\theta}\left([\bar{x} + B_1]^{\gamma}\hat{x} - \frac{[\alpha\hat{x} + \bar{x} - R]^{\gamma+1} - [\bar{x} - R]^{\gamma+1}}{(\gamma + 1)\alpha}\right)\right]^{1/(r+k)}$$

The owner's expected utility for the dichotomous contract is

$$\begin{aligned} E(U_0|a(B_1), \mathscr{C}^d) = {} & \xi[a(B_1)]^k - \alpha\xi[\alpha\xi[a(B_1)]^k\tfrac{1}{4}[\hat{s}(a(B_1))]^2 + R\tfrac{1}{2}\hat{s}(a(B_1)) \\ & -B_1(1 - \tfrac{1}{2}\hat{s}(a(B_1))) \end{aligned}$$

where $\hat{s}(a)=\hat{x}/\xi a^k$ is the state that yields outcome $\hat{x}$ if effort a is selected.

We now differentiate the owner's expected utility with respect to B_1:

$$\begin{aligned} \frac{\partial E(U_0|a(B_1), \mathscr{C}^d)}{\partial B_1} = {} & \xi k[a(B_1)]^{k-1}a'(B_1) - \alpha\xi k[a(B_1)]^{k-1}a'(B_1)\tfrac{1}{4}[\hat{s}(a(B_1))]^2 \\ & - \alpha\xi\tfrac{1}{2}[a(B_1)]^k[\hat{s}(a(B_1))]\hat{s}'(a(B_1))a'(B_1) + R\tfrac{1}{2}\hat{s}'(a(B_1))a'(B_1) \\ & - (1 - \tfrac{1}{2}\hat{s}(a(B_1))) + B_1\tfrac{1}{2}\hat{s}'(a(B_1))a'(B_1). \end{aligned}$$

Evaluating this at $B_1=\alpha\hat{x}-R$ and observing that $\hat{s}'(a)=-k\hat{x}/\xi a^{k+1}$ we obtain

$$\left.\frac{\partial E(U_0|\cdot)}{\partial B_1}\right|_{B_1=\alpha\hat{x}-R} = a'(B_1)[a(B_1)]^{k-1}\{\xi k - \alpha k\hat{x}^2/4\xi[a(B_1)]^{2k}\} - (1 - \tfrac{1}{2}(\hat{x}/\xi[a(B_1)]^k)$$

And since $\hat{x}=2f(a(B_1))=2\xi[a(B_1)]^k$ we have

$$\left.\frac{\partial E(U_0|\cdot)}{\partial B_1}\right|_{B_1=\alpha\hat{x}-R} = a'(B_1)[a(B_1)]^{k-1}\xi k(1 - \alpha) > 0 \quad \text{if } \alpha < 1 \quad \text{and} \quad a'(B_1) > 0$$

But

$$a'(B_1) = \left[\frac{k}{2\xi r\theta}\left([\bar{x} + B_1]^\gamma \hat{x} - \frac{[\alpha\hat{x} + \bar{x} - R]^{\gamma+1} - [\bar{x} - R]^{\gamma+1}}{(\gamma + 1)\alpha}\right)\right]^{1/(r+k)-1}$$

$$\cdot \frac{1}{r+k}\frac{k\hat{x}}{2\xi r\theta}[\bar{x} + B_1]^{\gamma-1}\gamma = [a(B_1)]^{1-r-k}\frac{1}{r+k}\frac{k\hat{x}\gamma}{2\xi r\theta}[\bar{x} + B_1]^{\gamma-1} > 0.$$

REFERENCES

Akerlof, G., "The Market for 'Lemons': Quality Uncertainty and the Market Mechanism," *Quarterly Journal of Economics* (August 1970), pp. 488–500.

Alchian, A. and H. Demsetz, "Production, Information Costs, and Economic Organization." *American Economic Review* (December 1972), pp. 777–795.

Argyris, C., *The Impact of Budgets on People* (Controllership Foundation, 1952).

Arrow, K. J., *The Limits of Organization* (Norton, 1974).

Becker, G. S. and G. J. Stigler, "Law Enforcement, Malfeasance, and Compensation of Enforcers." *Journal of Legal Studies* (January 1974).

Doeringer, P. and M. Piore, *Internal Labor Markets and Manpower Analysis* (Heath, 1971).

Gjesdal, Frøystein, "Accounting in Agencies" unpublished paper, Stanford University Graduate School of Business (1976).

Harris, M., and A. Raviv, "Optimal Incentive Contracts with Imperfect Information," unpublished working paper #70-75-76, GSIA, Carnegie-Mellon University (1976).

Hopwood, A. G., "An Empirical Study of the Role of Accounting Data in Performance Evaluation," *Journal of Accounting Research Supplement* (1972), pp. 156–193.

Itami, H., "Evaluation Measures and Goal Congruence under Uncertainty," *Journal of Accounting Research* (Spring 1975), pp. 73–96.

Jensen, M. C. and W. H. Meckling, "Theory of the Firm: Managerial Behavior, Agency Costs and Ownership Structure," *Journal of Financial Economics* (October 1976), pp. 305–360.

Kaplan, R., "The Significance and Investigation of Cost Variances: Survey and Extensions," *Journal of Accounting Research* (Fall, 1975), pp. 311–337.

Kihlstrom, R., and M. Pauly, "The Role of Insurance in the Allocation of Risk," *American Economic Review* (May 1971), pp. 371–379.

Mirrlees, J. A., "Notes on Welfare Economics, Information, and Uncertainty," in Balch, M., McFadden, D. and Wu, S. (eds.), *Essays on Economic Behavior Under Uncertainty* (North-Holland, 1974).

———, "The Optimal Structure of Incentives and Authority within an Organization," *Bell Journal of Economics* (Spring, 1976), pp. 105–131.

Radner, R., "Market Equilibrium and Uncertainty: Concepts and Problems," in M. D. Intriligator and D. A. Kendrick (eds.), *Frontiers of Quantitative Economics* Volume 2 (North-Holland, 1974).

Ridgeway, V. F., "Dysfunctional Consequences of Performance Measurement," *Administtative Science Quarterly* (September 1956), pp. 240–247.

Ronen, J. and J. L. Livingstone, "An Expectancy Theory Approach to the Motivational Impacts of Budgets," THE ACCOUNTING REVIEW (October 1975), pp. 671–685.

Rothschild, M. and J. Stiglitz, "Equilibrium in Competitive Insurance Markets: An Essay on the Economics of Imperfect Information," *Quarterly Journal of Economics* (November 1976), pp. 629–649.

Schiff, M. and A. Y. Lewin, "The Impact of People on Budgets," THE ACCOUNTING REVIEW (April 1970), pp. 259–268.

Spence, M., "Job Market Signaling," *Quarterly Journal of Economics* (August 1973), pp. 355–374.

Spence, M., and R. Zeckhauser, "Insurance, Information and Individual Action," *American Economic Review* (May 1971), pp. 380–391.

Stafford, F. P. and M. S. Cohen, "A Model of Work Effort and Productive Consumption," *Journal of Economic Theory* (March 1974), pp. 333–347.

Stedry, A. C., *Budget Control and Cost Behavior* (Prentice-Hall, 1960).

Stiglitz, J. E., "Risk Sharing and Incentives in Sharecropping," *Review of Economic Studies* (April 1974), pp. 219–255.

———, "Incentives, Risk, and Information: Notes Toward a Theory of Hierarchy," *Bell Journal of Economics* (Autumn 1975), pp. 552–579.
Swieringa, R. J. and R. H. Moncur, *Some Effects of Participative Budgeting on Managerial Behavior* (NAA, 1975).
Townsend, R. M., "Optimal Contracts and Competitive Markets with Costly State Verification," unpublished working paper, Graduate School of Industrial Administration, Carnegie-Mellon University (August 1976).
Williamson, O. E., M. L. Wachter, and J. E. Harris, "Understanding the Employment Relation: The Analysis of Idiosyncratic Exchange," *Bell Journal of Economics* (Spring 1975), pp. 250–278.
Wilson, R., "On the Theory of Syndicates," *Econometrica* (January 1968), pp. 119–132.

THE AMERICAN ECONOMIC REVIEW
VOL. 68 NO. 1 MARCH 1978

Some Results on Incentive Contracts with Applications to Education and Employment, Health Insurance, and Law Enforcement

By MILTON HARRIS AND ARTUR RAVIV*

When decision-making authority is delegated from one agent to another, contractual arrangements are often used to allocate resources and outputs. Such situations may be analyzed using the theory of principal-agent relationships. This theory seeks to characterize optimal contracts and explain observed arrangements. Examples which fit the "agency paradigm" include employer-employee, insurer-insured, and owner-manager relations. In this paper, we report some results which significantly extend the theory of agency to situations characterized by a divergence of incentives between the two parties and asymmetric information with opportunities for acquiring information. In addition, we discuss several applications of this theory.

The theory of optimal contracts under conditions of uncertainty has received considerable attention. Kenneth Arrow and Robert Wilson (1968) were concerned with the optimal sharing of purely exogenous risk. Wilson (1969) and Stephen Ross considered situations in which the risk could be affected by the actions of the agents. They analyze contracts which induce similar attitudes toward risk on the part of the agents, thus allowing the possibility that decentralized decision making will be optimal. Conditions under which such arrangements are indeed Pareto optimal are also investigated. In their models, incentive problems arise purely as a consequence of diverse attitudes toward risk among the agents. A. Michael Spence and Richard Zeckhauser, in the context of insurance contracts, introduced the problem of a divergence in incentives due to the action of an agent together with differential information among agents. More recently, Joseph Stiglitz (1975a) analyzed incentive contracts between employers and employees. With regard to differential information, both Spence-Zeckhauser and Stiglitz assume one of two extreme cases: either the agent's action is known by everyone with certainty (in which case there is no differential information), or no information about the agent's action is available to anyone except the agent himself. A somewhat intermediate case was analyzed by Robert Townsend in which the exact information possessed by one agent can be made available to the other at some cost.

Two important aspects of agency relationships are not fully explored in the literature on the theory of contracts. First, most agency relationships must deal with incentive problems which arise because the agent would prefer to work less, other things equal, while the principal is indifferent to the level of the agent's effort, other things (i.e., his share of the payoff) equal. This type of incentive problem is somewhat different from the one considered by Wilson (1969) and Ross in which a divergence in incentives results only from different attitudes toward risk. Second, in most instances an agent may acquire information about other agents' actions. This possibility was discussed in interesting papers by Armen Alchian and Harold Demsetz and by C. Michael Jensen and William Meckling. The quality of the information obtained through monitoring (or supervising) depends on the resources committed to this activity as well as on the available monitoring technology. Furthermore, as Stiglitz

*Carnegie-Mellon University. We would like to acknowledge helpful discussions with Ed Prescott and Rob Townsend, as well as suggestions of Stephen Ross, Martin Hellwig, an anonymous referee, and the managing editor of this *Review*.

points out, "... the amount (or quality) of supervision will affect both the optimal incentive scheme which will be used and the level of expected utility which the individual will attain" (1975a, p. 572). Consequently, the optimal incentive contract will depend on the available monitoring technology. In this paper, we explore these aspects of the agency problem.

Our analysis is based on a model in which there are two individuals: one, denoted the agent, takes an action which together with the realization of an exogenous random variable results in the payoff to be divided between the agent and the other individual, denoted the principal. Incentive problems arise because the agent has a disutility for the action while the principal does not. We distinguish two versions of this model. In the first, the agent is assumed to take his action without any information regarding the realization of the exogenous random state. In the second version, the agent is assumed to know the value of the random state before taking his action. In both versions, the object of the analysis is to discover the form of the Pareto optimal contract, that is, how the optimal sharing arrangement for the payoff depends on the observed variables. In particular, our analysis deals with the following issues: When would we expect to observe performance-contingent contracts, and what would be the form of such contracts; when performance is not observable, under what conditions would we expect contracts to depend on imperfect estimates of performance, what types of estimators would be used, and how would they be incorporated into the contract.

Our results are discussed in terms of the employer-employee relationship. They are, however, more general, and we discuss their implications for three other agency relationships.

The first application is to the analysis of employment contracts based on training or education and ability. Here we show under what conditions and in what form it is optimal to make employment contracts contingent on training or ability. In particular we show when the type of contract used in the "signaling literature" (see Spence, 1973, 1974, 1976; John Riley; Stiglitz, 1975b) is Pareto optimal.

The second application is to health insurance contracts. We show when indemnity insurance, that is, contracts in which the insurance payment depends only on the degree of illness, is optimal. We also show when the optimal policy provides payment contingent on the level of medical care chosen. The case in which the level of medical care chosen is not directly observable is also considered.

The third application of the analysis is to the problem of procuring the optimal amount of law enforcement, an issue which was addressed by Gary Becker and George Stigler. We exhibit conditions on the information structure under which the standard type of compensation arrangement for the enforcer (i.e., a salary) would lead to an inefficiently large degree of malfeasance or nonfeasance (shirking). We also show under what conditions these inefficiencies could be resolved by the use of contracts which we exhibit. In particular, we provide conditions under which some suggestions of Becker and Stigler would be optimal.

I. The Agency Model

In this section we describe the model with which we address the issues mentioned above (a more detailed and formal treatment may be found in the authors' working paper). In this model there are two individuals, "the principal" and "the agent." For concreteness, in describing the model and results, we refer to these individuals as the employer and worker, respectively.

The worker chooses a level of effort (or action) a, which together with the realization of some exogenous random variable θ determines the value of the worker's product x (the payoff). The random variable θ may be interpreted as the result of any exogenous uncertain event which affects the worker's productivity, for example, the weather, equipment failure, the price of the product, etc. We represent the relationship among the value of the worker's output, the worker's effort, and the realization of the random variable by a production function X, that is,

(1) $$x = X(a, \theta)$$

We assume that greater effort by the worker results in greater output for any value of θ (i.e., $X_1 > 0$ for all a, θ).

Two important cases may be distinguished regarding the information available to the worker when he decides upon his level of effort. First, in Model 1, we assume that he does *not* know the value of θ when he chooses his effort. For example, a sharecropper may not know what the weather will be when he plants his crop; a lawyer, when he prepares his case, may not know which judge will preside. Second, in Model 2, we assume that the worker *does* observe the value of θ and chooses his effort contingent on this observation. For example, a salesman may observe the state of demand before deciding how many calls to make.

The division of the product will be determined by a function which may depend on any variable which is observable by both parties, that is, whose value is known by both parties when the product is divided. This assumption rules out contracts which are not incentive compatible. The function and its list of arguments denoted $(S; z)$ will be called a *contract*. The value of $S(z)$ is interpreted as the worker's share of the product while the employer's share is $x - S(z)$. The product x is assumed always to be observable by both parties. In addition to x, the list z might include the effort a, provided, of course, that it is observable. If a is not observable, z might include an estimator, denoted α of a. For example, an estimator of the sharecropper's effort might be the amount of time he spends in the field. An estimator of the salesman's effort might be the number of miles he drives. When available, the estimator will be called a *monitor*, that is, a monitor is a random variable whose distribution is conditional on a. The class of available monitors is referred to as the *monitoring technology.*

Associated with the worker is a utility function U, whose first argument is the worker's share of the product and whose second argument is his effort. The worker is assumed to prefer less effort to more effort, other things equal. We therefore assume that

(2) $$U_1 > 0; \qquad U_2 < 0$$

We will often assume that the worker is risk averse, that is, that U is strictly concave in the first argument.

Given a contract $(S; z)$, in Model 1 the worker determines his effort by solving the following maximization problem:

(3) $$\max_a E_\theta U[S(z), a]$$

In Model 2, the worker chooses a as a function of θ to solve

(3') $$\max_a U[S(z), a]$$

In both models, the effort chosen will depend on the functional form of S; in Model 2, it will also depend on the realization of the exogenous random variable.

Associated with the employer is a utility function V, which is a function *only* of his share of the product. We assume V is monotone increasing, concave (i.e., the employer is either risk neutral or risk averse). Given a contract $(S; z)$, and a level of effort a chosen by the worker according to either (3) or (3'), the employer's utility is

(4) $$E_\theta V[X(a, \theta) - S(z)]$$

This concludes our presentation of the model. We turn in the next section to a description of our results.

II. Results

Our results characterize the Pareto optimal contracts under various assumptions concerning the availability of information. In particular, optimal contracts are investigated under alternative assumptions on the observability of the worker's effort and the random variable and on the existing tech-

[handwritten marginal note:] The principal determines S by solving $\max_S E_\theta V[X(a,\theta) - S(z)]$

nology for monitoring the worker's effort. We are interested in Pareto optimal contracts on the supposition that observed contracts will have the property that, given the availability of information, neither agent's expected utility can be increased without decreasing the expected utility of the other agent. Thus we seek to characterize the contracts which we expect to arise under various information structures. Our results are simply discussed here without formal derivations; these may be found in our earlier paper.

To begin, suppose that the realization of the random variable (also referred to as "the state of nature" or simply "the state") is freely observable by both employer and worker when the product is distributed. In this case, our first result implies that making the contract contingent on the worker's effort provides no gains over contracts which depend only on output and the observed value of θ. Therefore, if the state is freely observable, we would *not* expect to observe contracts contingent on worker effort. Thus *ex post* uncertainty as to the relationship between the effort and the product is essential if contracts based on worker performance are to be observed. For future reference we state this result as

PROPOSITION 1: *The expected utilities achieved under any contract which depends on the product, the effort, and the state can also be achieved under a contract which depends on the product and the state, but not on the effort. This result holds for both Models* 1 *and* 2.

The above result does not yield information as to the form of the optimal contract when the state is freely observable. This information is provided by

PROPOSITION 2: *The Pareto optimal contract which depends on the product and the state specifies a "standard" output contingent on the state. The worker receives an amount which depends on the standard output and perhaps on the state, plus the difference between the actual output and the standard. The employer receives an amount which depends only on the state and is therefore unaffected by the worker's level of effort. This result holds for both Models* 1 *and* 2.

To illustrate this result, consider the sharecropper example mentioned above. In this case, Propositions 1 and 2 imply that if the weather is the only exogenous random factor affecting the crop, we would expect to observe an arrangement in which the tenant "pays" the landlord an amount of output contingent only on the weather and keeps the remainder of the crop.

Note that Propositions 1 and 2 hold regardless of attitudes toward risk of the employer (landlord) and worker (tenant). Thus the determination of the variables on which the contract will depend (if all are observable) is independent of attitudes toward risk. For example, if output, effort, and the weather are all observable, the contract will depend only on output and weather. This result does depend, however, on the ability of both parties to agree *ex ante* on which types of weather are possible, what the probability attached to each type is, and how weather affects output. It also depends on the ability of both parties to observe *ex post* which type of weather occurred. Attitudes toward risk do play a role in determining the sharing function. For example, if the landlord is risk neutral, the contract will be such that if the tenant puts in sufficient effort to produce the (weather-contingent) standard output, then the tenant's share will be independent of the weather. If the tenant does not render the effort implicit in the standard output, however, his share may be weather-dependent. The landlord's share (i.e., rent) *will* depend on the weather, in general, if the tenant is risk averse.

Attitudes toward risk also play an important role in determining the variables on which the optimal contract will depend when the state is not observable, *ex post*. The next result states that risk aversion on the part of the worker is a necessary and sufficient condition for contracts which depend explicitly on effort to be superior to contracts which depend only on the output. Intuitively, if the worker is risk neutral, it will be optimal for him to bear all the risk associated with uncertain productivity. In this case, all effects of the worker's performance are internalized, and thus incentive problems are resolved without the use of performance-contingent contracts. When the worker is risk averse, optimality requires some sharing of risk, and therefore the employer bears some of the consequences of the worker's choice of effort. In this case, performance-contingent contracts are superior to contracts based only on output.

PROPOSITION 3: (i) *If the worker is risk neutral, any contract which depends only on output and effort can be dominated (in the Pareto sense) by a contract which depends only on output.*

(ii) *If the worker is risk averse, any contract which depends only on output can be strictly dominated by a contract which depends on both output and effort.*

(iii) *If the worker is risk averse, any contract which depends only on output can be strictly dominated by a contract which depends only on output and the state and is of the form given in Proposition* 2.

These results hold for Models 1 and 2.[1] Next we characterize the form of Pareto optimal contracts which depend on output and effort.

PROPOSITION 4: *Any Pareto optimal contract in the class of contracts depending only on output and effort has the property that the worker's share depends only on the output, provided his effort meets a prespecified criterion. If not, he receives nothing. This result holds for Model* 1.

Thus when the worker's effort is freely observable, and the worker is risk averse, we would expect to observe contracts which stipulate a particular choice of effort by the worker. Since the worker will always choose to meet the requirement, we refer to this contract as a forcing contract.[2]

With respect to the sharecropping paradigm, these results imply that if the tenant is risk averse, and output and effort, *but not the weather,* are observable *ex post,*[3] we would expect the sharing arrangement to include a stipulation of how much effort the tenant is expected to expend. If the tenant puts in the required effort (and he will if his effort is perfectly observable), he will receive a share of the product. This share will depend on the product and the attitudes toward risk of the landlord and tenant. For example if the landlord is risk neutral (and not the tenant), the tenant will get a fixed wage independent of output (or the weather). If, on the other hand, the tenant (and not the landlord) is risk neutral, contracts stipulating the tenant's effort are unnecessary; we expect to observe the landlord receiving a fixed rent with the tenant keeping the residual.

We now turn to some results regarding the use of imperfect estimators of effort as a contingency affecting the distribution of the product. Clearly we would not expect to observe the use of imperfect monitors of effort when there are no gains to using actual effort. We have exhibited above two situations in which there are no gains to acquiring information about the worker's effort (even if such information is available costlessly). Moreover we have shown that in all other cases there are gains to acquiring information, that is, if information of "sufficient quality" can be obtained at a "sufficiently low price," then both individuals can be made better off. The two conditions

[1] For Model 2 the utility function of the worker is assumed to be separable and the production function is one-to-one in the state.

[2] This terminology was suggested to us by Ross.

[3] With respect to the sharecropping example, one might question the assumption that the tenant's effort is observable while the weather is not. We agree that these assumptions are not particularly appropriate to sharecropping. Our model is, however, applicable to a large class of situations, and for many of these, the assumptions are appropriate (see Section III). We use the sharecropping example here only for the purpose of illustrating all our results with a consistent example.

under which there are no gains to monitoring the worker's effort are (a) when the realization of θ, the exogenous random variable affecting output, is observable, and (b) when the worker is risk neutral. From a methodological point of view, these results imply that it is not possible to simplify the analysis of monitoring by assuming away either exogenous uncertainty or risk aversion on the part of the worker.

In general, even when there are gains to perfect information on effort, these gains may be impossible to realize through imperfect monitoring. The introduction of imperfect information on the worker's effort into a contract produces two opposing effects on the welfare of the parties to the contract. First, since the information is imperfect, additional uncertainty is introduced. Since both the employer and worker are risk averse, this additional uncertainty tends to reduce welfare. Second, inclusion of monitoring can motivate the worker to choose a level of effort which, neglecting the first effect, would make both parties better off.

Because the minimum (necessary) conditions for monitoring to be valuable appear to be very difficult to formulate, we explore several sets of sufficient conditions. These results are derived using forcing type contracts. This type of contract specifies that the worker is paid only if the monitoring reveals his effort to be "acceptable," and the size of the payment does not depend on the results of monitoring in any other way. The forcing contract thus requires that a decision be made based on the realization of the monitor. This statistical decision problem is the test of the following hypothesis: the worker's level of effort is one of a set of acceptable levels. The precision of the monitor, in this case, is summarized by the probabilities of type I and type II errors. The conditions on the monitoring technology referred to below are assumptions as to the availability of monitors with various probabilities of type I and type II errors.

Our results regarding the use of contracts based on imperfect monitoring of worker effort can be summarized as follows:

i) First, we establish general sufficient conditions under which the potential gains to monitoring may be realized.

ii) Under additional assumptions on the monitoring technology, we show that any Pareto optimal contract can be approximated to any degree of precision by a forcing type of contract.

iii) Under another set of assumptions on the monitoring technology and the worker's utility function, we show that all the results achievable under perfect information can be obtained even when information is imperfect, using a forcing contract.

The above results are obtained only for Model 1.

III. Applications

In this section, three applications of the results of the previous section are analyzed. These results are used to describe the Pareto optimal contractual arrangements, and therefore the contracts we would expect to observe in some interesting situations. First, we analyze employment contracts based on education, training, or ability. We compare our results to those of the signaling literature (for example, Spence, 1973, 1974). Second, we consider optimal health insurance contracts and explain indemnity insurance. Finally, the problem of optimal compensation of law enforcers is discussed. Here we relate our results to those of Becker and Stigler.

A. *Ability, Training, and Employment Contracts*

There has recently been considerable interest in the relationship between education and other "signals" and the allocation of labor in job markets. For example, Spence (1973, 1974, 1976) stresses the use of education as a signal for native ability in the hiring of employees (see also Riley, Stiglitz, 1975b). In this literature, a particular payment structure for the worker, based on the signal, is assumed. This structure involves paying the worker a fixed wage which depends only on his education level. These papers provide no analysis to justify the use of such a payment schedule, nor do they consider the possibility that the use of the signal in this way may be Pareto inferior to some other contractual arrangement. The present section is devoted to a clarification of this issue. We characterize the Pareto optimal contract in several situations similar to those analyzed in the signaling literature. In particular we exhibit conditions under which an *optimal* contract will depend on the education level of the worker (as well as things like recommendations, transcripts, previous experience, etc.), even when education is not a perfect measure of acquired ability or productivity. Thus our results may be viewed as complementary with the signaling literature.

To apply our model to the present problem, we reinterpret the effort as the ability the worker has acquired to perform the task, and the state as his native ability. We assume that neither the worker nor his prospective employer knows the worker's native ability at the time the contract is agreed on. Finally, each worker is assumed to know his own *acquired* ability.

With this interpretation, our results of Section II are applicable and imply:

i) If native ability is known or observable *ex post*, it follows from Propositions 1 and 2 that the optimal contract specifies that the employer receives an amount which depends only on the worker's native ability. In particular, the employer specifies a standard output to be produced by the worker contingent on his native ability. The employer's payoff is a certain share (which may depend on the worker's native ability) of this "standard output" while the worker receives the remainder of the standard revenue plus any output generated in excess of the standard (or minus any shortfall of actual output from standard output). This arrangement is equivalent to specifying a standard level of acquired ability required from a worker in this particular job and allowing workers with different levels of acquired ability to participate and accept the full consequences if their acquired ability is different from the one required.

ii) If workers are risk neutral, from Proposition 3, the Pareto optimal contract will specify a given payoff to employers independent of output, the worker's acquired ability, or his native ability level. Therefore, the worker receives the entire output minus some constant, that is, the worker purchases the right to use the production function for a given price.

iii) If workers are risk averse, contracts which depend only on the output are inefficient relative to contracts which depend on the native ability and/or acquired ability of the worker as well as the output. Pareto-superior results can be obtained if the acquired ability is observable and is included in the contract. From Proposition 4 it follows that Pareto optimal contracts when only output and acquired ability are observable are of the form "workers with acquired ability level of (at least) a^* will be paid $S(x)$, others need not apply," where $S(x)$ is some function of the output. For example, if years of education is a perfect correlate of acquired ability, this result implies that it is Pareto inferior not to make employment and/or salaries contingent on the education of the worker. Even if acquired ability is not observable (nor is something perfectly correlated with it) there may be imperfect measures which are sufficiently precise to make using them Pareto efficient. Examples of such monitors include years of education, interviews, transcripts, recommendations, etc. In this case we have shown sufficient conditions under which it is Pareto inferior not to include such monitors of acquired ability. The contract used is of the forcing type and specifies a minimum required level of the observable monitor of acquired ability. The above analysis provides an explanation for compensation schedules which are functions of education level. According to our analysis it is optimal for workers to receive *fixed wages* contingent on education level when employers are risk neutral. If employers are risk averse, a worker's compensation will depend on his output if he meets the education requirement.

B. *Health Insurance Contracts*

It has for some time been recognized that when insurance payments depend on a decision of the insured as well as the state of nature, then an optimal allocation of resources and risk will not be achieved by a simple arrangement in which the insured pays a given price (premium) in return for various payments contingent on the state of nature. This problem arises because the insured has an incentive to "overspend" on insured expenses. It has been called "moral hazard" in the insurance literature (see, for example, Arrow, chs. 5, 8, 9; Pauly, 1968). One way to mitigate the inefficiency is to impose some of the cost of medical care on the insured. Zeckhauser illustrates the tradeoff between risk spreading and incentives. He suggests that insurance payments should depend on the degree of illness as well as the cost of the associated health care. Pauly (1971) refers to this type of insurance as "indemnity" insurance. The results of Section II can be applied to the case of health insurance to show under what conditions moral hazard causes inefficiencies and how appropriate contractual arrangements such as indemnity insurance can resolve this problem. Therefore, the results of Zeckhauser and Pauly (1971) can be obtained as special cases of our results.

To apply our results, we view the insurer as the principal and the insured as the agent. The random state θ is interpreted as the degree of illness. There are two possible interpretations of the agent's action, a. First, a may be the level of preventive care purchased by the insured or a general decision made by him *before* the state is realized as to the amount and quality of health care to be purchased when and if he becomes ill. The second interpretation of the agent's action is as a decision made *after* becoming ill on the amount and quality of health care to purchase. These two interpretations correspond to the assumptions of Models 1 and 2, respectively. The payoff x is interpreted as the amount spent on health care.[4]

Applying the results of Section II yields the following:

i) If the insurer can observe the degree of illness of the insured θ, then from Propositions 1 and 2 the optimal insurance contract specifies a given amount to be paid by the insurer for each possible degree of illness, that is, indemnity insurance. The amount paid by the insurer is thus independent of the choice of medical care taken by the insured. The insured under this contract can choose a level of medical care which costs more or less than the amount which the insurer agrees to pay. Moreover, since the insured is obviously risk averse, Propositions 1, 2, and 3 imply that indemnity insurance is *strictly* Pareto superior to insurance based only on the cost of the medical care. All of the above results hold whether the choice of medical care is taken before or after the occurrence of an illness.

ii) If the degree of illness cannot be observed by the insurer, but the insured's choice of medical care can be observed, then from Proposition 3 there are contracts which depend on both the cost of medical care and the insured's choice of medical care which are *strictly* Pareto superior to contracts which depend only on the cost. This result holds whether the choice of medical care is taken before or after the occurrence of illness. Furthermore, when the insured chooses his level of medical care *before* the occurrence of an illness, from Proposition 4, the Pareto optimal contract (when only the total cost and the insured's choice of care are observable) stipulates that the insurer pays some share of the cost *provided that the insured chooses some prespecified level of medical care.* Otherwise, the insurer pays nothing. Even when the insured's choice of medical care is not itself

[4]Note that these interpretations of a and x require opposite assumptions on the signs of the first derivatives of U and V than were made in Section I. It is easy to check that all the results continue to hold.

directly observable, it may be optimal to employ some indirect and imperfect measure of the level of care (for example, frequency of visits to a doctor). When these measures are sufficiently precise estimates of the insured's actual choice of medical care, the optimal policy will be essentially the same as when the choice is directly observable.

C. *Compensation of Law Enforcers*

In a very interesting paper, Becker and Stigler analyze the law enforcement problem and suggest two alternative methods for improving the incentives given enforcers. Here we recast the law enforcement problem in our framework and employ the results of the previous section to obtain the optimal contract between the state and enforcers. Our results provide a firm foundation for the suggestions of Becker and Stigler. In particular, we show explicitly under what conditions each suggestion is Pareto optimal.

Becker and Stigler explore the economic incentives for malfeasance in law enforcement. They conclude that officials responsible for enforcement might lack sufficient incentives to enforce certain laws. Moreover, there may also be incentives for them to engage in malfeasance. Becker and Stigler suggest two methods for improving the incentives given enforcers. The first suggestion discourages malfeasance and lack of proper enforcement by penalizing the enforcer if such behavior is detected. The penalty is set such that it more than offsets the gain from malfeasance. This method is made operational by requiring the enforcers to "post a bond equal to the temptation of malfeasance, receive the income on the bond as long as they are employed, and have the bond returned if they behave themselves until retirement" (Becker and Stigler, p. 9). If the state detects malfeasance on the part of the enforcer, he is fired and loses the bond he posted. The second suggestion is to allow free entry into the enforcement industry. Enforcers would be rewarded based on their performance. Becker and Stigler argue that the amount of enforcement would be optimal if successful enforcers were paid the fines levied against convicted violators. These fines would equal the damages to society caused by the violator divided by the probability of conviction.

The situation described by Becker and Stigler can be stated in terms of Models 1 and 2 of Section I. The state (society) and the enforcer can be viewed as the principal and agent, respectively. The payoff x to the law enforcement activity is the revenue generated via the fine levied on convicted violators net of the costs associated with trying the accused. These latter costs include both costs borne by the accused (for example, time lost) and those borne by the state (for example, court costs). As is the case in the Becker-Stigler paper, we are not concerned with the problem of *crime prevention* or the effects of law enforcement on the level of criminal activity. In fact, we assume here that the level and type of criminal activity is completely exogenous. The schedule of fines is also taken to be exogenous. The state is interested in the degree of law enforcement as measured by the revenue generated from fine collection.

Two important aspects of the incentive problem for law enforcers may be distinguished. These aspects correspond to two distinct interpretations of the agent's action a, and the exogenous random variable θ (recall that a and θ jointly determine the payoff x). In the first, the effort of the enforcer can be interpreted as his level of investment in crime detection and apprehension capabilities and the levels of activities such as patrolling, etc. These decisions must occur *before* θ, *the level of crime activity, is known.* In this case, the problem is to provide, in an efficient contract, the proper incentives for investment in crime detection and apprehension capabilities. This problem may be analyzed using Model 1, since the agent's action (investment and patrolling) is taken before the realization of the exogenous random state (level of criminal activity).

In the second interpretation, the random state θ is the type of crimes committed, the identities of the criminals, and other details associated with the crimes (for example, evidence, etc.). The action of the enforcer *a* is the effort expended in apprehending the criminals, creating cases, and the extent to which the enforcer refrains from engaging in malfeasance (for example, taking bribes, etc.). We assume for the purpose of this analysis that the enforcer knows all the details of the crimes (including the identities of the criminals) before taking his action. Society, as represented by the state, may or may not know these details. In any case, we assume contracts are agreed upon before crimes are committed. This version of the problem can be analyzed using Model 2.

Our results indicate the following:

i) With regard to the first problem, suppose the level of criminal activity can be observed *ex post*, both by the state and by enforcers. In this case, it follows from Propositions 1 and 2 that the optimal contract specifies that the state receives an amount which depends only on the level of criminal activity. In particular, the state specifies a standard for the revenue generated by enforcement activities contingent on the level of criminal activity. It then receives a certain share of this standard revenue while enforcers receive the remainder of the standard revenue plus any revenues generated in excess of the standard (or minus any shortfall of actual revenue from standard revenue). Essentially, the optimal arrangement is equivalent to one in which the state specifies a given level of investment in enforcement capability and enforcers accept full responsibility for any deviations from this level.

Regarding the second problem, when both the state and enforcers can observe the particulars of the crimes which occur, Propositions 1 and 2 imply essentially the same result but with a slightly different interpretation. Here the state specifies a total amount to be recovered by the enforcer, contingent on the particular circumstances of the crimes which have occurred. The state receives a share of this specified amount, independent of the enforcer's action. The enforcer receives the remainder of the specified amount, plus or minus any deviation of the actual amount recovered from the specified amount. All consequences of malfeasance are borne by the enforcer.

ii) If law enforcers are risk neutral, as assumed by Becker and Stigler, the Pareto optimal contract in both interpretations specifies that enforcers receive the entire payoff minus, perhaps, some constant. This follows directly from Proposition 3 and is similar to Becker and Stigler's second suggestion. In this case, enforcers purchase for a fixed amount the right to enforce laws and collect fines. There is no point in observing either the enforcer's action or the random state when the enforcers are risk neutral.

iii) If law enforcers are risk averse, contracts which depend only on the revenue generated may be inefficient. In the second interpretation, by Proposition 3, Pareto-superior results can be achieved if the particulars of the crimes committed can be observed by both parties. In this case the particular form of the Pareto optimal contract is as described in (i). Also, if there is a one-to-one relationship between the payoff and the crimes committed for any given action by the enforcer, then Pareto-superior results can be obtained if the enforcer's action can be observed.

In the first interpretation, Pareto-superior results can be achieved if either the action or the level of criminal activity can be observed by both parties. Moreover there are potential gains to monitoring (imperfectly) the activities of enforcers including detection of shirking. Under certain conditions on the monitoring technology, forcing contracts will be Pareto optimal. Under this type of contract, the enforcer would receive an amount which depends on the payoff if monitoring reveals that his action is "acceptable" (for example, there was no shirking). If his action is found to be unacceptable, he would receive a smaller amount or pay a penalty. This contract is similar to the first method suggested by Becker and Stigler, in which enforcers are required to post a bond. In order for such an arrangement to be Pareto superior to compensation which depends only on the revenue, the state must possess means of detecting unacceptable performance by enforcers which have low probabilities of error. The restrictions on the quality of the detection mechanism needed to guarantee Pareto superiority of the Becker-Stigler proposal are quite severe.

REFERENCES

A. Alchian and H. Demsetz, "Production, Information Costs, and Economic Organization," *Amer. Econ. Rev.*, Dec. 1972, *62*, 777–95.

Kenneth J. Arrow, *Essays in the Theory of Risk Bearing,* Chicago 1970.

G. S. Becker and G. J. Stigler, "Law Enforcement, Malfeasance, and Compensation of Enforcers," *J. Legal Stud.*, Jan. 1974, *3*, 1–18.

M. Harris and A. Raviv, "Optimal Incentive Contracts with Imperfect Information," Grad. Sch. Ind. Adm., work. paper no. 70-75-76, Carnegie-Mellon Univ., April 1976.

C. M. Jensen and W. H. Meckling, "Theory of the Firm: Managerial Behavior, Agency Costs and Ownership Structure," *J. Finan. Econ.*, Oct. 1976, *3*, 305–60.

M. V. Pauly, "The Economics of Moral Hazard," *Amer. Econ. Rev.*, June 1968, *58*, 531–37.

———, "Idemnity Insurance for Health Care Efficiency," *Econ. Bus. Bull.*, Fall 1971, *24*, 53–59.

J. G. Riley, "Competitive Signalling," *J. Econ. Theory*, Apr. 1975, *10*, 174–86.

S. A. Ross, "The Economic Theory of Agency: The Principal's Problem," *Amer. Econ. Rev. Proc.*, May 1973, *63*, 134–39.

A. Michael Spence, *Market Signaling: Information Transfer in Hiring and Related Processes*, Cambridge, Mass. 1973.

———, "Competitive and Optimal Responses to Signals: An Analysis of Efficiency and Distribution," *J. Econ. Theory,* Mar. 1974, *8*, 1296–332.

———, "Competition in Salaries, Credentials, and Signaling Prerequisites for Jobs," *Quart. J. Econ.*, Feb. 1976, *90*, 51–74.

——— **and R. Zeckhauser,** "Insurance, Information, and Individual Action," *Amer. Econ. Rev. Proc.*, May 1971, *61*, 380–87.

J. E. Stiglitz, (1975a) "Incentives, Risk and Information: Notes Toward a Theory of Hierarchy," *Bell J. Econ.*, Autumn 1975, *6*, 552–79.

———, (1975b) "The Theory of 'Screening', Education, and Distribution of Income," *Amer. Econ. Rev.*, June 1975, *65*, 283–300.

R. M. Townsend, "Efficient Contracts with Costly State Verification," Grad. Sch. Ind. Admin., work. paper no. 14-77-78, Carnegie-Mellon Univ. 1976.

R. B. Wilson, "On the Theory of Syndicates," *Econometrica*, Jan. 1968, *36*, 119–32.

———, "The Structure of Incentives for Decentralization Under Uncertainty," in *La Decision*, Paris 1969.

R. Zeckhauser, "Medical Insurance: A Case Study of the Tradeoff between Risk Spreading and Appropriate Incentives," *J. Econ. Theory*, Mar. 1970, *2*, 10–26.

III

Application to Financial Accounting

THIRD LECTURE

JOEL S. DEMSKI

Our goal in this final session of the seminar is to extend our analysis to financial reporting questions. The principal-agent model remains a central idea, but in general we have multiple agents, multiple principals, and multiple periods.

The discussion proceeds in three stages. Initially we reflect on "qualitative" concerns that arise when we begin to look seriously at a market for information. We then review what is known about incentives for private versus public production of information, such as financial statistics. Regulatory concerns and the Arrow Paradox conclude our discussion.

The Market for Information

To develop our intuitive understanding, consider several allocation scenarios. If a large decentralized firm centrally produces some important factor such as power we would not be surprised to see a transfer price mechanism being employed. Similiar comments apply to technical engineering services, but not to economic analysis. Likewise, we would be quite surprised to see a sophisticated management information system in which managers were directly charged for each query. Conversely, we feel comfortable with a market-based allocation of management consultants; and we also prefer a market mechanism in personal health (we prefer to pick our family physician). Yet we were deeply distressed (I hope) by the information market assumption in the Kihlstrom [1974] paper.

At a casual level, then, we are suspicious of market solutions to information production decisions when resale of information is a possibility. (There is also a tendency to think that value is problematic because you never observe the signal until after you have paid, but our earlier discussions should have dispelled this concern.) We also become suspicious of market solutions when "unfair" advantage is taken. We tend, for example, to frown on insider trading. And the idea of "protecting" unsophisticated investors is far from novel in our literature (see Beaver [1977], for example). Other concerns could also be mentioned, but this is sufficient to motivate our discussion. The thought I want to leave you with here is that we have begun to carefully examine these concerns using the basic ideas expressed in our previous sessions, but (as usual) much work remains.

To begin reviewing our progress, recall the standard neoclassical-based market failure story (as in Appendix 8.1 of Demski and Feltham [1976]). We used the example in which consumption by one individual of, say, beer produces an unwanted external effect on another.[1] Without joint negotiation, creation and enforcement of pollution rights, corrective taxation, central allocation, or some sort of corrective "mechanism," the unaided-market solution is inefficient. Both individuals can be made better off by, say, having the second pay the first to consume less beer. And we summarize the situation with the somewhat casual comment that the unaided-market solution results in overconsumption of the offending good.[2]

One observation that we can make immediately is to apply this to the production of information. Public dissemination of financial information may benefit "outsiders." If so, we would (by applying the above analysis) expect underproduction of financial information. Similarly, our patent policy has been defended on grounds of providing incentives to produce a public good. Beaver's [1977] discussion is excellent here, and the point should be clear: by applying the standard market failure analysis, we confirm the underproduction suspicion. (Note, however, that no empirical analysis has been offered, and the argument has proceeded by analogy—an equilibrium model has not been formally massaged in producing this conclusion.)

The next step in the story is Hirshleifer's [1971] discovery of a possible distributive effect. The basic idea is probably best illustrated by Hirshleifer's example, an economy of *identical* individuals and three commodities:

(1) current corn: x_0;

(2) future corn if s^1 obtains: x_1^1;

(3) future corn if s^2 obtains: x_1^2.

With $\phi(s^1) = .6$, $E(U|x) = lnx_0 + .6ln\,x_1^1 + .4ln\,x_1^2$. Letting the price vector be $P = (P^0, P^1, P^2)$, each consumer's allocation problem is then described by

$$\max ln\,x_0 + .6\,ln\,x_1^1 + .4ln\,x_1^2$$
$$\text{s.t. } x_0 P^0 + x_1^1 P^1 + x_1^2 P^2 \leq W,$$

where $W = P^0 \bar{x}_0 + P^1 \bar{x}_1^1 + P^2 \bar{x}_1^2$ in the pure exchange economy at hand. Further, suppose the endowments are:

$$\bar{x}_0 = 100,$$
$$\bar{x}_1^1 = 200,$$
$$\bar{x}_1^2 = 80.$$

Equating supply and demand we readily see that

$$x_0^* = \bar{x}_0 = 100, \quad \text{with} \quad P^0 = 1,$$
$$x_1^{1*} = \bar{x}_1^1 = 200, \quad \text{with} \quad P^1 = .3,$$
$$x_1^{2*} = \bar{x}_1^2 = 80, \quad \text{with} \quad P^2 = .5,$$

and $E(U|x^*) = \underline{\underline{9.537.}}$

Now suppose that perfect and costless information is revealed to *all* individuals before the market opens. If s^1 obtains, the resulting price vector is (1, .5, 0), while if s^2 obtains it is (1, 0, 1.25). No trade occurs in either case. Hence, $E(U|\eta^P) = 9.537$.

Alternatively, suppose *one* individual obtains costless and perfect information before the market opens. The equilibrium price vector will be (1, .3, .5) and the optimal consumption schedule is given by

	s^1 obtains	s^2 obtains
x_0	100	100
x_1^1	333 1/3	0
x_1^2	0	200

with $E(U_i|\eta^i) = 10.210 > 9.537$.

How do you interpret this? In this example, the value to society of producing public information is surely zero, while the value to individual i of private information is not. You therefore have information production incentives; and the incentive in this extreme example comes from what has become labeled a distributive effect.

Note that speculating on the information would increase the private returns to individual i.[3] Also ask yourself what would happen if individual i could sell his information. Now combine this thinking with our earlier argument on possible underproduction of financial

→ Stock market: If s^1 occurs we cannot really say that the resulting vector is such and such but we can only say that the ordering of the sequence of prices will change. ↓ we are dealing w/ sequences $\langle E_n \rangle = \langle s_n, \langle P_n \rangle \rangle$ and we are interested in some type of lexicographic choice here.

information. You now have two concerns moving in opposite directions. Indeed, this is the basic point of Hirshleifer's [1971] paper (see his analysis of patent policy).

Finally note that other insights are available here. Suppose we add *one* individual to the basic economy. His only endowment is $\bar{x}_1^2 = 100$ and he believes s^1 will obtain for certain. What happens if public information is produced before the market opens? You should interpret this in light of the Blackwell Theorem. In this example, the opportunity set may vary with the signal; however, that possibility is assumed away in the theorem.

Another variation on this theme is demonstrated in Table 8.8 of Demski and Feltham [1976]. All individuals in the economy *oppose* the production of information before trading because such information destroys mutual insurance possibilities. (In a casual sense, suppose two of you are willing to bet on a horse race but a third wants to reveal the outcome *before* you bet. . . .) Indeed, when you consider asymmetrically informed agents you encounter this insurance phenomenon because the trades you will agree to may (if you aren't careful) reveal what you know and thereby destroy whatever advantage knowing it conferred.

By way of summary, we have established Theorem 7:

THEOREM 7. *Consider an economy and three costless information structures: η^o (null), η^i (private to individual), and η^P. Then*

$$E(U_i|\eta^i) \geq E(U_i|\eta^o); \quad \textit{and}$$
$$E(U_i|\eta^P) \lesseqqgtr E(U_i|\eta^o).$$

Note, however, that η^i is strictly private here. Others do not know i is accessing η^i (see Baiman [1975], for example).

This leads to the next step which is *market efficiency,* as the term is used in the finance literature. The casual idea here is that the market is efficient with respect to some information if that information is fully reflected by the equilibrium prices—which gives rise to the fair game interpretation. A more precise explanation is to say that the market is efficient with respect to some information if the prices are the same as in the case where everyone possessed their existing information as well as the information in question.

Two questions now come to mind. First ask yourself what this means. I think a more precise interpretation is as follows: we have some *mechanism* (casually called the market) that produces an equilibrium. Individuals access private information structures, η^i. The mechanism is then efficient with respect to η if the prices that would prevail under the η^i structures are identical to those that would prevail under the (η^i, η) structures. Do you agree with this?

Second, ask yourself how this could ever happen. To convey the idea of recent work, I offer here the following example that is inspired by the Kihlstrom and Mirman article [1975].

We have an economy of identical *pairs* of individuals. The structure is the same as in our previous example from Hirshleifer [1971], except that the current period is irrelevant and the endowments are:

	$i = 1$	$i = 2$
$\bar{x}_0$	0	0
$\bar{x}_1^1$	10	0
$\bar{x}_1^2$	0	10

with $\phi(s^1) = \phi(s^2) = 1/2$ and $E(U_i|x) = \phi(s^1)\, ln\, x_1^1 + \phi(s^2)\, ln\, x_1^2$.

It is readily apparent that with no information (η^0), the equilibrium holdings are (5, 5) and $P^1 = 1$, $P^2 = 1$ is the equilibrium price vector.

Now suppose that public information can be produced before the market opens. If y^1 is observed, $i = 1$ shifts his beliefs to $\phi(s^1|y^1, \eta^P) = .8$, while under y^2, $\phi(s^1|y^2, \eta^P) = .2$. $i = 2$ moves in the same direction, but not as far: $\phi(s^1|y^1, \eta^P) = .6$ and $\phi(s^1|y^2, \eta^P) = .4$. ($Y = \{y^1, y^2\}$ and you may interpret the story in terms of $\phi(y^1) = \phi(y^2) = .5$ for $i = 1, 2$, etc.)

If y^1 obtains, the price vector will be $P^1 = 1$, $P^2 = 1/3$; however, if y^2 obtains the equilibrium price vector will be $P^1 = 1$, $P^2 = 2$, with the following pattern of consumption:

	y^1 obtains		y^2 obtains	
Prices	1	1/3	1	2
$i = 1$ (consumption)	8	6	2	4
$i = 2$ (consumption)	2	4	8	6

Now suppose $i = 1$ obtains the information, while $i = 2$ remains uninformed. Both continue in the mode of classic price takers. If y^1 obtains, the price vector will be $P^1 = 1$, $P^2 = .4$, while under y^2 we would have $P^1 = 1$, $P^2 = 1.6$, with the following pattern of consumption:

	y^1 obtains		y^2 obtains	
Prices	1	.4	1	1.6
$i = 1$	8	5	2	5
$i = 2$	2	5	8	5

Note the pattern that emerges. If $i = 1$ becomes informed and behaves in the usual price-taking manner, the equilibrium prices will reveal (perfectly in this case) his private information. The mechanism here could be efficient with respect to private information produced by the $i = 1$ individuals. Two implications should be pondered. First, the Hirshleifer analysis raises the question of possible overproduction of information. This suggests that individuals attempting to capitalize on private gains may indeed reveal their information. (In fact, this is in some sense the idea of a rational expectations equilibrium.) Second, individuals may learn from prices (and prices don't condition beliefs in Demski and Feltham [1976, Chapter 8] or in Hirshleifer's [1971] paper). You should now ask what this does to our overall information production analysis. Does price reveal quality? (E.g., consider a wine shop. . . .)

Finally, notice the relative "cleverness" of the two groups in the above story: $i = 1$ is a price taker while $i = 2$ is actually using the equilibrium price to reveal $i = 1$'s information. You may interpret this as $i = 1$ having private information but not knowing that $i = 2$ knows of such access. So the next question is whether something more "sophisticated" can be said. This is an open question, but the idea is illustrated by the Ponssard and Zamir [1973] work summarized in Appendix 8.2 of Demski and Feltham [1976]. A simple zero-sum game is being played, but the outcome structure is uncertain:

	s^1 obtains			s^2 obtains	
	c	d		c	d
a	2.5	−2	a	1	10
b	12	0	b	0	4

where the illustrated payoffs go to the row player.

The catch here is that row goes first *and* column observes row's move before making his move. Also, row has perfect information. He would like to pick b under s^1 and a under s^2, but this reveals his information. Can he do better? What do we do in poker? It turns out that our casual bluffing, bluff-calling idea is an equilibrium in this game. In particular, let $\phi(s^1) = 1/8$. The equilibrium solution is for row to play "honestly" 4/7 of the time, and 3/7 of the time to pick b regardless of which state obtains. In response, column's best play is to "believe" that row's choice signals the state 1/4 of the time and simply select c 3/4 of the time. Contrast this with the above price story. That is, suppose the $i = 1$ group knew that all market participants knew they were informed. Is price-taking behavior optimal at this point? To my knowledge this is an open question.

We see, then, that introducing information production possibilities into a general equilibrium setting raises numerous questions. The analysis is far from complete (such as precise modeling of an efficient market) and the work to date is ambiguous on the issue of allocative efficiency. Equally sparse is the empirical side. With this in mind, we conclude with a review of regulatory questions.

Information and Regulation

The regulation story has two chapters, loosely referred to as "goals" and "mechanism." The goals question is simple to state and impossible to solve. In a very simple sense suppose we have convinced ourselves that efficiency gains are available through some sort of cooperative effort. We might, that is, be at point x, as shown in Exhibit 3.1. The goal question is where, on the PO surface, should we aspire to be. To fall short of the surface is foolish and to go beyond the surface is infeasible. (Further note that, in the limit, a pure equity issue could be involved here.) Similarly, staying within the distinguished area of the surface leads both participants to more preferred circumstances. But *where* should we aspire to be?

We approach problems at the individual level by measuring preferences and then applying optimization theory. Indeed, we have filled many hours (and academic careers) doing just that. But accepting Arrow's [1963] *formulation* of the problem and his *axioms* denies us the route at the social choice level.

The setting is straightforward. We have a set of choices A and distinguish the set of all complete and transitive binary relations

Exhibit 3.1

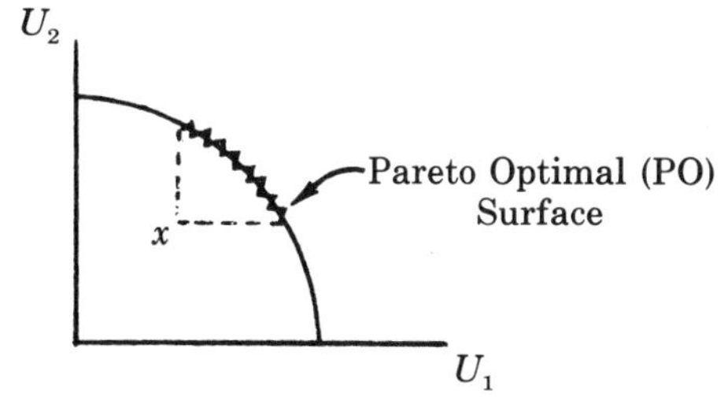

$\mathcal{R}$ = {binary relations on A|complete and transitive}. We then have a finite set of individuals $i = 1, \ldots, n$, each characterized by $\succcurlyeq \in \mathcal{R}$. $\succcurlyeq$ is interpreted as i's preference ranking, but note that we say nothing about whether i is selfish, whether a is a lottery, etc. Finally, we characterize *social preference* with a function $f\colon \times_{i=1}^{n} \mathcal{R} \rightarrow \mathcal{R}$.[4]

We now impose four axioms in an effort to rule out some of the possibilities.

Universal Domain (UD). With $|A| \geqslant 3$ and $n \geqslant 2$, f must provide a complete and transitive ranking regardless of $\succcurlyeq_i \in \mathcal{R}$.

Pareto Optimality (PO). $x \succcurlyeq_i y \ \forall_i \rightarrow x \succ_i y$.

Universal domain and pareto optimality specify that a solution must exist and must be on the Pareto surface. The next two axioms address the equity question of where on that surface we should be.

Independence of Irrelevant Alternatives (IIA). Let $C(A) = \{a \in A | a \succcurlyeq a^1 \ \forall a^1 \in A\}$. Consider $(\succcurlyeq_1, \ldots, \succcurlyeq_n)$ and $(\succcurlyeq'_1, \ldots, \succcurlyeq'_n)$ and respective choice sets $C(\bar{A})$ and $C'(\bar{A})$ for $\bar{A} \subset A$.

$a^1 \succcurlyeq_i a^2 \leftrightarrow a^1 \succcurlyeq^1_i a^2$;
$\forall_i = 1, \ldots, n$; and
$\forall a^1, a^2 \in \bar{A}$.

Then $C(\bar{A}) = C'(\bar{A})$.

Nondictatorship (ND). There does not exist some individual j such that $\succcurlyeq_j = \succcurlyeq$ for all $(\succcurlyeq_1, \ldots, \succcurlyeq_n) \in \mathcal{R} \times \ldots \times \mathcal{R}$.

THEOREM 8 (ARROW). *The set of collective choice rules $f(\cdot)$ that satisfies these four axioms is null.*[5]

Working through the proof is an excellent exercise. *Pareto optimality* guarantees that there is some *decisive group* which always gets its way when the $\succcurlyeq_i$ line up. And as everything is finite there is, in fact, a minimum decisive group. Now exercising *independence of irrelevant alternatives* and *universal domain* implies that one individual is decisive for everything.

We could, at this point, engage in extensive discussion concerning various alternative attempts to rationalize social choice. It seems worthwhile, however, to briefly mention one tack, the dropping of universal domain. Somewhat casually, we appear to have a situation in financial reporting in which interest groups get their way if they are sufficiently "powerful." This is the central idea in the Watts and Zimmerman [1978] "positive theory" article. Can we represent such behavior?

Let $I = \{1, \ldots, n\}$ be the set of individuals and $c \subset I$, a *coalition.* We say that $a \succsim_c a'$ if $a \succsim a'$ for all $i \in c$. Now let $\bar{c}(a, a')$ be the set of all coalitions that have sufficient "power" to force choice or ranking of a over a'. We assume $\bar{c}(\cdot)$ is nonempty for all a, a'. The idea, then, is to focus on the conjunction of *power* and *preference*:

$$a \succsim a' \leftrightarrow a \succsim_c a' \quad \text{for some } c \in \bar{c}(a, a'). \qquad (*)$$

That is, $\succsim$ is defined by $a \succsim_c a'$ only if some powerful coalition has aligned member preferences. This has (in my mind) considerable descriptive appeal at the anecdotal level, but it nevertheless sounds *ad hoc.* It turns out, however, that it is equivalent to a "reasonable" set of axioms. In particular, let the social preference for (a, a') under $\succsim_1, \ldots, \succsim_n$ be denoted $F(\succsim_1, \succsim_2, \ldots, \succsim_n; a, a')$ where $F(\cdot)$ is either $a \succ a'$, $a \sim a'$, $a' \succ a$, or a and a' noncomparable. The axioms are:

PO': $a \succsim_I a' \rightarrow a \succsim a'$ and $a \succ_I a' \rightarrow a \succ a'$.

IIA': If $a \succsim_i a' \leftrightarrow a \succsim'_i a'$ for all i, then $F(\succsim_1, \ldots, \succsim_n; a, a') = F(\succsim'_1, \ldots, \succsim'_n; a, a')$.

(This is not quite as strong as IIA.)

Nonpositive Responsiveness (NPR): Suppose $a \succsim a'$ obtains under $\succsim_1, \ldots, \succsim_n$. If the set strictly preferring a' over a does not grow in $\succsim'_1, \ldots, \succsim'_n$, then $a \succsim' a'$.

THEOREM 9 (BLOOMFIELD, 1976):[6] *Social choice is represented by (*) if and only if it respects PO', IIA', and NPR.*

The structure of the proof is not difficult. For necessity, if $a \succsim a'$ obtains, we have some $c \in \bar{c}(a, a')$ such that $a \succsim_c a'$ and this readily provides the three axioms. (Note that coalitions behave in a "normal" way: $a \succsim_c a'$ and $a \succsim_{\hat{c}} a' \rightarrow a \succsim_{c \cup \hat{c}} a'$ as well as $a \succsim_d a'$ for any $d \subset c$.)

For sufficiency, if $a \succsim a'$ obtains we must have $a \succsim_c a'$ for some c. Otherwise $a' \succ_i a$ for all i. In turn, the maximal such coalition is surely decisive and we easily move from here to arrive at (*). We see more of this structure in our discussion of the Beaver and Demski [1974] objectives paper.

The mechanism question is, in many respects, intertwined with

$\succsim$. It is, of course, important to remember to include the cost of any mechanism in our thinking. But more important, I suspect, is the information question. Somewhat narrowly, suppose we agree somehow on $F(\cdot)$ and then rely on some group such as the FASB to implement it. We must then somehow communicate $\succsim_i$. This gets us back to the problems discussed in the second lecture as well as to moral hazard auditing on the regulations themselves.[7]

Notes

1. See Demski and Feltham [1976], Table 8.2.
2. The extreme public good version of this phenomenon is illustrated in Table 8.3 of Demski and Feltham [1976].
3. You should study Hirschleifer's [1971] article and Appendix 8.3 in Demski and Feltham [1976] before concluding that this result is driven by a lack of production or an absence of homogeneous beliefs. A paper by Hakansson, Kunkel, and Ohlson [1979] conclusively answers the question of information value in pure exchange settings.
4. An example from Luce and Raiffa [1957] may be instructive. Consider a society of two individuals, 1 and 2, whose preferences for two alternatives, x and y, are listed in columns 1 and 2. Columns f_1, f_2, f_3, and f_4 represent possible ways of combining the individuals' choices into a social preference pattern. For example, in procedure f_3, the choice of the society depends only upon individual 1's choice, and individual 2's choice has no impact.

Domain

$i = 1$	$i = 2$	f_1	f_2	f_3	f_4
$x > y$	$x > y$	$x > y$	$y > x$	$x > y$	$y > x$
$x > y$	$y > x$	$x \sim y$	$y > x$	$x > y$	$x \sim y$
$x > y$	$x \sim y$	$x > y$	$y > x$	$x > y$	$y > x$
$y > x$	$x > y$	$x \sim y$	$y > x$	$y > x$	$x \sim y$
$y > x$	$y > x$	$y > x$	$y > x$	$y > x$	$x > y$
$y > x$	$x \sim y$	$y > x$	$y > x$	$y > x$	$x > y$
$x \sim y$	$x > y$	$x > y$	$y > x$	$x \sim y$	$y > x$
$x \sim y$	$y > x$	$y > x$	$y > x$	$x \sim y$	$x > y$
$x \sim y$	$x \sim y$	$x \sim y$	$y > x$	$x \sim y$	$x > y$

5. See Arrow [1962], Quirk and Saposnik [1968], and Sen [1970].
6. Also see Bloomfield and Wilson [1973].
7. Also see Groves [1973] and Green and Laffont [1979] for discussions of incentive issues.

References

Arrow, K. *Social Choice and Individual Values,* Cowles Foundation Monograph #12. New York: John Wiley & Sons, 1963.

Baiman, S. "The Evaluation and Choice of Internal Information Systems within a Multiperson World." *Journal of Accounting Research,* Spring 1975.

Beaver, W. "The Relevance of a Mandated Disclosure System." In *Report of the Advisory Committee on Corporate Disclosure.* Washington, D.C.: Securities and Exchange Commission, 1977.

Beaver, W. H., and Demski, J. S. "The Nature of Financial Accounting Objectives: A Summary and Synthesis." *Studies on Financial Accounting Objectives: 1974, Journal of Accounting Research Supplement,* 1974.

Bloomfield, S. "A Social Choice Interpretation of the von Neumann-Morgenstern Game." *Econometrica,* Jan. 1976.

———, and Wilson, R. "The Postulates of Game Theory." *Journal of Mathematical Sociology,* July, 1973.

Demski, J., and Feltham, G. *Cost Determination: A Conceptual Approach.* Ames, Iowa: Iowa State University Press, 1976.

Green, J., and Laffont, J. *Incentives in Public Decision Making.* New York: North Holland, 1979.

Groves, T. "Incentives in Teams." *Econometrica,* July 1973.

Hakansson, N.; Kunkel, J.; and Ohlson, J. "Sufficient and Necessary Conditions to Have Social Value in Pure Exchange." Unpublished working paper. Berkeley: University of California, 1979.

Hirshleifer, J. "The Private and Social Value of Information and the Reward to Inventive Activity." *American Economic Review,* Sept. 1971.

Kihlstrom, R. "A Bayesian Model of Demand for Information about Product Quality." *International Economic Review,* Feb. 1974.

———, and Mirman, L. J. "Information and Market Equilibrium." *Bell Journal of Economics,* Spring 1975.

Luce, R. D., and Raiffa, H. *Games and Decisions.* New York: John Wiley & Sons, 1957.

Ponssard, J., and Zamir, S. "Zero-Sum Sequential Games with Incomplete Information." *International Journal of Game Theory,* 1973.

Quirk, J., and Saposnik, R. *Introduction to General Equilibrium Theory and Welfare Economics.* New York: McGraw-Hill, 1968.

Sen, A. K. *Collective Choice and Social Welfare.* San Francisco: Holden-Day, 1970.

Watts, R., and Zimmerman, J. "Towards a Positive Theory of the Determination of Accounting Standards." *The Accounting Review,* Jan. 1978.

Journal of Accounting Research
1974 Supplement

The Nature of Financial Accounting Objectives: A Summary and Synthesis

WILLIAM H. BEAVER AND JOEL S. DEMSKI*

The nature and the specification of financial accounting objectives are issues that recently have received considerable attention. Nontrivial resources have been expended by public accounting firms and by the AICPA Objectives Committee, among others, in attempting to specify what these illusive objectives might, or should, be.

There seems to be a consensus that the primary purpose of financial reporting is to provide information to financial statement users. Yet, the basic, fundamental role of objectives within this utilitarian, user-primacy framework remains obscure—largely, we speculate, because the problem of heterogeneous users has not been forcefully addressed. That is, explicit recognition of irreconcilable conflicts of interest among user classes (or users) provides the key element in defining the objectives issue.

A basic purpose of this summary and synthesis, then, is to offer a view of the nature and role of financial accounting objectives that explicitly rests on heterogeneous users. The argument is presented in six stages. Initially, we provide a summary description of the problem of selecting among competing financial accounting alternatives. In the second section we explicitly formulate the user-primacy or utilitarian notion. Following this is a discussion of the basic nature of objectives. We then discuss the role of accounting research in this scheme, analyze the papers presented at this conference in terms of the framework developed, and finally explore some areas for further research on the objectives issue.

* Stanford University

Choice Among Financial Reporting Alternatives

Numerous alternative financial accounting procedures are often available and, presumably, the role of a policy agent, such as the FASB, is to single out those alternatives that are "desirable" or "acceptable."[1] Recognizing that different alternatives may produce different outcomes, we view this determination of the desirable or acceptable alternatives as a decision problem. Further recognizing that numerous individuals may be affected by these choices, we view this decision problem as a multiperson or social choice problem.

To pursue this orientation, we provide a brief description of the outcomes that may be associated with adoption of one financial reporting procedure as opposed to another. This, of course, requires initially a focus on individual users of financial reports.

THE INVESTOR-DECISION SETTING

For obvious reasons, we term the financial statement user an investor. The individual investor faces a multiperiod consumption-investment decision where his opportunity set is constrained by his wealth. Adopting a conventional expected utility characterization of this decision process, we view the investor as assessing a probability distribution over future states of nature.

Within this setting are a variety of reasons why investor consensus or unanimity may not exist regarding which information should be produced. For example, the precise incidence of the cost of producing a particular set of public information is an open question; investors may agree on the information's relevance but are likely to disagree as to who should bear its cost. At a more fundamental level, heterogeneous opinions may ensure disagreement as to what is relevant. And, in such an event, providing special purpose reports to those in disagreement may lead to more disagreement, because the value of information to one individual may depend on what information other individuals possess.

As becomes evident, we cannot rely on a single, isolated investor in our description of the investor setting. In a multiperson setting, financial statement information may affect both production and exchange sectors of an economy. In the exchange setting, information manifests itself in at least two respects: (1) the exchange of securities among individual investors and (2) the prices at which those securities trade (which in turn determines the wealth of each investor). The manner in which financial statement information will be reflected in trading and in prices will be a function of

---

[1] We initially focus on a policy group such as the FASB for expositional convenience. At a very fundamental level, the question of what institutional mechanism should be employed remains unsettled (and unresearched).

the structure of the securities market; it will involve such factors as transaction costs, information costs, and alternative sources of information.[2]

In the productive sector we note that financial statement information may affect the choice of productive alternatives and, therefore, the aggregate supply in the economy.[3] From our standpoint, it is sufficient to recognize that these productive consequences must be addressed in choosing among alternative financial reporting schemes. (Disclosure issues provide a ready illustration.)

To sum up, tracing the possible outcomes associated with alternative financial reporting policies requires a focus on production and exchange sectors. Different individuals may be affected in differing ways by alternative policies. Indeed, noninvestors, as well as nonusers, may be affected. Since our goal is to provide a view of the objectives problem that explicitly recognizes outcomes associated with these individuals, we require a convenient, compact description of their relevant individual characteristics. This is provided in the following subsection.

ALGEBRA OF CHOICE

One way to describe individual characteristics is to represent preferences with a binary preference relation. We let I denote the set of individuals and $\mathcal{H}$ the set of financial reporting alternatives. Consider any pair of alternatives, η and $\eta' \in \mathcal{H}$. If individual $i \in I$ regards reporting alternative η as at least as good as alternative η', we denote this $\eta V_i \eta'$. A ready mnemonic characterization is η is "as valuable as" η' to individual i.[4]

To illustrate, suppose individual i regards price level adjusted income (η) as at least as valuable as a conventional income measure (η') in selecting among alternative investment options. We denote this fact by $\eta V_i \eta'$. Observe, now, that this V_i representation device encodes all of the individual's opinions about the financial reporting alternatives. Precisely how these opinions are formed, or what their major determinants are, need not concern us for the moment; our basic concern is representation of these, essentially exogenous, preferences.

Moving on, we employ the same basic representation device at the social level. If alternative η is at least as desirable, or valuable, as alternative η', we represent this by $\eta V \eta'$. Alternatively, if η is *not* as desirable as η', we represent this by *not* $\eta V \eta'$. Quite clearly, then, for any two alternatives

[2] The structure of the market will also bear on the issue of the optimal form of information regulation (e.g., whether the market mechanism should be used to make information decisions in the economy).

[3] The nature of these productive effects and their impact on the incentives for information production have been discussed by Arrow [1962], Hirshleifer [1971], and Demsetz [1969], among others.

[4] More formally, V_i is a subset of $\mathcal{H} \times \mathcal{H}$. We can think of it as encoding the individual's preferences in terms of pair-wise comparisons of all $\eta, \eta' \in \mathcal{H}$. Further discussion can be found in Arrow [1963], Ijiri [1967], and Sen [1970].

we have one regarded as as good as the other and vice versa (*indifference*), one regarded as as good as the other but not vice versa (*strict preference*), or neither regarded as as good as the other (*noncomparability*).

Suppose, now, that we must decide some specific issue, such as the acceptable or desirable method(s) for measuring a land development firm's income. We let $\bar{\mathcal{H}} \subset \mathcal{H}$ denote the set of viable alternatives and $\bar{\bar{\mathcal{H}}} \subset \bar{\mathcal{H}}$ the set of acceptable or desirable methods. This set of desirable methods is, of course, represented by the V relation. If alternative η is one of the methods singled out as desirable, it must (by definition) be as good as the other viable alternatives. Hence,

$$\bar{\bar{\mathcal{H}}} = C(\bar{\mathcal{H}}, V) = \{\eta \in \bar{\mathcal{H}} \,|\, \eta V \eta' \text{ or not } \eta' V \eta \text{ for all } \eta' \in \bar{\mathcal{H}}\}$$

where the $C(\bar{\mathcal{H}}, V)$ notation explicates the fact that we are selecting the best members of $\bar{\mathcal{H}}$ with respect to the primitive desirability ordering represented by V.

Whatever opinions individuals hold, or whatever desirability pronouncements regulatory agencies or accounting theory make, then, can be represented with an appropriate binary relation.

We now use this representation device to formulate, in the next two sections, the financial accounting objectives issue.

Utilitarianism

It is generally agreed that financial accounting ought to provide useful information to those who use the resulting data. The AICPA Objectives Committee Report on *Objectives of Financial Statements* [1973], for example, states:

> The basic objective of financial statements is to provide information useful for making economic decisions. (P. 13)

In a simplistic sense, the information must be useful to those who use it (otherwise it will not be used and its production would needlessly consume resources).

However, the usefulness edict cannot be regarded as monolithic in formulating the problem of choosing among financial accounting methods. In particular, it seems clear that we must be more inclusive in our analysis and look beyond those who actually receive the accounting data. For example, it is a straightforward exercise to demonstrate a setting in which all who receive the data are indifferent between η and η' but those who do not receive the data will be severely harmed if η as opposed to η' is used. Hence, we regard I as encompassing all individuals, regardless of their user status. Directly or indirectly they may be affected by choice between η and η'; and we therefore recognize individual preferences between η and η', regardless of whether they actually receive the respective data.

Whether one system is more valuable than another to some individual depends, of course, on a variety of factors. What choice options are available, what resource dispositions may be affected, and the individual's beliefs and attitudes are all relevant at this point. Extensive discussion of the determinants of value to individual i is beyond our present scope.[5] Rather, our concern is with the relationship between individual value, encoded in V_i, and the public reporting alternatives that are deemed appropriate. In short, V must—in some basic sense—depend on the V_i. If everyone were to regard cash basis accounting as useless for financial reporting then it ought not to be used.

This as yet unspecified dependence or relationship between V and the V_i can be represented by a function, f:

$$V = f(V_1, \ldots, V_i, \ldots, V_I) .$$

Precisely how V should depend on the individual V_i is an open question. Pareto optimality is, of course, a close to unassailable requirement. That is, if $\eta V_i \eta'$ holds for *all* I individuals it would certainly be capricious to deny $\eta V \eta'$. Indeed, this would amount to a resource allocation scheme based on systematically denying people what they want.

Pareto optimality is, therefore, a relatively acceptable notion to impose on the specification of $f(\cdot)$. It may well be that many existing controversies can be resolved by invoking this criterion alone. Unfortunately, however, this does not completely resolve our problem because choice among many alternatives harms some individuals and benefits others. For example, many disclosure issues fall into this category. Such cases are strictly noncomparable from a Pareto optimality point of view. These types of choices must, however, be made; and it is in guiding these types of choices that objectives have a significant role to play.

Role of Objectives

A utilitarian view requires that V depend in some manner on value at the individual level, or V_i. Pareto optimality is a natural, though incomplete, requirement to impose on the relationship between the V_i and V. Beyond these noncontroversial observations we must be more specific in addressing the question of how V should depend on the V_i.

Further specification of the relationship between V_i and V can take a number of forms. We might, for example, insist that whatever relationship is specified must not result in any indeterminant cases. This requires that V be such that $C(\bar{\mathcal{H}}, V)$ be nonempty for all nonempty subsets of $\mathcal{H}$. Al-

---

[5] With consistent behavior represented by the expected utility hypothesis, we model information use in terms of individual probability revision. The demand for information is, therefore, a derived demand, reflecting—ultimately—the information's ability to increase the individual's (primitive) well-being. Discussion of the basic theory is available in Demski [1972] and Marschak and Radner [1972]. Application to a setting of possibly heterogeneous individuals in a market setting can be found in Hirshleifer [1971], Radner [1968 and 1972], and Demski [1974a and 1974b].

ternatively, we might require that choice between any two alternatives not be influenced by preferences among other alternatives (independence of irrelevant alternatives).

Restriction to a *complete* and *transitive* ordering of $\mathcal{H}$ can, however, cause difficulties. Arrow's impossibility theorem guarantees that restricting all preference relations to weak orders (without further restriction) and imposing nondictatorship, independence of irrelevant alternatives, and Pareto optimality conditions are mutually inconsistent conditions.[6] The set of all $f(\cdot)$ satisfying these conditions is null. As a result, any method of movement from the V_i to V we select is guaranteed to violate some subset of Arrow's conditions. The question, of course, is which condition(s) to violate; presumably the role of objectives is to address this question.

More specifically, the role of objectives is to specify the relationship between the V_i and V that will form the basis for resolution of financial reporting controversies. At a very fundamental level this requires value or ethical judgments as to whose well-being will be traded off—and in what dimensions—for whose. For example, the AICPA Objectives Report states:

> An objective of financial statements is to serve primarily those users who have limited authority, ability, or resources to obtain information. . . . (P. 17)

Precisely which tradeoffs are desirable is, of course, an open question. But the nature of the problem and the fundamental role of objectives seem clear. Objectives are neither necessary nor sufficient conditions for optimality in a narrow sense. Rather, they specify or define the relationship between V_i and V. It is, for example, difficult to conceive of the FASB's making consistent choices without some fundamental conception of the relationship between V_i and V.[7]

Policy Making and the Role of Evidence

With the relationship between V_i and V specified, the financial accounting choice problem becomes more structured. In particular, it assumes a form of appropriately evaluating alternatives and assimilating these evaluations.

An important issue at this point concerns the role of research in movement from the analysis or evidentiary domain to the policy domain. Recent empirical research has, for example, investigated the association between financial statement data and security prices. Such analysis cannot, however,

---

[6] Arrow [1963].

[7] In fact, many possible ways of moving from V_i to V take the form of appropriate constitutional games. See Demski [1974b]; using such an approach, for example, we know the necessary and sufficient conditions for the *form* to be one of a group, such as the FASB. In fact, Bedford [1974] has suggested that the AICPA Objectives Committee Report may be viewed as the constitution defining the role of the FASB. In this respect, it seems anomalous that the FASB has been financed and appointed prior to construction of its constitution.

in and of itself imply or dictate a preference for one reporting practice over another. The role of such evidence is to alter probability assessments;[8] it carries no preference encoding per se. Indeed, adherence to the Savage axioms ensures such a decomposition of beliefs and preferences.

To further develop this point, consider a particular association metric such as the API (abnormal performance index). Careful assimilation of any study relying on such a metric would address specification issues,[9] the necessary movement from an ex post metric to an ex ante probabilistic assessment, and the costs of the reporting alternatives. With proper specification and appropriate environmental regularity, we then interpret the API as a measure of the private value of advance information. But, in general, private value and social value of information do not coincide.[10] The conclusion, of course, is that empirical research does not, in general, resolve the fundamental choice problem.[11]

Another important issue at this point concerns the testing of conjectural hypotheses. We do not view such hypotheses as the efficiency of security markets as objectives. These hypotheses relate to the determinants of individual value, not to the relationship between individual and social value. [12] This does not, however, render testing of these hypotheses unimportant. For example, it may be valuable to produce information on the consequences of alternatives prior to making policy pronouncements. Observe, moreover, that these types of studies, whether directly or indirectly related to individual consequence determinations, may simplify the consequence domain. Hence, it may prove to be desirable to specify guidelines (or secondary objectives) to help make these essential simplifying as-

---

[8] Put another way, we face a choice problem and these studies represent additional information being brought to bear on the problem at hand. This issue has been discussed in an external reporting context in Beaver [1973 and 1974]. See Demski [1973] for an elaboration of this theme in a managerial context.

[9] Issues of risk measurement, specification of the ex post relationship between risk and return, and specification of the appropriate weighting across securities are important examples.

[10] See Akerloff [1970], Demski [1974a and 1974b], Fama and Laffer [1971], Hirshleifer [1971], Kihlstrom and Pauly [1971], Rothschild [1973], and Spence [1973].

[11] Simplifications, of course, do exist. In the restricted setting of interperiod tax allocation, one of the authors has advanced an efficiency argument in which the API metric and social values are likely to agree. See Beaver and Dukes [1972 and 1973]. This issue constitutes a special case where all of the informative alternatives constitute part of publicly available information and each can be provided at essentially zero cost by the firm. Given these conditions and the finding that earnings under deferral are more highly associated with the information set used by the market, it would appear to be Pareto optimal to report deferral. As noted earlier, Pareto optimality provides an incomplete ordering; as a result, it will not always resolve the issue. The above argument implicitly assumes that the price domain remains constant and that the issue is merely one of cost. If the price domain is affected then Pareto optimality may no longer be invoked.

[12] Moreover, they do not have the "first principle" or primitive notion of an objective. The likelihood of their truth will vary with the production of evidence.

sumptions. Harberger [1971], in fact, made such a proposal for research in applied welfare economics.

Other Approaches

We would characterize the approach outlined above as a decision-theoretic approach to problems of social choice where the existence of heterogeneous users of financial reports is explicitly admitted. Contrasting views tend to fall into one of two schools: (1) the "truth" or "objectivist" approach and (2) the "decision-model" approach.[13] The first asserts the existence of true values and views the purpose of accounting as reporting the true values as accurately as possible.[14] The second suggests that we examine how investors actually do or *should* make decisions and produce information which will provide assessments of the parameters of that actual or idealized model.[15]

The problems with the truth approach center around its suppression of individual differences and relegation of cost considerations to secondary importance. Focusing on truth (an imposition in Arrow's utilitarian framework) denies the existence of differing opinions about which public information will be most valuable. For example, to the extent that truth involves reporting past events, it does not allow for differing opinions as to which events are relevant and hence worth reporting (e.g., the historical cost of an asset). Similarly, to the extent that truth implicitly involves a prediction of the future (e.g., depreciation for the past year), it does not allow for heterogeneous expectations over future states. Rather, heterogeneity is suppressed under the guise of a search for truth. Even with presumed unanimity, however, the typical analyses do not explicitly recognize the cost of producing true measures. The resulting framework is therefore incomplete.

The decision-model approach also suffers from suppression of heterogeneity and cost considerations. It does admit to heterogeneity across classes of users but strict intraclass homogeneity is maintained. In the limit, of course, we could have I classes of one member each; and in this sense heterogeneity is allowed. Interclass externalities, however, are not admitted to in the typical analysis and the central problem of heterogeneous users is therefore ignored.[16]

Indeed, this approach assumes that knowledge of the decision model will automatically reveal what information is needed.[17] This typically is

---

[13] See Chapter 1 of Demski, *et al.*, [1972] for a similar classification.

[14] E.g., MacNeal [1939].

[15] Bierman [1974], Revsine [1973], and Sterling [1970] provide three recent examples.

[16] It is, in fact, often felt that specific reports for specific classes will completely resolve the reporting choice problem in an acceptable manner. Individual class determination, now, is a form of liberalism, and it is well known that no amount of liberalism will repair the Arrow paradox. (See Sen [1970], Chapter 6*.)

[17] For example, see Sterling [1970], p. 454.

not the case. Consider the investor-decision model and assume that a specific model can somehow be singled out. The parameters to be predicted are the probabilities that the various state-dependent cash flows will occur. No amount of inspection of that model alone will reveal what (if any) financial statement data may be useful in assessing these probabilities. Both approaches, in fact, speak of information needs, as opposed to optimal information in some cost-benefit context; and both, therefore, constitute forms of impositions.

The nature of the financial reporting problem when heterogeneity is admitted can be further explored by examining the papers presented at this conference.

SORTER AND THE AICPA OBJECTIVES REPORT

The Objectives Report presents twelve objectives designed to assist policymakers by providing a means for evaluating desirable goals and helping to achieve them. Four of them (the first, second, and last two) represent objectives in the sense of specifying how movement from V_i to V is to be accomplished. The remaining items, though termed objectives, actually represent disguised policy decisions.

The first and last two objectives call for production of *useful* information:

> The basic objective of financial statements is to provide information useful for making economic decisions. (P. 13)

> An objective of financial statements for governmental and not-for-profit organizations is to provide information useful for evaluating the effectiveness of the management of resources in achieving the organization's goals. (P. 46)

> An objective of financial statements is to report on those activities of the enterprise affecting society . . . and which are important to the role of the enterprise in its social environment. (P. 55)

We interpret these statements, in broadest terms, as requiring that Pareto optimality be observed in movement from V_i to V. As previously mentioned, this is a close to unassailable requirement.

Beyond this call for efficiency, we still face the problem of which types of movements along an efficient surface are to be permitted or whose well-being will be traded off for whose. The key to resolving such issues appears to lie in the introduction of the power of various individuals to enforce their wishes over the wishes of others. And at this point the second objective is quite explicit:

> An objective of financial statements is to serve primarily those users who have limited authority, ability, or resources to obtain information and who rely on financial statements as their principal source of information about an enterprise's economic activities. (P. 17)

Under the assumption that such a set of individuals is nonempty, this objective requires, in effect, that when conflict situations arise, the disadvantaged individuals are to have sufficient power to achieve their wishes.[18] Whether these individuals should possess such power is an ethical question that we are not prepared to address at this time. But some such set of tradeoffs is essential if we are to admit to movement along an efficient surface.

Observe, however, that market efficiency raises an interesting question of how stringent this preferential treatment is likely to be. In particular, if the market is efficient with respect to publicly available information then investors are playing a "fair game" with respect to all public information, including financial statement information. Hence, it is not obvious how serving this constituency would differ from serving the larger set of investors who rely upon other sources of published information.

The remaining statements in the Report deal with the nature of preferred accounting methods, rather than with the relationship between individual and social preference. Moreover, these policy choices are established within a decision-model analysis and are, therefore, subject to the general criticisms detailed above (apart from whether they are consistent with the Pareto optimality and preferential treatment to disadvantaged individuals' objectives).

The Report, for example, notes that all investors need to know the timing, magnitude, and riskiness of future cash flows.

> Thus, the information needs of creditors are essentially the same. Both groups are concerned with the enterprise's ability to generate cash flows to them and with their own ability to predict, compare, and evaluate the amount, timing, and related uncertainty of these future cash flows. (P. 20)

Extant models of the investor-decision process under uncertainty are virtually unanimous in suggesting that, at a minimum, the investor's outcome description should include a specification of the (state-dependent) future cash flows. But having said this in no way identifies which set of costly measures should be employed for this purpose or solves the problem of heterogeneous users.

Though we may appear to be quibbling over semantics, use of the term user "needs" reflects an inherent difference in philosophy. The term creates the implication that without the needed information, decision making would be infeasible. Furthermore, the cost of this needed information is not discussed in the Report.[19] The role of information is to alter investors' assessments of the probability distribution over future states of the world.

---

[18] Let c be the disadvantaged subset of I. This objective then requires that $\eta V_i \eta'$ for all $i \epsilon c \Longrightarrow \eta V \eta'$. In Bloomfield's [1971] axiomatization of cooperative game (and social choice) theory, this objective specifies a *constitution*. Addition of responsiveness and independence of irrelevant alternative conditions ensures that all choice processes admit to the constitutional interpretation. Note, however, that if we admit to conflicts within the disadvantaged class, the sound objective still provides an incomplete ordering.

[19] Interestingly, the Report chooses to model firm behavior according to a sacrifice-benefit dichotomy (see page 28). Yet, it does not apply the same simple paradigm to the analysis of information decisions.

Probabilistic assessments are always feasible in the absence of any particular set of information under consideration. In fact, the decision-theoretic approach to the information-choice problem presumes such assessments exist in the form of prior distributions. Information has value if it is expected to induce a revision of probabilities and actions that imply a greater expected utility (with cost considered) to the investor. This is one way to place a meaningful interpretation on a term like *user needs*. However, such an interpretation of user needs is inconsistent with the manner in which it is applied in the Objectives Committee Report.

The decision-model approach and its attendant user-needs dictum also create a false impression of unanimity. For example, consider the two major classes of users identified in the Report—creditors and investors. The payoff-relevant partition of future states will vary considerably between these two classes. The creditor is concerned with two basic events: default and no default, with finer partitions on the former. The investor, on the other hand, is concerned with finer partitions of the no default event. Even within these major classes of users, lack of unanimity may exist because of heterogeneity of preferences for future consumption and heterogeneity of expectations.

Another example of where disguised policy decisions are offered within a decision-model framework is in the Report's reaffirmation of the importance of income determination. The basis for such a statement is that in order to assess future cash flows the investor needs to know past earnings. Moreover, the term *income determination* is used as if it were some unambiguous, monolithic concept (such as true earnings) devoid of any measurement error.

Apart from its ambiguity of meaning, we view such an "objective" as an implicit policy decision and one that is questionable in light of evidence on market efficiency. The Report, by its reaffirmation of the primacy of accounting earnings, adopts the position that considerable interpretation of events (in terms of earnings effects) is required in financial statement reporting. In an efficient market the justification for such a position is unclear. In an inefficient market that does not fully reflect the information publicly available it might be argued that the financial statement data must be carefully interpreted for the investor, lest he be misled and purchase an overpriced security (or sell an underpriced one). However, in an efficient market such paternalism is even more questionable. Put another way, income measurement is not precluded in an efficient market—but it cannot be automatically assumed either. Management may have a comparative advantage in interpreting the effects of certain events on future cash flows. In such instances, reporting their interpretations (i.e., earnings measurement) may be quite appropriate.

Finally, the committee Report, reflecting the information constraint of primarily relying upon financial statements, leaves the impression that financial statements must be self-contained. In a market efficient with respect to published information, the investor who relies upon financial statement data is still playing a fair game, even though prices may reflect a much broader information set. In such a setting, it may not be cost-effective (in a Pareto optimality sense) to have financial statements convey all of the firm-specific information, but rather report only that portion in which it has a comparative advantage relative to other information sources. The issue of comparative advantage is essentially ignored by the Report, with the possible exception of management forecasts, where cost considerations are still omitted.

In short, the Report offers two classes of statements: objectives and policy choices. The policy choices are founded on a decision-model philosophy of information production and therefore cannot be taken as ultimate, unchallengeable guides to resource commitment. Rather, they represent the combined judgment of the committee as to what broad rankings will be reflected in V. Given that their arguments are debatable at several points, we do not view these disguised policy choices as the central theme of the Report. Instead, its central thrust lies in a noncontroversial call for Pareto optimality and a controversial call for preferential treatment for disadvantaged individuals. It is this (second) objective that constitutes the essence of the Report. The unanswered questions, of course, are what the consequences of such power are likely to be and whether they are, in some ethical sense, desirable.

CYERT-IJIRI

Cyert and Ijiri offer a view of the financial reporting environment that explicitly recognizes a limited amount of heterogeneity. Three classes of individuals are distinguished: users, corporations, and the profession. Conflicts among the three groups are admitted, but intragroup conflicts are not. Denoting the three groups' preference relations V_U, V_C, and V_P, the objectives issue is now (re)expressed as specifying the function:

$$V = f(V_U, V_C, V_P) .$$

In elaborating their view, Cyert-Ijiri make two observations that deserve reinforcement. First, they explicitly recognize (limited forms of) conflict among the individuals. Hence, usefulness in a narrow sense of value to those who receive the data is not viewed as necessarily specifying the unanimity or Pareto efficient surface. That is, nonusers are acknowledged as having a stake in the determination of financial reporting methods.

Second, movement along the efficient frontier is explicitly entertained and alternative power configurations are admitted to. The Objectives Report grants such power to users (and, in particular, to disadvantaged users). But other alternatives are available—the extremes in the Cyert-Ijiri tripartite being acquiescence to either the corporation or the profession groups.

In short, the role of objectives is specification of the relationship between V and the individual V_i. Whether one class of movements along the Pareto surface is more desirable than another is a distinctly ethical question; and the basic, fundamental purpose of objectives is to delineate these choices. Again, though, the unanswered questions are what the consequences of various power configurations are likely to be and whether they are, in some ethical sense, desirable.

GONEDES-DOPUCH

Gonedes and Dopuch offer a view of the financial reporting environment that explicitly allows for heterogeneity (with the exception of constraints introduced in section 5 to ensure a nonempty core). Unlike the Objectives Committee or Cyert and Ijiri, however, they confine themselves to the unanimity criterion of Pareto optimality and thus do not entertain movements along an efficient surface.

More specifically, they postulate complete and perfect markets and then examine the financial information production problem with a conventional market solution, as well as one based on the core of the corresponding cooperative game. [20] And, in a more narrow sense, they address the question of when the laissez-faire approach will be efficient (in the sense of inducing Pareto optimal information production decisions). Here they document the market failure case when information of a public good nature cannot be excluded from nonpurchasers (the free rider problem), and thereby conclude that the laissez-faire approach cannot be entirely relied upon. Indeed, the market failure possibilities are far deeper than those associated with the free rider problem. Issues of adverse selection (Akerloff [1970]), signalling (Spence [1973]), and the effect of information on the completeness of markets and efficient risk-sharing arrangements (Kihlstrom and Pauly [1971] and Radner [1968 and 1972]) are also relevant. Informational differences may lead to noncooperative pathologies of adverse selection, fraud, moral hazard, cheating, bluffing, and punishing; and the attendant market failure possibilities are indeed immense.[21]

Several additional aspects of the Gonedes-Dopuch analysis are worth noting. First, their analysis of movement from the evidentiary to the policy domain is less than complete and creates the impression that, barring free rider problems, such movement is straightforward. In a literal sense, however, the behavioral assumptions in their analysis (as well as in ours) confine the role of evidence to that of providing information; evidence per se carries no inherent preference encoding.

---

[20] The former is, essentially, a unanimity game that admits to a constitutional interpretation (Bloomfield [1971]). The core approach, in turn, is consistent with the usual constitutional restrictions along with Wilson's [1970] core property being imposed on the $f(\cdot)$ function (Bloomfield [1971]). And, as the number of actors increases, the core approaches the perfect competition solution.

[21] See Baiman [1974] and Rothschild [1973] for additional discussion.

Second, Gonedes-Dopuch do conclude that price domain analysis is sufficient for assessing consequences (as opposed to ordering consequences). Perfect and complete markets, as assumed by Gonedes and Dopuch, are sufficient to support this argument; but incompleteness or imperfection tends to negate it. In fact, the theory of the firm under incomplete markets is close to being in a state of disarray.[22] In short, consequences may manifest themselves in manners far beyond those of immediate security price movements.

Third, Gonedes-Dopuch conclude in the final section, after observing market failure, that some nonmarket approaches to settling the financial information-production issue may be desirable. This strikes us as an important point to reinforce. Market failure renders a market solution suspect, but not necessarily deficient. The real issue is how a market solution compares with the nonmarket alternatives; and in this sense the efficacy of market-based studies as either consequence or evaluation devices is an unsettled question. Rejection of the market approach is, therefore, premature at the least and incorrect at the worst. That is, we presently lack evidence on how well market and nonmarket evaluation schemes compare, as well as on how complete market-based consequence measures are.

Finally, we return to the reliance on unanimity. The central difference between the Objectives Report and the analysis of Gonedes-Dopuch is the former's reliance on disadvantaged individuals to move along the Pareto surface. Nondisadvantaged individuals are not, in the Objectives Report approach, permitted to block or prevent the realization of the disadvantaged individuals' wishes. At a most fundamental level, then, the central issue among the approaches proferred here is how movement from V_i to V is to be accomplished. Where, admitting to Pareto optimality, is power to reside? Herein lies the central role, and central importance, of financial accounting objectives. Unfortunately, we know very little about this issue.

Implications for Future Research

As indicated above, research plays at least two roles: (1) to provide evidence on various aspects of V_i (e.g., security-price research provides information on certain aspects of the consequence space that will in part determine individual preference for an information alternative); and (2) to provide evidence on the consequences of various mappings from V_i to V. In these respects the papers and subsequent discussions at the conference have called for additional research of one form or another. Gonedes-Dopuch provide the most elaborate attempt to take stock of the current body of knowledge and suggest ways in which the evidence-gathering process might be improved. However, most of the expressed concerns for future research are directed toward the first role cited above. One of the implications of the framework developed here is that we should consider generating

[22] Ekern and Wilson [1974] and Radner [1972].

evidence on the issue of objectives itself. There has been essentially no recognition of this second role of research thus far; hopefully, one of the results of the conference will be to suggest directions for research into this area. Tentatively, we offer the following (incomplete) list:

(1) What are sources of market failure in addition to the free rider problem? What are the consequences of these failures? What are the costs associated with attempting to remove market failure?

(2) What institutional arrangements and attendant mappings from V_i to V are to be considered and what are the (costs and) consequences of these solution forms as opposed to those of a market solution?

(3) If we are willing to violate Arrow's assumption of unrestricted domain, under what restrictions on beliefs and/or preferences are forms of unanimity attainable? (See Ohlson [1974], Lintner [1969], Wilson [1968], and Ekern and Wilson [1974] for some aspects of this issue.)

(4) If we view the problem in a game-theoretic context, what mechanisms are needed to ensure that the game will be cooperative, and what are the costs of implementing such mechanisms (e.g., costs of detecting and litigating contract violations)?

(5) If we relax the assumptions sufficiently to ensure a cooperative solution, what forms of noncooperative behavior can occur and what are the consequences associated with such behavior (e.g., adverse selection, moral hazard, signalling, fraud, bluffing, cheating, etc.)? In this broader context, the role of certification can be formally introduced and analyzed; and in such a setting we may arrive at a more precise notion of what Cyert-Ijiri imply by moving objectives toward the P circle.

(6) If we admit to incomplete and/or imperfect markets, what additional dimensions of the consequence space become relevant? Consider the issue of forecasts by management. Instituting mandatory forecasting may affect the incidence of risk borne by management vis-à-vis investors. In complete markets management may insure against such risks and the consequences of such a policy may be relatively straightforward. However, in incomplete markets such policies represent implicit attempts at wealth redistribution and objections by management become better understood. Moreover, since the incidence of the risk cannot be fully insured, management may respond with forms of forecasting behavior that considerably affect the value of forecasts. In any event, these are dimensions of the consequence space that we have only begun to admit to.

(7) Finally, what is the role of accounting information in supporting the existence of more complete markets?

Of course, none of this research will—in and of itself—resolve the fundamentally ethical question of how preferences should be weighted across individuals in determining financial reporting policies. We are, however, hopeful that it will provide some information on what the consequences of alternative choices may be. On the other hand, though, we must admit to a certain philosophical reservation in suggesting this research. At a basic level, the major focus of our paper is the problem of providing a social ordering for alternative public information systems. Yet research is also a form of information; and, in the limit, our analysis applies with equal force to financial accounting and financial accounting research.

Conclusion

In conclusion, we have offered a view of the nature and role of objectives that explicitly rests on heterogeneous users. This view incorporates the usual utilitarian statement. But explicit consideration of heterogeneous users raises the inherent difficulties in delineating the relationship between conflicting individuals and the choices that must be made. This is the area, it seems to us, in which objectives have a vital role.

Our presentation, however, stops far short of the refined specification that often accompanies statements of objectives. We have not, for example, structured our analysis on an assumption that financial reporting policies need to be regulated by some agency. This can only be an outcome of the analysis; it does not serve as an acceptable assumption.

Similarly, we have not issued a call for forecasts, more disclosure, or presentation of a statement of financial activities. There is no general economic law or theorem that will support either contention. Again, these requirements can only be the product of analysis; and the role of objectives is to specify the nature of the tradeoffs in such analysis.

BIBLIOGRAPHY

AKERLOFF, GEORGE A. "The Market for 'Lemons': Quality Uncertainty and the Market Mechanism," *Quarterly Journal of Economics* (August 1970).

AICPA OBJECTIVES COMMITTEE. *Objectives of Financial Statements*. New York: American Institute of Certified Public Accountants, 1973.

ARROW, KENNETH J. "Economic Welfare and the Allocation of Resources for Invention," in *The Rate and Direction of Economic Activity: Economic and Social Factors*. Princeton: National Bureau of Economic Research, 1962.

———. *Social Choice and Individual Values*. New York: John Wiley, 1963.

BAIMAN, STANLEY. "Optimal Forecasting in Selected Organization Models." Ph.D. dissertation, Stanford University, 1974.

BEAVER, WILLIAM H. "Implications of Security Price Research for Accounting: A Reply to Bierman," *The Accounting Review* (July 1974).

———. "The Behavior of Security Prices and Its Implications for Accounting Research (Methods)," *AAA Committee Reports*. Supplement to *The Accounting Review* (1972).

———. "What Should Be the Objectives of the FASB?" *Journal of Accountancy* (August 1973).

———, and DUKES, R. E. "Interperiod Tax Allocation and δ-Depreciation Methods: Some Empirical Results," *The Accounting Review* (July 1973).

———, and ———. "Interperiod Tax Allocation, Earnings Expectations, and the Behavior of Security Prices," *The Accounting Review* (April 1972).

BEDFORD, NORTON M. "Discussion of 'Establishing Financial Accounting Standards—The Plan and the Performance.'" Stanford Lectures in Accounting, Stanford University, April 1974.

BIERMAN, HAROLD. "The Implications of Efficient Markets and the Capital Asset Pricing Model to Accounting," *The Accounting Review* (July 1974).

BLOOMFIELD, STEFAN. "An Axiomatic Formulation of Constitutional Games." Ph.D. dissertation, Stanford University, 1971.

———, and WILSON, ROBERT. "The Postulates of Game Theory," *Journal of Mathematical Sociology* (1973).

DEMSETZ, HAROLD. "Information and Efficiency: Another Viewpoint," *Journal of Law and Economics* (April 1969).

———. "The Private Production of Public Goods," *Journal of Law and Economics* (October 1970).

DEMSKI, JOEL S. "Choice Among Financial Reporting Alternatives," *The Accounting Review* (April 1974a).

———. "Comments on 'Some Fruitful Directions for Research in Management Accounting,'" in N. Dopuch and L. Revsine, eds., *Accounting Research 1960–1970: A Critical Evaluation*. Urbana: Center for International Education and Research in Accounting, University of Illinois, 1973.

———. *Information Analysis*. Reading, Mass.: Addison-Wesley, 1972.

———. "The Value of Financial Accounting." Working paper, Stanford University, 1974b.

———; FELTHAM, G.; HORNGREN, C.; and JAEDICKE, R. "A Conceptual Approach to Cost Determination." Manuscript, 1972.

EKERN, STEINAR, and WILSON, R. "On the Theory of the Firm in an Economy with Incomplete Markets," *Bell Journal of Economics and Management Science* (Spring 1974).

FAMA, EUGENE F. "Perfect Competition and Optimal Production Decisions Under Uncertainty," *Bell Journal of Economics and Management Science* (Autumn 1972).

———, and LAFFER, ARTHUR. "Information and Capital Markets," *Journal of Business* (July 1971).

HARBERGER, ARNOLD. "Three Basic Postulates for Applied Welfare Economics: An Interpretative Essay," *Journal of Economic Literature* (September 1971).

HIRSHLEIFER, JACK. "The Private and Social Value of Information and the Reward to Inventive Activity," *American Economic Review* (September 1971).

IJIRI, YUJI. *The Foundations of Accounting Measurement*. Englewood Cliffs, N.J.: Prentice-Hall, 1967.

JENSEN, MICHAEL, and LONG, J. "Corporate Investment Under Uncertainty and Pareto Optimality in the Capital Markets," *Bell Journal of Economics and Management Science* (Spring 1972).

KIHLSTROM, RICHARD and PAULY, M. "The Role of Insurance in the Allocation of Risk," *American Economic Review* (May 1971).

LINTNER, JOHN. "The Aggregation of Investors' Diverse Judgments and Preferences in Purely Competitive Security Markets," *Journal of Financial and Quantitative Analysis* (September 1969).

MAC NEAL, KENNETH. *Truth in Accounting*. Philadelphia: University of Pennsylvania Press, 1939.

MARSCHAK, JACOB, and RADNER, R. *Economic Theory of Teams*. New Haven: Yale University Press, 1972.

OHLSON, JAMES. "The Complete Ordering of Information Alternatives for a Class of Portfolio-Selection Models." Working paper, Stanford University, 1974.

RADNER, ROY. "Competitive Equilibrium Under Uncertainty," *Econometrica* (January 1968).

———. "Existence of Equilibrium of Plans, Prices, and Price Expectations in a Sequence of Markets," *Econometrica* (March 1972).

REVSINE, LAWRENCE. *Replacement Cost Accounting*. Englewood Cliffs, N.J.: Prentice-Hall, 1973.

ROTHSCHILD, M. "Models of Market Organization with Imperfect Information: A Survey," *Journal of Political Economy* (November-December 1973).

SEN, A. K. *Collective Choice and Social Welfare*. San Francisco: Holden-Day, 1970.

SPENCE, M. "Job Market Signalling," *Quarterly Journal of Economics* (August 1973).

STERLING, ROBERT R. "On Theory Construction and Verification," *The Accounting Review* (July 1970).

WILSON, ROBERT. "The Finer Structure of Revealed Preference," *Journal of Economic Theory* (December 1970).

———. "The Theory of Syndicates," *Econometrica* (January 1968).

DISCUSSION SUMMARY

The basic purpose of financial reporting is to provide information that is useful to financial statement users. However, because of the heterogeneous nature of these users, information that is useful to one user may be worthless (or worse) to another. This causes the role of financial reporting objectives to remain unclear. This paper examines the nature and role of financial accounting objectives and presents a view that takes into account the heterogeneous nature of financial statement users.

Financial statement information may affect both the production and exchange sectors of an economy. Heterogeneity among the group of users may cause individual users to be affected in different ways. Both users and nonusers may be affected. In selecting from among financial accounting alternatives, policy makers should take into consideration the heterogeneous nature of the individuals affected. The criterion of Pareto optimality, although a very noble one, usually does not help in choosing an alternative because some individuals may benefit from a particular alternative and others may be harmed by it.

Arrow's impossibility theorem guarantees that restricting all preference relations to weak orders and imposing nondictatorship, independence of irrelevant alternatives, and Pareto optimality conditions are mutually inconsistent conditions. Which condition or conditions should then be violated? The answer to this question should be the role of accounting objectives.

The paper examines the role of research in aiding policy decisions and concludes that it cannot determine whether one reporting alternative is preferable to another. An examination of the AICPA Objectives Report concludes that "the central thrust lies in a noncontroversial call for preferential treatment for disadvantaged individuals."

The Cyert-Ijiri view of the financial reporting environment and the Gonedes-Dopuch view are discussed. Cyert and Ijiri allow for a limited amount of heterogeneity (interclass, not intraclass) among users. They fail to answer questions about what the consequences of various power configurations will be and whether these configurations are desirable. Gonedes and Dopuch explicitly allow for heterogeneity but confine themselves to the Pareto optimality criterion.

Finally, the authors present a series of questions which provide some direction for research in the area of the nature and role of financial reporting objectives.

THE VALUE OF FINANCIAL ACCOUNTING

JOEL S. DEMSKI

It has been over a decade since Feltham [1968] first rigorously defined the concept of "value of information" in the accounting literature. Numerous elaborations and extensions have followed, and new insights have been gleaned (e.g., Butterworth [1972], Feltham [1972], Itami [1977], and Hilton [1979]). But extension of the value concept to the multiple user setting of financial reporting remains largely unaccomplished.

In one sense, we do not envision a direct extension from individual style to social "cost-benefit" analysis. Arrow's celebrated Impossibility Theorem[1] precludes such an approach (provided we accept his formulation and axioms). In another sense, we also do not envision an application of results concerning the value of information to an individual in a single person setting to the value of the same information to the same individual in a multiperson setting. For example, it may be rational to pay to suppress free information in a multiperson setting, though such payment would never be rational in a single person setting [Baiman, 1975; Demski, 1974; and Ponssard, 1976]. Blackwell's well-known theorem[2] does not necessarily apply in a multiperson setting.

This research was sponsored by the Stanford Program in Professional Accounting, major contributors to which are: Arthur Andersen & Co.; Arthur Young & Co.; Coopers & Lybrand; Deloitte, Haskins & Sells; Ernst & Ernst; Peat, Marwick, Mitchell & Co.; and Price Waterhouse and Company. Helpful comments of Bill Beaver, George Foster, Chuck Horngren, Ron Marshall, and Mark Wolfson are gratefully acknowledged.

The purpose of this paper is to explore the concept of value of information, with particular emphasis on the multiperson setting of external financial reporting. We begin with a brief review of the value of information concept. Both individual and social value are considered. We then propose a social value concept, based on a class of cooperative games, termed *constitutional value*. This has the advantage of accommodating "political" aspects of the financial reporting scene as well as providing an explicit example of how the choice aspects of financial accounting theory can be formulated in light of the Arrow conundrum.

Value of Information

Individual value

The usual and familiar notion of "value of information" is based on the acquisition of information by a single economic agent (household or firm) in order to improve the quality of some decision.[3] Broadly viewed, in other words, information is a factor of production (that is, production of good decisions); and we have learned to examine its demand and use within the confines of the usual economic analysis. In particular, we have examined accounting systems from this perspective.

The only difficulty is that for the information to be useful we must confine our analyses to the economics of uncertainty. Otherwise, with subjective certainty posited, the consequences of all conceivable decisions are known in advance, and as a result there is hardly any demand for information. For example, there is no reason to measure a firm's income in an economy characterized by subjective certainty; all parameters or outcomes of interest are, by assumption, known (see Beaver and Demski [1979]).

Admitting to uncertainty, the value of information concept turns out to be quite straightforward. One information system—such as one accounting system—is more valuable than another if and only if, from the particular agent's perspective, it is more desirable or preferred to the other. Value and rational preference, in other words, are coextensive.

In turn, we typically measure such value with an expected utility measure. System 1, then, is more valuable than system 2 if and only if the agent's expected utility measure with system 1 is higher than with system 2. Alternatively, we may elect to measure value in monetary units by focusing on the certain cash equivalent or selling price that makes the individual agent indifferent between proceeding with the information or proceeding without it (but in possession of the selling price). Note that one must be careful here because in general buying and selling prices of lotteries are not equal. (Appendix 1 contains an example, and LaValle [1968] and Hilton [1979] should be consulted for extensive discussions of cash equivalents and the value of information in a single person setting.)

Finally, we reiterate that this value is very much a personalistic concept. Whether one accounting system is more valuable than another depends, in general, on the choice problem, tastes, and beliefs at hand. Blackwell,[4] in turn, has provided us with necessary and sufficient conditions for one accounting system to be more valuable than another *regardless* of the problem, tastes, and beliefs. These conditions, unfortunately, cover but a limited set of possibilities, and we must therefore proceed with a personalistic notion of value. Different agents in different circumstances will generally value accounting systems differently.

Social value: market allocation mechanisms

Now consider an economy of individual agents. With a thoroughly conventional (neoclassical) setting we are able to extend this notion of individual value to the social level. With all goods tradeable in complete event-contingent markets, we know that, at equilibrium, for any pair of event-contingent commodities, each consumer equates his marginal rate of substitution (in consumption) for the two commodities to their price ratio. Similarly, each producer equates their marginal rate of transformation (in production) to the same price ratio. And in this sense *and setting,* prices reflect value at the social level.

Application of these ideas to accounting systems is straightforward. Suppose all types of systems and event-contingent commodities are traded in perfect markets (which implies that no interuser or producer external effects are present).[5] At equilibrium, then, consumers and producers have adjusted their plans so that the marginal rates of substitution equal the marginal rates of transformation (equal the price ratios). And we thereby arrive at a setting in which accounting system prices reflect the value of such systems. For example, each individual will acquire information up to the point of indifference between more information and more of some specific (current period, certain) consumption good, given prevailing terms of trade. And at this point the price ratio, the prevailing terms of trade, equals the rate at which the agent is willing to substitute the one for the other. (See Gonedes and Dopuch [1974] for a similar analysis, based on costless bargaining among consuming and producing agents.)

The major drawback with this story is the assumption that accounting systems, and in particular financial reporting systems, do not give rise to market failure possibilities. But market failures are easy to envision here. With nontrivial production cost and trivial transmission cost, a monopoly producer of the information may exist. Similarly, a public good story (recognizing that information is a factor of production and not the usual consumption good associated with public good arguments) may emerge. The information, when produced, is made available to all agents in the society. This, in turn, raises the possibility of the use of a nonmarket allocation mechanism to sort out the preferred set of financial reporting systems. We surely face such an institutional structure in financial reporting. And numerous reasons for the use of nonmarket allocation mechanisms in the determination of financial reporting policy have been advanced. (See Gonedes and Dopuch [1974], Demski and Feltham [1976], Beaver [1977], and Foster [1979] for summarizations of these various arguments.) This provides a sufficient set of reasons to explore the value concept in a regime of non-market-based allocation.

Social value: nonmarket allocation mechanisms

Movement into the regime of nonmarket allocation mechanisms, such as the FASB, SEC, and CASB reporting requirements, raises the question of explicitly specifying an objective function. Value remains an euphemism for preference; and if society selects one system of public reporting over another, we presume the first is more valuable than the second (speaking net of cost). Note, however, that this concept of social value is now used to guide nonmarket allocation decisions, just as the individual value concept is used to guide individual decisions. This is in sharp contrast with the interpretation of social value as a revealed manifestation of individual decisions in the completely neoclassical setting discussed earlier. Social value becomes, in other words, a guide to action in this setting.

Unfortunately, Arrow's Paradox raises fundamental questions as to how strong or useful a guide to action it can provide. In particular, if we respect the conditions of Pareto optimality and independence of irrelevant alternatives, and refuse to admit a dictator, Arrow has shown that we cannot—*in general*—construct a complete and transitive guide to nonmarket allocation decisions. In other words, respecting these conditions on the relationship between individual and social value, we are not able to provide a complete and transitive guide to action. Thus, and in this sense, the concept of social value of financial reporting remains ambiguous.

Of course, we always have the option of restricting ourselves to special cases or of discarding some of the conditions Arrow imposed on the value relationship. The former approach has the advantage of respecting the Arrow conditions *provided the special circumstances are satisfied.* Thus, the social value concept becomes well defined if we restrict the preferences of the individual agents in various ways. Examples are provided in Demski [1973], Ohlson [1975], Cushing [1977], and Scott [1977]. (In turn, Mueller [1976], Sen [1977], and Kelly [1978] provide recent reviews of this entire literature.) The difficulty is that in one way or another these are specific cases.[6]

Dropping at least one of Arrow's other conditions is also less than completely appealing. Removal of Pareto optimality would amount to basing a theory of the value of financial reporting on the primitive concept of systematically denying individual agents what they—in their self-perceived best interests—want. On the other hand, removal of the nondictatorship condition surely runs afoul of Western ideals. Finally, removal of the independence of irrelevant alternatives restriction commits us in one way or another to interpersonal utility measurements. This, however, is inconsistent with the degree of uniqueness established in the typical utility representation theorems. (The Savage [1954] expected utility representation, for example, is unique only to a positive linear transformation.)

Are we, then, confined to a list of special cases or less than pleasing assumptions on which to build a value concept to guide the regulation of financial reporting? The answer is no, provided we do not ask too much. This is pursued below, where we focus on a particular cooperative game formulation of the nonmarket allocation process.

Constitutional Value

The purpose of this final section is to examine the idea of a particular type of game, termed a *constitutional game,* and the social value of information concept to which it gives rise. Several motives underlie the exercise. One is to illustrate the types of analyses that are possible with a game theory approach. As noted above, relying on special cases or the dropping of Arrow's nondictatorship, Pareto optimality, or independence of irrelevant alternatives axioms lacks appeal. By a process of elimination, we arrive at the avenue of not insisting on a complete and transitive definition of social value of information. Society's choices may, in this view, be intransitive; or society may be unable to choose between two particular financial reporting systems. This is the topic of game theory, which can be broadly viewed as the theory of social choice without insistence on Arrow's universal domain axiom.

A second motive is to offer a formalism that provides some insight, at an anecdotal level, into recent events in the history of our regulation of financial reporting. A third is to present a social choice interpretation of the Watts-Zimmerman work on "positive accounting."

The constitutional approach is deceptively simple. We focus on the conjunction of *power* and *preference* and define social value accordingly. More precisely, in this view we define one financial reporting system as more valuable than another when some group of individual agents (1) unanimously regards the one as more valuable than the other in terms of individual value and (2) has the *power*—socially speaking—to guarantee this choice in the social sphere (when operating from the strength of unanimity). For example, returning to APB days, if members of the insurance industry prefer historical to current valuation of marketable securities and if they have sufficient power to enforce this desire, we then regard the former as more valuable than the latter.

This *characterization* is consistent with recent suggestions that "political" aspects of financial reporting be explicitly recognized [Horngren, 1972 and 1973; Gerboth, 1973; Cyert and Ijiri, 1974; and May and Sundem, 1976]. It is also consistent with the underlying theme in the recent "positive" approach that suggests the interpretation of our financial reporting environment ". . . as resulting from interaction among . . . maximizing individuals in both markets and the political process" [Watts, 1977, p. 54; see also Watts and Zimmerman, 1978 and 1979].

Quite clearly, the key element in the characterization is the set of individual agents having sufficient power to ensure choice of one reporting scheme or requirement over another. That is, the system depends on a defined constitution (or listing of "powerful" groups of individual agents). Unfortunately, specification of the constitution is essentially exogenous. The power structure is reflected in, not determined by, this concept of value.

Nevertheless, the characterization appears to capture the concern of recent authors. Moreover, its axiomatic foundations are known and we are therefore able to be quite explicit about what is being characterized.

To pursue this, we envision a function or assignment procedure that for any set of individual values and pair of financial reporting requirements or methods assigns one of four possible social outcomes: (1) the first method is superior to the second; (2) the second method is superior to the first; (3) society is indifferent between the two; or (4) society is unable to express a preference between the two.

Three requirements are now placed on this assignment procedure. First, Pareto optimality is maintained: if all individuals weakly (strongly) value one system over another system then so does society. Second, independence of irrelevant alternatives is maintained: if two alternative sets of individual value rankings agree, then their respective social value rankings must also agree. Finally, a responsiveness condition is also observed: suppose that one system is as socially valuable as another and then consider any alternative set of individual values. If the set of individual agents strictly opposed to the first over the second does not increase in this altered configuration, then the one remains as socially valuable as the other.

These three conditions are necessary and sufficient for the constitutional value interpretation to obtain. That is, the social choices can be described here (and only here) as if:

(1) For each pair of reporting alternatives there exists a set of possible groupings of individuals (or coalitions) who have the power when acting in unison to force choice of the one reporting alternative over the other.

(2) One method is socially more valuable than another if and only if the members of one such coalition are unanimous on this point.

This result, due to Bloomfield [1976] and Bloomfield and Wilson [1972], is more formally described in Appendix 2.

Numerous interpretations and implications are available at this point. Consider the "positive theory" work. Two themes are present here: the importance of indirect contributors to information value, such as through political costs and regulatory concerns; and the conjunction of preference and power in the political arena. Focusing on the latter theme, a direct implication is that political activities will be correlated with individual value. Watts and Zimmerman [1978] conduct precisely such a test by examining firms' submissions to the FASB on general price level accounting. Overlaid with the constitutional game interpretation, however, the preference-power characterization is completely equivalent to a social choice process that respects Pareto optimality, independence, and responsiveness conditions. Hence, another avenue for empirical investigation of the theory is the testing of these (axiomatic) conditions.

On an anecdotal level, APB and FASB activities are also interpretable with this conjunction of power and preference characterization. Many, such as Gerboth [1973], contend the APB was disbanded because it ran afoul of powerful interest groups; and it surely was overruled on the investment credit issue. An equally vivid example is its foray into marketable securities reporting (Armstrong [1977]; also see FASB Statement No. 12). Similarly, under interest group pressure the FASB waived short-run compliance with its lease reporting requirement. And the FASB was surely unable to express a preference in oil and gas accounting until a rather powerful group of individual agents acted! In a similar vein, the Trueblood Objectives Report, the Metcalf Report, the FASB's Conceptual Foundations Project (culminating in the *Financial Accounting Concepts* series), and the Arthur Andersen suit over ASR150 can all be interpreted in terms of attempts to specify the constitution—or which coalitions have the power when acting in consort to force what choices in the political arena.

In short, the constitutional value characterization of social choice that emerges from a conjunction of power and preference can be used to catalogue and interpret current research and current events in financial reporting. At the same time, however, it should be emphasized that only a characterization has been offered. If the social choice process obeys the identified axioms, it can be described *as if* choices are based on the conjunction of power (delineated in a constitution) and preference. But what mechanism might or should be at work here adds another dimension to the issue. How, for example, are individual values to be solicited or learned? (See Green and Laffont [1979].)

Summary

The concept of value of information is somewhat elusive and problematic in the multiperson setting of financial accounting. Ideally, when faced with market failure and allocation decisions being made by some nonmarket allocation mechanism, we would guide that allocation mechanism with a well-defined objective function. And, presumably, in the sphere of nonmarket allocation decisions on financial reporting, that objective function would be the social value of the information whose production is being regulated.

In turn, Arrow's Theorem structures the specification of such a value concept in terms of which subset of his mutually inconsistent axioms to abandon. One particular avenue, dropping the requirement of a complete and transitive social preference relation, was examined under the concept of constitutional value, or the conjunction of power and preference in the political process. This appears to account for the political anecdotes associated with the regulation of financial reporting and to provide added insight into the positive theory work of Watts and Zimmerman. But precisely what the implications of these observations are for accounting theory remains to be seen. An essential feature of financial accounting—movement from individual to social value—is largely unresearched.

Appendix 1

The purpose of this appendix is to provide an example of individual information value measurement and the difference between buying and selling prices of lotteries.

Outcome Structure:

	States:		
Acts:	S_1	S_2	S_3
a_1	\$50	\$50	0
a_2	0	0	\$60

Probabilities: $\phi(S_i) =$ 1/3 1/3 1/3

Preferences: $U(x) = ln(100 + x)$

Information Structures:	*State Partition*	*Cost*
η^0 :	$\{S_1, S_2, S_3\}$	\$0
η^1 :	$\{\{S_1, S_2\}, \{S_3\}\}$	\$5
η^2 :	$\{\{S_1\}, \{S_2, S_3\}\}$	\$3

Expected Utility Analysis:

$$E(U|\eta^0) = \frac{2}{3}\, ln(100 + 50) + \frac{1}{3}\, ln(100) = 4.88$$

$$E(U|\eta^1) = \frac{2}{3}\, ln(100 + 50 - 5) + \frac{1}{3}\, ln(100 + 60 - 5) = 5.00$$

$$E(U|\eta^2) = \frac{1}{3}\, ln(100 + 50 - 3) + \frac{1}{3}\, ln(100 - 3) + \frac{1}{3}\, ln(100 + 60 - 3) = 4.87$$

Selling Prices:

$$ln(100 + 31.04) = 4.88 = E(U|\eta^0)$$
$$ln(100 + 48.26) = 5.00 = E(U|\eta^1)$$
$$ln(100 + 30.82) = 4.87 = E(U|\eta^2)$$

Buying Prices:

$$ln(100) = \frac{2}{3}\, ln(100 + 50 - \underline{\underline{30.26}}) + \frac{1}{3}\, ln(100 - \underline{\underline{30.26}})$$

$$ln(100) = \frac{2}{3}\, ln(100 + 50 - \underline{\underline{53.22}}) + \frac{1}{3}\, ln(100 + 60 - \underline{\underline{53.22}})$$

$$ln(100) = \frac{1}{3}\, ln(100 + 50 - \underline{\underline{32.86}}) + \frac{1}{3}\, ln(100 - \underline{\underline{32.86}}) + \frac{1}{3}\, ln(100 + 60 - \underline{\underline{32.86}})$$

Appendix 2

The purpose of this appendix is to more rigorously specify the constitutional value concept and its axiomatization. We summarize Bloomfield's [1976] result. A slightly different version is in Bloomfield and Wilson [1972]. And both papers provide extensive work on the link of these axioms and strengthened versions thereof to game theory.

We focus on a nonnull, finite set of n individuals, denoted I, and a nonnull set of financial reporting alternatives, denoted H. Individual preferences are represented with a binary relation defined on H, and denoted $V_i \subset H \times H$ (where any subset of $H \times H$ is a binary relation defined on H). We then interpret $\eta V_i \eta'$ as individual $i \in I$ regards alternative $\eta \in H$ as at least as valuable as $\eta' \in H$. Each V_i is regarded as complete and transitive. We then recognize indifference (or equal value) as $\eta V_i \eta'$ and $\eta' V_i \eta$ and strict value as $\eta V_i \eta'$ and *not* $\eta' V_i \eta$. Indifference will be denoted $\eta IV_i \eta'$ and strict value will be denoted $\eta SV_i \eta'$.

Now consider any nonnull subset of I, termed a coalition. We then define $\eta V_c \eta'$ when $\eta V_i \eta'$ for all $i \in c \subset I$. A coalition regards η as at least as valuable as η' when *all* of its members individually rank η and η' in this manner. We also assume the coalitions behave in a "normal" manner—if $\eta V_c \eta'$ and $\eta V_{c'} \eta'$, then $\eta V_{c \cup c'} \eta'$ and $\eta V_{c''} \eta'$ for any $c'' \subset c$. Similar remarks apply to SV_c and IV_c.

Finally, we represent society's regarding η as at least as valuable as η' by $\eta V \eta'$. And our problem is to specify V (and the derivative IV and SV relations) as a function of $V_1, V_2, \ldots, V_n$.

Arrow, recall, insists that V be complete and transitive and imposes Pareto optimality, universal domain, independence of irrelevant alternatives, and nondictatorship conditions on the relationship between V and $V_1, V_2, \ldots, V_n$. Here a related set of conditions is imposed, but V is not required to be complete and transitive. Thus, for any $\eta, \eta' \in H$ we envision one of the following possibilities:

(1) $\eta SV \eta'$ (η strictly more valuable than η')

(2) $\eta' SV \eta$ (η' strictly more valuable than η)

(3) $\eta IV \eta'$ (η indifferent to η')

(4) not $\eta V \eta'$ and not $\eta' V \eta$ (η and η' noncomparable).

Somewhat more precisely, we seek a function $F(V_1, V_2, \ldots, V_n; \eta, \eta')$ that assigns (for *any* combination of complete and transitive V_i) one (and only one) of the above possibilities to each $\eta, \eta' \in H$.

Besides imposing the innocuous requirement that $\eta IV \eta$, three axioms will be considered:

Pareto Optimality ($\overline{PO}$): $\eta V_I \eta' \rightarrow \eta V \eta'$ and $\eta SV_I \eta' \rightarrow \eta SV \eta'$.

Independence of Irrelevant Alternatives ($\overline{IIA}$): Suppose $\eta V_i \eta' \leftrightarrow \eta V_i' \eta'$ for all $i \in I$. Then $F(V_1, \ldots, V_n; \eta, \eta') = F(V_1', \ldots, V_n'; \eta, \eta')$.

Nonpositive Responsiveness ($\overline{NPR}$): Suppose $F(V_1, \ldots, V_n; \eta, \eta') = \eta V \eta'$ and $V_1', \ldots, V_\eta'$ are such that $\eta V_i \eta' \rightarrow \eta V_i' \eta'$ for all $i \in I$. Then $F(V_1', \ldots, V_n'; \eta, \eta') = \eta V' \eta'$.

$\overline{PO}$ is slightly stronger than Arrow's axiom, which only requires $\eta SV_I \eta' \rightarrow \eta SV \eta'$. $\overline{IIA}$, in turn, is slightly weaker than Arrow's counterpart, which requires identity of choice sets over subsets of H that V_i and V_i' agree upon. The major difference between the two structures, though, is the use of $\overline{NPR}$ in lieu of nondictatorship and universal domain (with V complete and transitive). On the surface, $\overline{NPR}$ appears nearly innocuous: if $V_1, \ldots, V_n$ results in $\eta V \eta'$ and if the V_i are perturbed so that the set of individuals strictly opposed to $\eta V \eta'$ does not grow, then we continue to have $\eta V \eta'$. But nontrivial structure is implied here. To see this more precisely, *suppose* $n = 5$, $\eta S V_i \eta'$ for $i = 1,2,3$, $\eta' S V_i \eta$ for $i = 4,5$, *and* $\eta V \eta'$. Now change the V_i to $\eta I V_i' \eta'$ for $i = 1,2,3$ and $\eta' S V_i' \eta$ for $i = 4,5$. $\overline{NPR}$ requires that the first conclusion commits us to $\eta V' \eta'$ in the second case. Of course, we might move from $\eta S V \eta'$ in the first to $\eta I V' \eta'$ in the second, but the first result nevertheless commits us to a not entirely pleasing conclusion in the second case. On the other hand, suppose in the second case we have $\eta' S V \eta$. Then $\overline{NPR}$ precludes $\eta V \eta'$ in the first. In other words, *if* some coalition with $\eta V_c \eta'$ is able to "force" $\eta V \eta'$ even though $\eta' S V_{I-c} \eta$, $\overline{NPR}$ renders the $I - c$ coalition somewhat powerless.

These axioms are, of course, intimately associated with the *constitutional value* concept used in the text. Let $\bar{c}(\eta, \eta')$, which will be assumed nonempty for all η, $\eta' \in H$, consist of all nonnull subsets of I, any one of which, when acting in unison, has the power to ensure $\eta V \eta'$. We then define $\eta V \eta'$ if and only if the members of some coalition with sufficient power to enforce such a ranking are unanimous in exercising that power:

$$\eta V \eta' \quad \text{if and only if} \quad \eta V_c \eta' \quad \text{for some} \quad c \in \bar{c}(\eta, \eta'). \tag{1}$$

We term the listing of coalitions $\{\bar{c}(\eta, \eta')$ for all $\eta, \eta' \in H\}$ a constitution (or power catalogue). Also note that V may be incomplete, intransitive (or even dictatorial).

Though *ad hoc* in appearance because of the exogenous specification of $\bar{c}(\eta, \eta')$, we have the following:

THEOREM (BLOOMFIELD [1976]). *Social choice is represented by the value concept in (1) if and only if the relationship between V and V_i respects $\overline{PO}$, $\overline{IIA}$, and $\overline{NPR}$.*

That is, under this axiomatic structure society behaves *as if* it had a power catalogue and made choices in a manner consistent with the alignment of preference and power.

A rigorous proof is available in Bloomfield [1976], and Bloomfield and Wilson [1973] provide a slightly different axiomatization. The outline of the logic is, however, straightforward. For necessity, if the constitutional value definition in (1) obtains with $\eta V \eta'$, we have a coalition with $\eta V_c \eta'$ and this directly provides the three axioms. For sufficiency, suppose $\eta V \eta'$ obtains. $\overline{PO}$ provides that the set of all individuals with $\eta V_i \eta'$ is nonempty. Exercising $\overline{NPR}$ and $\overline{IIA}$ establishes that this particular set is decisive for η over η'.

Notes

1. Arrow [1963].
2. Blackwell's theorem gives necessary and sufficient conditions for one costless information system to be as valuable as another costless system, regardless of the setting. One implication of the theorem is that if we have two costless systems η and η', but η is a garbling of η', η would never be more valuable than η'. See Marschak and Miyasawa [1968], Feltham [1972], McGuire [1972], or Demski and Feltham [1976].
3. The decision improvement may be direct, as when we consult with a market expert prior to launching a new product, or indirect, as when we acquire monitoring information to provide a better basis for motivating a subordinate or to provide a better basis for sharing the risk of that decision. See Gjesdal [1978] and Demski [1979].
4. See Arrow [1963]. Also see Gjesdal [1978] for extensive discussion of the related problem in an agency setting.
5. Being able to unambiguously measure the "amount" of information and thereby meaningfully speak of buying different amounts in a market places restrictions on the types of information we are able to envision in the story. Basically, we work with the Blackwell condition. See Kihlstrom [1974], for example.
6. To be sure, "the general problem" arises in all multiperson settings. In the laissez-faire story we are concerned with questions of distribution, while in the market failure setting we are concerned with questions of efficiency and distribution.

References

Armstrong, M. "The Politics of Establishing Accounting Standards." *Journal of Accountancy,* Feb. 1977.

Arrow, K. J. *Social Choice and Individual Values,* Cowles Foundation Monograph 12. New York: John Wiley & Sons, 1963.

Baiman, S. "The Evaluation and Choice of Internal Information Systems within a Multiperson World." *Journal of Accounting Research,* Spring 1975.

Beaver, W. H. "The Relevance of a Mandated Disclosure System." In *Report of the Advisory Committee on Corporate Disclosure.* Securities and Exchange Commission, 1977.

Beaver, W. H., and Demski, J. S. "The Nature of Income Measurement." *Accounting Review,* Jan. 1979.

Bloomfield, S. "A Social Choice Interpretation of the von Neumann-Morgenstern Game." *Econometrica,* Jan. 1976.

Bloomfield, S., and Wilson, R. "The Postulates of Game Theory." *Journal of Mathematical Sociology,* July 1972.

Butterworth, J. "The Accounting System as an Information Function." *Journal of Accounting Research,* Spring 1972.

Cushing, B. E. "On the Possibility of Optimal Accounting Principles." *Accounting Review,* April 1977.

Cyert, M., and Ijiri, Y. "Problems of Implementing the Trueblood Objectives Report." *Studies on Financial Accounting Objectives: 1974, Journal of Accounting Research Supplement,* 1974.

Demski, J. S. "Rational Choice of Accounting Method for a Class of Partnerships." *Journal of Accounting Research,* Autumn 1973.

———. "Choice among Financial Reporting Alternatives." *The Accounting Review,* April 1974.

———. "A Simple Case of Indeterminate Financial Reporting." *Accounting Journal,* in press.

———, and Feltham, G. A. *Cost Determination: A Conceptual Approach.* Ames, Iowa: Iowa State University Press, 1976.

Feltham, G. A. "The Value of Information." *Accounting Review,* Oct. 1968.

———. *Information Evaluation.* Studies in Accounting Research #5. American Accounting Association, 1972.

Financial Accounting Standards Board. *Tentative Conclusions on Objectives of Financial Statements of Business Enterprises.* FASB, 1976.

Foster, G. "Externalities and Financial Reporting." Paper presented at American Finance Association Meeting, Dec. 1979.

Gerboth, D. "Research, Intuition, and Politics in Accounting Inquiry." *Accounting Review,* July 1973.

Gjesdal, F. *Stewardship Accounting: Controlling Informational Externalities.* Ph.D. diss., Stanford University, 1978.

Gonedes, N. J., and Dopuch, N. "Capital Market Equilibrium, Information Production, and Selecting Accounting Techniques: Theoretical Framework and Review of Empirical Work." *Studies on Financial Accounting Objectives: 1974, Journal of Accounting Research Supplement,* 1974.

Green, J. R., and Laffont, J. *Incentives in Public Decision Making.* New York: North Holland, 1979.

Hilton, R. "The Determinants of Cost Information Value: An Illustrative Analysis." *Journal of Accounting Research,* Autumn 1979.

Horngren, C. T. "Accounting Principles: Private or Public Sector?" *Journal of Accountancy,* May 1972.

———. "The Marketing of Accounting Standards." *Journal of Accountancy,* Oct. 1973.

Itami, H. *Adaptive Behavior: Management Control and Information Systems.* Studies in Accounting Research #15. American Accounting Association, 1977.

Kelly, J. S. *Arrow Impossibility Theorems.* New York: Academic Press, 1978.

Kihlstrom, R. "A Bayesian Model of Demand for Information about Product Quality." *International Economic Review,* Feb. 1974.

LaValle, I. H. "On Cash Equivalents and Information Evaluation in Decisions under Uncertainty, Parts I, II, and III." *Journal of the American Statistical Association,* March 1968.

McGuire, C. B. "Comparisons of Information Structures." In *Decision and Organization,* ed. by C. B. McGuire and R. Radner. New York: North Holland, 1972.

Marschak, J., and Miyasawa, K. "Economic Comparability of Information Systems." *International Economic Review,* June 1968.

May, R. G., and Sundem, G. L. "Research for Accounting Policy: An Overview." *Accounting Review,* Oct. 1976.

Mueller, D. C. "Public Choice: A Survey." *Journal of Economic Literature,* June 1976.

Ohlson, J. A. "The Complete Ordering of Information Alternatives for a Class of Portfolio Selection Models." *Journal of Accounting Research,* Autumn 1975.

Ponssard, J. "On the Concept of the Value of Information in Competitive Situations." *Management Science,* March 1976.

Savage, L. J. *The Foundations of Statistics.* New York: John Wiley & Sons, 1954.

Scott, W. R. "Group Preference Orderings for Audit and Valuation Alternatives: The Single-Peakedness Condition." *Journal of Accounting Research,* Spring 1977.

Sen, A. K. "Social Choice: A Re-Examination." *Econometrica,* Jan. 1977.

Watts, R. L. "Corporate Financial Statements, A Product of the Market and Political Processes." *Australian Journal of Management,* April 1977.

Watts, R. L., and Zimmerman, J. L. "Towards a Positive Theory of the Determination of Accounting Standards." *Accounting Review,* Jan. 1978.

———. "The Demand for and Supply of Accounting Theories—The Market for Excuses." *Accounting Review,* April 1979.

IV

Reading List for the Seminar

READING LIST FOR THE SEMINAR

The purpose of this seminar is to examine the question of how we might analyze accounting as an economic good. This list provides an outline of the topics to be covered each session, as well as appropriate readings for each. The last part of the list contains suggested background material that the student should be familiar with before attempting the primary (or secondary) readings. Readings designated by an * are included in this book.

Session 1. Basic ideas in the economic analysis of information.

A. Information as an economic good and Blackwell's Theorem

Demski and Feltham, *Cost Determination* (Iowa State University Press, 1976), Chapters 1 and 2.

*Marschak and Miyasawa, "Economic Comparability of Information Systems," *International Economic Review* (June 1968).

Marschak and Radner, *Theory of Teams* (Yale University Press, 1972).

B. "Value" of information, learning, and demand for information

LaValle, "On Cash Equivalents and Information Evaluation in Decisions under Uncertainty," *Journal of the American Statistical Association* (March 1968).

Grossman, Kihlstrom, and Mirman, "A Bayesian Approach to the Production of Information and Learning by Doing," *Review of Economic Studies* (October 1977).

*Kihlstrom, "A Bayesian Model of Demand for Information about Product Quality," *International Economic Review* (February 1974).

Session 2. Application to managerial accounting.

A. Cost "assessment" and performance evaluation

Demski and Feltham, *Cost Determination* (Iowa State University Press, 1976), Chapters 3, 4, 5, 6, and 7.

*Harris and Raviv, "Some Results on Incentive Contracts . . . ," *American Economic Review* (March 1978).

*Demski and Feltham, "Economic Incentives in Budgetary Control Systems," *Accounting Review* (April 1978).

B. Communication incentives, stewardship reporting, and beyond

*Loeb and Magat, "Success Indicators in the Soviet Union: The Problem of Incentives and Efficient Allocations," *American Economic Review* (March 1978).

Groves and Loeb, "Information, Incentives, and Interdivisional Transfers" (unpublished).

*Demski, "A Simple Case of Indeterminate Financial Reporting," *The Accounting Journal* (in press).

Mirrlees, "The Optimal Structure of Incentives and Authority within an Organization," *Bell Journal of Economics* (Spring 1976).

Session 3. Application to financial accounting.

A. Equilibrium analysis, market efficiency, and regulation of information production

Demski and Feltham, *Cost Determination* (Iowa State University Press, 1976), Chapter 8 and Appendices 8.1, 8.2, and 8.3.

Beaver, "The Relevance of a Mandated Disclosure System," in *Report of the Advisory Committee on Corporate Disclosure* (Securities and Exchange Commission, November 1977), Chapter XX.

B. Consistent choice among financial reporting alternatives

*Beaver and Demski, "The Nature of Financial Accounting Objectives: A Summary and Synthesis," *Journal of Accounting Research Supplement 1974.*

Bloomfield and Wilson, "The Postulates of Game Theory," *Journal of Mathematical Sociology* (July 1973).

*Demski, "The Value of Financial Accounting."

C. Conclusions and critical analysis

Demski and Feltham, *Cost Determination* (Iowa State University Press, 1976), Chapter 9.

Slovic, Fischoff, and Lichtenstein, "Behavioral Decision Theory," *Annual Review of Psychology* (1977).

Background readings.

A. Measure theory

Coombs, Dawes, and Tversky, *Mathematical Psychology* (Prentice-Hall, 1970), Chapter 2.

B. Preference measurement and expected utility

Kassouf, *Normative Decision Making* (Prentice-Hall, 1970).

Coombs, Dawes, and Tversky, *Mathematical Psychology* (Prentice-Hall, 1970), Chapter 5.

C. Multiperson choice

Luce and Raiffa, *Games and Decisions* (Wiley, 1957), Chapter 14.

Arrow, *Social Choice and Individual Values* (Wiley, 1963).

D. Markets under uncertainty

Mossin, *The Economic Efficiency of Financial Markets* (Heath, 1977), Chapters 1, 2, 3, and 4.

Arrow, *Limits of Organization* (Norton, 1974).